Philip Durdey works as a saturation diver and lives at the end of a creek in South Devon with his wife Sophie and two sons. This is his first book.

$500,000,000 and Some Goats

Philip Durdey

$500,000,000 and Some Goats

Vanguard Press

VANGUARD PAPERBACK
© Copyright 2016
Philip Durdey

ISBN 978 17845 133 6

*Vanguard Press is an imprint of
Pegasus Elliot MacKenzie Publishers Ltd.*
www.pegasuspublishers.com

First published in 2016

Vanguard Press
Sheraton House Castle Park
Cambridge England

Printed and bound in Great Britain

To my Sophie, James and Jacques.

Acknowledgements

My Mum and Dad who should have turned their backs on me but never did. My wife for her patience, her love and advice during the writing of this book. Roger Martin who helped no end.

CHAPTER ONE

CONTACT

It was six in the morning on the 22nd of May, 2007, and a warm sun was already climbing into the clear blue African sky. I was on board a pipe-laying barge just off the oil-rich coast of Nigeria, in the disputed Delta region. An ocean swell was gently rocking my bunk and keeping me in a lazy slumber. I was tired, on the last day of a ninety-day contract, and in just a few hours would be looking forward to making my way home; but my world was about to change

'Pssst! Phil, Phil, for fuck's sake wake up, I think we're being attacked. Is that gunfire I can hear?' The voice – soft, quiet and laced with a large helping of panic – was perfectly pitched to penetrate my ear drums but nothing beyond. It belonged to my room-mate and dive supervisor, a thirty-six-year-old South African named Du Plooy; I knew him simply as Plooy. As the sleepy fog cleared in my mind, I began to make out the rattle of shots from sustained machine-gun fire. I struggled to gather my wits and said, 'I'm rather afraid it is.' Even to myself I sounded stupid – to Plooy I must have sounded like a right stuck-up Brit.

We were both sitting bolt upright, staring at each other dumbstruck, listening to bullets bouncing around various parts of the barge. 'Fuck…' I said in a slightly rougher, deeper tone. 'What shall we do?' Plooy held the highest rank in our room so I looked to him for guidance; I could see his mind turning over and hoped he was forming a plan to get us out of this. His reply now, though, made *him* sound like the stiff Brit. 'I think we should get up, get dressed and brush our teeth.'

Doing anything is better than doing nothing. After I had dressed in an old pair of coveralls and slipped on my work boots, we mustered side by side in a not-so-nice *ensuite* shower room, brushing our teeth and glancing at each other in the mirror. Real fear comes from the eyes, and I could see it there, dancing in our reflections. In fact, the situation on the barge was sliding downhill very fast. We could hear the rounds pinging, zipping and crunching into things. We had six armed Navy guys on board for security, and a gunboat never too far away, so we could only assume that the pirates running amok on the lower decks were pretty serious dudes.

Plooy turned to me with his mouth bubbling with toothpaste, looking like a rabid dog, and gargled, 'This is no good, Phil, I'm ringing the office.' He spat out the foam, turned and headed back to the bunks, wiping his mouth with the back of his hand as he went. I was one pace behind him and closing. We sank back on our bunks as Plooy grabbed his Nokia and hit speed dial. While he waited for the connection, it became pretty clear from the sounds of shooting that whoever had attacked the barge was now overrunning it and taking control.

'It's ringing,' Plooy whispered to me across the gap between our bunks. 'Hello, its Plooy and Phil. We've got pirates on board and shots are being fired!' There was a long pause while the office digested our information. I couldn't hear the reply, but Plooy spat back: 'What do you mean, you'll get us off? I don't think you're grasping what I'm trying to tell you. They're on board right now, shooting the shit out of the place...' Short pause, gunfire getting closer still. 'We're fucked, we're on our own,' moaned Plooy as he tossed the phone aside. To be fair, there was nothing the office could have done anyway.

Our bunks were next to each other, with about a metre of space between them; that gap was filled with a very dark, foreboding calm.

It was as scary as hell. We were both lying on our backs, trying to sink down as low as possible into the spongy mattress, listening to the unfolding chaos and exchanging nervous, twitchy glances whenever the noise sounded closer. Suddenly there was a change in the rate of gunfire; lots of uncontrolled sporadic shots gave way to controlled single pops. That was also when we graduated from being shit-scared to downright terrified. It sounded as if they were executing people on the lower landings, probably the locals, I thought; we white men were far too valuable to them for a simple bullet in the back of the head. But then again, since working in West Africa I had learnt never to try and second-guess the Nigerians.

'My heart is beating so fast,' Plooy hissed to me.

'Just got to keep calm, mate, and when they're gone we'll have a right old chuckle and a nice cuppa tea….Be a good story to tell the wife.' I don't know whether I was trying to convince Plooy or myself, but things were pretty far from all right; they were bad, and they were about to get a whole lot worse. The rate of fire had gone up again and they were right outside the door to our cabin, firing like lunatics up and down the corridor. The butts of their rifles were used to hammer on our door, and then we heard their voices. 'Open fucking door.' I managed to sink even lower into the mattress, just my nose exposed.

'Fuck, Plooy, what do we do?' I whispered.

'What *can* we do?' he hissed back.

'No come out, we fire!' shouted the pirate from outside.

'Look, if we don't open the door these fuckers will just shoot straight through it, and I don't fancy getting shot just yet. We have to open it and give ourselves up.' I had worked with Plooy now for the last three months, and I had grown to trust him without question, but he was asking quite a lot of us this time.

13

'You first,' I mouthed. I was beyond scared. Plooy hesitated, swallowed hard, tensed up and then cracked open the door before slipping out. I followed him with my head down. I honestly didn't know you could be so afraid and still function in a controlled manner. As we entered the corridor we adopted a submissive posture and put our hands above our heads. The man waiting for us was a shiny-looking black colour, about six and a half feet tall, and just as wide. He was clutching a hot, smoking AK47. A quick sideways look told me he was focused and determined, but there was something else, he also seemed to be having fun.

Thrusting and jabbing the barrel, he screamed for us to make our way down to the other end of the corridor. I was now wishing I had gone before Plooy, because the unsociable end of his Kalashnikov, that small steel circle of maiming and death, was being poked vigorously into my spine. We were halfway down the corridor when Noor, a Brit and another dive supervisor, was led out of his room by more pirates, also with his hands in the air and the compulsory look of fear slapped across his face. We all got some rough treatment to help us down the corridor to the bullet-riddled door, the morning sunlight streaking through the holes. The door crashed open and on the other side was another pirate, a smaller one this time, with ill-fitting sneakers on his feet and weird-looking strips of torn red, white and black material tied around his head, biceps and knees. But with an AK47 in his hands he was still looking and playing his part.

Outside in the sunshine it took a few minutes for our eyes to adjust to the brightness and the horrors before us. We were at the bow of the barge, outside the accommodation block, two decks up. I could see two more pirates, one on the stairwell and one on the walkway on the lower deck. Both of them were pointing their weapons at us, firing at the sky, then aiming back at us and screaming. We were half running and half being bundled down the stairwell in single file, with myself bringing up the rear. As we reached the main deck, they started to herd us over towards the port side, where a waiting gunboat was pitching in the swell just a few metres into the distance. I could see yet more pirates, all clutching guns and dressed in the same mix-and-match battledress consisting of odd combats, strips of black, red and white material, ill-fitting shoes or bare feet. They snarled at us nastily and glowered with alert, merciless eyes.

Two American crew members were being driven across the deck, a tower operator and a night-shift barge foreman. The foreman had a smashed face that was bleeding badly, and the tower operator was limping with a bloody hole in his calf. Things were starting to get a little sporty here now and there was still no sign of the cavalry, which was maybe just as well. If Nigerian security forces – not known for their professionalism – had returned fire, there would have been a massacre.

We three divers made it to the port side of the barge without taking any incoming hits. We had a pirate on each flank making sure we stuck to the script, and two more pushing us from the rear through the carnage of the main deck that had now gone all to hell. Overhanging the port side of the barge are fenders – rows of about half a dozen super-size tyres with a long steel shaft running through the middle. A chain on each end of the shaft secures them to the barge; they're designed to prevent damage to the barge when ships are moored alongside. Plooy, Noor and I were forced on top of the fender by the gunmen to our rear, with the gunboat still waiting in the swell dead ahead.

The gunboat had a big, belt-fed, 'get in amongst it' machine gun, mounted on a bi-pod in the bow, which was spitting flames and all sorts of obscenities at us. The pirate behind it was struggling to control the gun's delinquent behaviour, whilst firing wildly above our heads into the crane. The sound of this weapon was much more brutal than the AK's; it just rattled straight through you, almost making your knees buckle and forcing you into the foetal position. At the stern of the boat was the helmsman, another pirate, who was sitting between two very powerful 115hp outboard engines. All three of us were standing side by side on top of the fender. Even the swell of the ocean was angry; it had been building steadily for the last two days. The gunboat was trying to dock against the fender so that they could load us on board, but the pitch and swell were making this manoeuvre a near impossibility.

At this point, time seemed to stand still for me. It was a 'Matrix' moment, I was frozen on top of this rubbery fender with the feel of supersonic bullets slicing past my head. I took stock of the situation. The barge had been overwhelmed and was showing signs of damage, black smoke was billowing out of the main winch room and bullet holes were peppered all over the superstructure. My two mates and I were being forced into a boat that I really didn't want to get into, and as of that moment I knew my leave had been cancelled.

CHAPTER TWO

THE GETAWAY

I expected a bullet from the heavy machine gun to smash into me at any minute, for the man behind it was way out of control. He looked deranged and was trying to fire above our heads into the crane, but with the pitch and roll of both vessels the incoming fire was getting dangerously close – so close in fact that I could feel and hear the zip, zip of the bullets past my ears. He was completely off his nut, and we were expected to jump into his boat and join him. I chanced a nervous glance at Plooy and Noor and I just knew that they were thinking the same thing as me. 'Fuck this for a game of soldiers!'

The gunboat edged in closer and for a brief moment the crazy man ceased fire; the gun had jammed. With a final prod from the AKs we jumped, all three of us at the same time, arms and legs windmilling through the air until our toes found purchase on the side of the gunboat. You don't have to be a seafarer to know that all the weight combined on one side of a boat is no good thing, and we were now in danger of capsizing it. This would have been the best thing that could have happened as most Nigerians can't swim, but we were in survival mode as never before: Noor dived across instantly to redistribute the weight, and Plooy pulled me in because I was still wobbling about on the gunwale as the boat rocked dangerously from side to side.

The pirate in the stern in charge of the outboards had a face like a mutated frog; I was being kidnapped, and all I could think of was how ugly this man was. I don't know whether it was the look of disgust on my face, but he jumped out of his seat, shouting and slapping me around the head, until I cowed down with the others. The crazy guy up front in the bow had just cleared his stoppage and had resumed firing up into the boom of the crane. He was incredibly small, about the size of a European twelve-year-old, but was unrelenting in his rate of fire.

Another gunboat came tearing around the port bow, also firing into the barge; they had hostages on board, and if our faces looked anything like theirs we must have looked very, very scared. I counted and recognised three: an American from our barge, one skipper and a deckhand from the tugboat that assisted us with our anchor movements. I looked for the tugboat and spotted it drifting about a hundred metres away from the barge's port stern; even from this distance I could see it had suffered a fair amount of damage to the bridge, with most of the windows shot out and a run of bullet-holes along the hull.

My attention was drawn back to our barge to see three more hostages being lined up on the fender: the two Americans, Shane and Bob, whom I'd seen earlier with their injuries, and a Nigerian rigger I didn't recognise. They were surrounded by half a dozen pirates, all of whom were celebrating their morning's work, firing their AKs one-handed up into the sky whilst punching the air with the other. They had done what they had come to do, with no resistance whatsoever from the navy which was here to protect us from just such an attack. They had overrun both our vessels – which had plenty of security on board – and had captured nine hostages without so much as one of their men getting a splinter from our hard wooden decks.

As we moved forward to pick up the last three hostages and the remaining pirates, I started to feel very weird indeed. I felt slightly pathetic, vulnerable, cold, scared and very depressed. There was always that feeling that I should have done something – found somewhere to hide, fought them off or at the very least shown some resistance; but it was way too late for that now. All my concentration from now on had to be focused on what lay ahead, whatever it was and for however long. I was just about sharp enough at that moment to know that this was just the beginning; it could be a long time before I reached home, and things were more than likely going to get a great deal worse.

Bob, the old American guy with the bloody nose, was bundled in with us along with three more pirates. There were now four hostages and five pirates in our boat. Shane and the rest of the pirates waited for the other gunboat. As soon as everyone was aboard old Frog Face gunned the engines and headed for shore. Powered by the twin 115hp engines the gunboats did forty-plus knots, and they were going flat out. We were forced to crouch down low in the bilge, in amongst sloshing water, spilt fuel and spent bullet casings. I could feel every knock the boat took at this speed – it felt as if we were skimming over concrete. The stench of fuel was stinging my nostrils and my coveralls were drenched in it, causing me to shiver from the cold even though it was a bright, hot tropical morning. I folded my arms across my chest for some comfort, and shuffled in a little closer to Plooy who was crouched down next to me.

Looking up to stretch my neck, I took a quick glance at my cramped surroundings. Noor and Bob were both in the same position as me and Plooy, crouched down, arms folded and huddled together for warmth and protection. The small crazy pirate in the bow was facing forward with his back to me, and was making determined sweeps across the blue horizon with that big ugly gun. Even though I couldn't see his face, I just knew those big crazy bug-eyes were staring unblinkingly out into the distance. The two pirates on either side of him were bending down into the wind and covering both flanks. Even like that they both dwarfed the little crazy guy. These two were passing a bottle of clear liquid to each other; I guessed it was kai-kai, the cheap spirit favoured by the unemployed and working class of Nigeria. There was one more pirate just behind the front three; he was facing us and sharing a cigarette with Frog Face. They were calmly chatting, shouting to be heard above the engine noise. I locked eyes with him momentarily and he flashed me a vicious smile which held zero compassion and then drew a long, bony finger across his throat. I instantly recoiled and returned my eyes to the bottom of the boat, picking out a shell casing which was lolling around in the bilge water. My whole world had now been reduced to the tiny but deadly confines of this gunboat.

The boat slowed down as we reached the beach. The surf was ferocious, about eight feet high and messy. As Frog Face lined up the boat for his first run in, I made a quick calculation to try to judge how far we had come. I figured we had been travelling for just over half an hour, and at approximately forty knots that was roughly twenty nautical miles so far, in an estimated nor-by-nor-west direction.

Frog Face may not have been much of a looker, but he could certainly handle a boat. I could only watch in awe as he slipped the vessel in through a gap in the surf, holding back on the throttle then gunning it with split-second timing, sending us crashing through the waves to the safety of the river mouth. The crunching surf acted like a defensive barrier and, once through, the gunboat stopped and bobbed to and fro like a cork in the gentle swell. As Frog Face sat back against his outboards the other pirates relaxed and engaged in excited conversation, congratulating and cheering each other and mocking us. I couldn't tell what the conversation was about; it was too fast and tribal, but I did know that the atmosphere was changing. I was just about to check on my companions when one of the bigger pirates lunged at Bob, his forearm flicking out and sending a slosh of kai-kai from the opened bottle into Bob's face. Bob instantly recoiled, holding his hands up to protect himself from the assault, but the pirate knocked Bob's hands away before pouring more kai-kai over his face and shouting at him. The rest of us made to protest, but got several guns aimed at us and a berating from Frog Face.

It soon became clear that the pirates wanted Bob to wash the blood from the wound on his face. The rest were all laughing, jumping up and down and enjoying our discomfort, even egging on the medic to splash more kai-kai over Bob. He was the largest of the group, with thick arms and a barrel chest, and he was now pouring the kai-kai over Bob's head, making a big show and laughing as he did so. It was a worrying new development, as all the pirates appeared to be very drunk and losing control as they celebrated their victory. Just when I started to wonder how things could get any worse, they all started firing their AK47s into the water and falling over each other, pushing us captives back down into the bottom of the boat with the butts of their guns. The little crazy guy took the huge machine gun from its mount, held it over his head and began firing that, too, into the water.

There was nothing left for us to do but crouch low in the bilge and hope that we didn't get hurt. The noise from the heavy machine gun was destroying my faith in human nature, and my confidence in getting out of this situation alive was fading with it. As the bullets whacked into the sea, bucketfuls of water were hurled into the air. The sheer volume of water being kicked up by the bullets and falling down upon us was phenomenal. As the little crazy guy continued to fire, the kick from the gun finally became too much for him to handle and he fell over backwards, landing on top of us with the gun still spewing out bullets. From a distance it must have looked as though some sort of alternative circus of mayhem was in town: guns, bullets, water and pirates flying here and there, and a bunch of stupid terrified white men underneath it all. What appeared to have begun as a professionally executed sea-assault was fast turning into a dysfunctional getaway.

I didn't think I would ever say that I was pleased to see a boatful of bloodthirsty pirates coming my way, but that morning I was. As the other gunboat pulled alongside, the pirates in our boat ceased their over-zealous celebrations, and were now fully occupied with swapping tales of bravado with the newcomers who were also full of piss and vinegar. We picked ourselves out of the bilges, and Bob was left to nurse his own nose and wipe the searing kai-kai and blood from his eyes. I quickly made eye contact with Shane in the other gunboat, and we exchanged a look of united fear and a desolate smile before the boats pulled away.

Both gunboats made passage up the river together, the other boat just in front and to the left of ours, chugging along at a more conservative speed. As we were now on the pirates' home turf of Rivers State, they pulled us out from the bilge to sit up on a wooden slat that ran like a bench across the breadth of the boat. Not only was this because they were no longer in danger of having us rescued, but they also wanted to show off their valuable plunder to all the local villagers, who lived in the communities dotted up and down these stretches of the river.

I felt scared and hopelessly depressed. Happy cheering villagers of all ages had come out to line the banks of the river to witness our humiliation. I checked to see how the others were doing, and they all looked as miserable as I felt. At least the pirates weren't paying us any attention at the moment; they were too busy showing off to the natives. Up and down they paraded us, to the absolute delight of the river people.

'You see, you see this, this how we live, we suffer, no? It's all your fault.' This was said with venom by the big medic guy; he was wearing a shiny green vest top with 'PRADA' printed on the front, so that was what we later named him. It was the first time we were blamed for all the problems the communities faced in the Niger Delta – and there were many – but it wouldn't be the last. The oil men who worked these waters were considered by the locals to be responsible for all the poverty and pollution they endured.

Noor tried to reason with Prada that it really wasn't all our fault; we worked side by side with his own kind, Nigerians from these very same communities. He even went on to say that he ate the same food as they did and enjoyed it. It was a very brave try by Noor, but I thought it was going to take a bit more than the same taste in food to get pally with Prada.

The show was at an end. The locals had had a great time, the pirates were all swelled up with pride and topped up with a bit more kai-kai, and we were cold and wet, scared shitless and completely exhausted. I for one had the start of a banging headache.

Frog Face cranked up the throttle and the outboard dug into the dark brown river water, speeding our boat away from the villages and into the maze of creeks and swampland. The green jungle scenery was spectacular against the bright blue sky and the murky brown of the river. The pirates were all quiet, staring straight out into the bush, so I seized the opportunity to gain some idea of the direction in which we were being taken.

The river was very full and fat; it was snaking left and right and had smaller rivers arcing off in all directions. From the air it would have looked like a disorganised gravy trail interspersed by fields of fresh broccoli. It was very hard not to get disoriented, and I had to stay highly focused to keep my bearings. As the crow flew they hadn't taken us very far from the barge, but I had a feeling we were quite close to their hide-out; they all felt very comfortable and at home in this territory. It wasn't the distance they could put between the location of the kidnapping and their hide-out that would keep them safe, it was geology and the nature of the area we were now in. Much of the delta is made up of a complex labyrinth of rivers and swamps covering a massive 70,000 square kilometres, a pirate's desert island for hiding booty and hostages.

We soon split up from the other gunboat and continued on our own. We had no idea where that boat went, and that was the last we saw of them. I thought we had been travelling for about another forty-five minutes, give or take, at about twenty knots. So I calculated we had travelled twenty to twenty-five nautical miles approximately, but I had really lost all sense of compass direction, which was a concern.

What worried me most, though, was the fact that we hadn't been hooded. It was good that I could see what was going on, but it made me wonder what sort of people had taken us. Why would the pirates let us know where we were going? Not only did it help in any escape plan, but when we were released and debriefed we could give the authorities some idea of where we had been held. I couldn't shake off the thought that maybe we would never leave this jungle alive. My mind was racing with these melancholic thoughts, and my banging headache was getting worse.

The pirates opened up with their guns again, startling me and firing blindly into the jungle. We knew now what to do when they started firing, and that was to bow our heads, cover them with our hands and try to pretend we were someplace else. Anyone out for a walk in the jungle that morning would have been cut to ribbons by mindless erratic small-arms fire, and no one would have been held accountable, for we were now in one of the most lawless places on the planet.

The firing stopped again as we skirted around one last bend and slowed to a crawl, drifting with the flood tide as we arrived at our final destination. I lifted my head and made a sweep from right to left, soaking up as much of these new surroundings as I could. To my right the solid green jungle wall continued, breaking only for another waterway that branched off and away.

On my left the imposing green wall had given way to a clearing stretching to and extending beyond the approaching left-hand bend. We passed a dangerously crooked jetty where a couple of guards sat smoking. My heart jumped as they both looked my way; they stared for the briefest of moments before turning and running. I looked further up the river bank and counted three large huts spaced evenly apart, that looked as if they had been transported straight from Auschwitz – our new home, maybe? Some mango trees nearby provided a little cover. Just before the left-hand bend there was a second jetty, newer and strong-looking, with a couple of boats tied alongside and some more guards looking our way with excited interest. Again my heart skipped and a little more fear seeped in. Round the bend I spotted several blue plastic fifty-five-gallon fuel drums stacked at random on the river bank, and beyond them an overflowing heap of rubbish nearly two metres tall. Just on the higher side of the rubbish dump, and a few metres further inland, was a rickety lean-to with a small smoking fire. More black faces peered out as the noise of the gunboat approached. Once past, we did a victory handbrake turn just before the irrepressible jungle continued its journey up river, and then turned back the way we had come.

Shots were being fired, and I looked into the camp again at the most terrifying picture I had ever witnessed. A gang of thirty-plus semi-naked, dust-caked black men had assembled and were streaking across the jungle clearing *en masse*, all cheering and screaming hatred, waving menacing-looking machetes and firing weapons above their heads. I was crushed and looked away, crept back down to the bilge and whispered the only words that came to mind: 'Oh, shit.'

CHAPTER THREE

CAMP HORRID

The river bank erupted into madness as soon as the gunboat docked. We were totally mobbed, with a cluster of hands clamouring to grab at us. The pirates all jumped out onto solid ground to be congratulated as the victorious warriors they had proved themselves to be. We were hauled over the side of the boat on to the bank and then pulled across the dirt on our backsides, our heels working double time to keep up. I was dragged up the track towards a man who was holocaust-thin, his eyes so sunken back in his skull that for a second I was filled with superstitious dread.

This was the moment that made me realise just how far over the rainbow we had come. I had never met one before, but I knew instantly that this was the 'juju' man or witchdoctor as I watched him cast spells over Noor and Plooy. We learned later that he was here to make magic, to kill any evil spirits that were hitching a ride on the white man.

I was keeping my head low, trying not to look at anyone, just letting myself be pushed, pulled and kicked towards the witch. It was my turn to be de-spirited, and I caught a drop of kai-kai on my bottom lip that he flicked over me with his magic paintbrush. As my tongue reached out to gather it up I realised just how bad the stuff tasted. I was held in front of the witch while he flicked more kai-kai over me and muttered his incoherent spell, before being pushed past him into the inner fringes of the camp.

All four of us had been separated by the baying mob, each one abused and manhandled towards a hut on the other side of the

26

clearing. I tried to keep my head down, looking at a mixture of several pairs of old, dirty training shoes and bare feet, all shuffling in different directions. Small home-made hand grenades were going off all around us, shocking the air clean out of my lungs; I had read enough Andy McNab books to know this was the time to play the 'grey man'. That meant not looking the bad guys in the eye. I was to act scared, non-threatening, submissive, but equally I must not beg for my life or cry. I was very convincing in my first stint of acting the 'grey man'; I just hoped I could pull off the much harder second part.

Noor and Plooy came back into view as we were all marched up to a hut – the one next to the lean-to, the cook house – and then Bob was shoved in to join us. We were pushed back against the outside wall of the hut as the excited mob pulled back a fraction and began to quieten down. Leaning back against the hut as far as I could, I slowly raised my head and made a quick survey of my surroundings. I saw the other two huts behind a small clearing filled with men of various sizes and states of dress. The men seemed to be aged anywhere between fifteen and thirty; they were drunk, stoned and much wired. They stared at us with complete and utter hatred.

My blood felt like ice in my veins as I scanned the multitude of faces that were inching towards us. Some were covered in dark tattoos; others had self-inflicted scars on the foreheads and cheeks. All were black, grubby and very hostile.

We stood leaning on each other through fear and exhaustion. I was on the outside next to Bob, with Plooy on Bob's other side and Noor next to him. The seconds ticked by, with nobody doing anything, when Plooy screamed 'Poes!' at the top of his voice and reached for his foot. This caused the pirates to jump back a step and then a second later to thrust all manner of weapons at us: guns, knives, machetes and spears. A horrible-looking insect the size of a small bird buzzed clear of Plooy's foot, leaving a smear of blood. He rubbed the blood away and placed his foot gently back on the ground. All the pirates started to laugh and moved in closer once again, baying and squawking at us like a murder of crows.

Mr Crazy bellowed an order and the mob settled down and fell back behind him, leaving the four of us once again standing alone with our backs still pressed up against the hut. From where I stood I was looking straight into the menacing barrel of Mr Crazy's big ugly gun, and from this angle it looked as though I would be shot straight in the face; he was the man we had come to fear the most. He seemed about as unhinged as was humanly possible, and he was pointing a gun at me. Behind him were the rest of the mob who I could only assume were egging him on, barking and grunting words of encouragement, drawing their long, bony fingers across their throats at us, stamping their feet and jumping up and down in hysterical excitement. I felt at that moment about as hopeless as I've ever been.

Mr Crazy grinned, flexed his trigger finger, lowered his head down to the gun and lined up one bloodshot eye along the sights. This was it. All the other noises faded away and everything slowed down. I could see the natives' mouths opening and closing and all their limbs moving as if in slow motion, but no sound came to me. All the colours around me grew much brighter: the giant green leaves against the sharp blue sky, the whiteness of the men's eyes and teeth against their dusty ebony skin. Lots of information should have been racing through my brain right then. Should I make a run for it, should I run at them and take one or maybe even two of them with me? Could I talk some sense or reason into these guys and stop this madness? Or should I just spare a thought for my girlfriend back home?

But none of these things passed through my mind. I was in shock. Cold, defeated and the most tired I had ever been, with the worst

28

headache I had ever known, I had no fight in me. I am ashamed to admit that the only thought to enter my mind at that moment was, 'Is this going to hurt?' I could feel the tension all around me. I didn't want to look, but I stole a glance as a skinny finger squeezed down on the trigger.

An explosion of noise punches me and instantly the human body tries to defend itself, starting from the feet. The toes curl up and a foot lifts off the ground, with one knee moving across to cover the other one. The thighs squeeze together, offering protection to the genitals. The stomach muscles tense up and the chest tightens; the elbows bend so the arms draw in closer to the body, with the hands bunching up, fingers locked. The chin tucks down on the chest while the head turns away. Mouth and nose screw up into a dreadful face and the eyes shut tight. All these movements are completed sooner than the blink of a rat's eye.

It was a couple of seconds after the gun shot when I realised there was no pain, no warm patch where blood was leaking, and in actual fact I hadn't been shot. I didn't want to open my eyes just yet, as I felt more comfortable with them closed. I was wondering which of the four of us had been shot, and waited for the screams to come, and the other three bullets I was sure would follow. I was still standing there waiting with my eyes shut when I heard the laughter start. The laughter soon turned into a guffaw. I slowly opened one eye to see the natives killing themselves; they were creasing up, slapping each other on the back and pointing at us. I could actually see tears rolling down their cheeks. One of the other pirates had fired his AK straight up, so we heard the bang but didn't get the bullet. I looked across at Plooy, Bob and Noor, who both flashed me very concerned and confused grimaces.

I had never felt so small and pathetic in my life. The game was repeated a few more times, and the more frightened we looked the

29

funnier they found it. After nearly pissing their pants the pirates tired of this game and pushed us inside the hut where we found a sort of rec room, a place where they would normally chill out drinking, taking drugs and watching war movies through a DVD player that was connected to a TV. These and a couple of bare light bulbs dangling from the rafters were powered by a petrol generator, which was just outside. Today's movie was playing in the background: it was Blood Diamond, the story of a big diamond in war-torn Sierra Leone.

The rec room was part of the main hut and measured about five square metres; there was a corridor leading off to some other rooms. Our prison cell was one of them. The four of us were all made to sit on a crudely constructed bench with just enough room if we squashed up tight, which suited me fine. Now that they had shaken us up a bit it was time for them to shake us down. It was time for our interrogation.

As we sat on the bench we were all told to empty our pockets on to a dirty, flimsy plastic table. The rec room was crammed full, with lots of pirate-looking people trying to see what sort of treasures the white men had in their pockets. The younger pirates, who were lower down in the pecking order, had to stand outside and lean through the holes in the timber walls that passed for windows. They were going to be very disappointed, as all I had in my pockets were a packet of smokes, a lighter and a short length of twine. A united chorus of groans sounded around the room as each of my friends also produced similarly useless items. They let me keep the smokes and my piece of twine, but took the mobile phones from the other guys.

A different man seemed to be taking control now. He wasn't on the raiding party that was sent to fetch us, but seemed to command respect from all around him. He was tall and slim, with weak, gangly limbs and large clown feet pointing at ten to two; his face was confident and handsome but cold and cruel. He handed us each a piece of tatty torn paper and a pencil to share, and asked us to write down our personal details. He wanted to know our nationalities, names, ages, ranks and the name of the company we worked for, as well as our immediate family members. I wrote down my name and rank, which was diver, but I had no wife or kids at that time, though I didn't want to say so; I thought the only one among us not to be married or have kids would surely be the first to get a bullet in the head. So I scribbled down that my girlfriend was in fact my wife and that my two Jack Russells, Max and Scrappy, were my kids. I also offered one more lie, that I was South African. The half-joke, half-rumour at that time among us divers was that South Africans made worthless hostages and were consequently set free without fuss. I noticed that both my dive supervisors had dropped their rank and were now just divers. I wasn't the only one telling tales.

We handed him back the scraps of paper and he seemed satisfied with his admin so far. As he was so good with the paper side of the business we later named him 'The Secretary'. Next he wanted to extract intelligence about our vessel, and if there was anything of value left on board.

They say that when men are captured in theatres of war and interrogated, they all break in the end and tell their captors what they want to know and more; it's just a question of time. If we were in a theatre of war, and it felt as if we were, we would have just set a new world record for the fastest tattle-tellers.

Midway through the interrogation excitement swept through the camp, and I had a look round to see what was going on. The first glimpse I caught of the 'General' made me do a double-take. The sea of pirates parted to admit a tall man of slight build; he was almost sashaying across the jungle clearing. Four or five burly bodyguards, all carrying the more modern version of the AK, shadowed his every

31

move. He was wearing black three-quarter-length cords with winkle-picker boots, a fresh white T-shirt beneath a black denim jacket, and a black French beret at a jaunty angle on his head. He was very tall – over six feet – and very slim. He was also quite young, in his early twenties. He had striking features with high cheek bones and flawless skin. I thought Mr Crazy was unhinged, but he had nothing on this character. This chap was definitely a heavy hitter and just oozed warlord credibility. Watching him breeze into camp gave me the willies.

The Secretary and the rest of the pirates had separated respectfully to let the General through to the inner circle. His bodyguards leant or sat in spaces nearby that had been hastily vacated by lower-ranking members of the gang. A sudden cold fear once again gripped me as the General stood before us, one hand on his hip, the other clutching a small semi-automatic handgun that now and again he would point to his own temple while he eyed us all up and down. He looked as if he was doing a psychopath's impression of the little teapot. He was a curious-looking fellow all right; in the jungle gloom just beneath the canopy his flawless skin gave way to a vile twist of the features that did nothing to hide his hatred for us. I was wondering whether this man was a bona fide flesh-eating warlord, or just the son of one.

The silence was unnerving and I fidgeted uncomfortably on the hard bench, waiting for his next move. I expected a damn good pistol-whipping, or a shot to the kneecap, and readied myself for one or the other. But when the General finally made his move it was both unexpected and rather civilised. He thrust forward the hand that rested so delicately on his hip, to shake it with each of our own.

'How far now?' he asked.

'No wahahla,' we answered quietly, which means 'no problem' – the correct response to his question of 'How's it going?'

With the unexpected introductions out of the way, the General turned back to the Secretary and his bodyguards and shouted a few rapid commands in his mother tongue. We were then pulled roughly from the bench and pushed back out through the door into the yard. I turned to face them, as did Plooy, Noor and Bob, only to be shoved round again and pushed towards a jungle area some way from the main yard. This was the direction that the General was indicating by waving his pistol. We slowed down as much as we could, and again we were prodded with rifle butts towards the jungle. There was a lot of excitement and commotion behind my back, but I couldn't make out any of it; the voices were too fast and too many, and all I could really hear was the blood thumping in my ears.

I looked across to see Bob, Plooy and Noor all looking like dead men walking, slowly making passage to the woods, heads bowed and shoulders slumped. I knew and they later confirmed that they were thinking the same as me – that we were being led to our execution. I struggled to put one sorry foot in front of the other and found myself walking with the grim determination of a cripple who knows he's going to be shot in the head for his efforts. I wanted to reach out to my mates, shake their hands and tell them that it had been nice working with them and knowing them, but I didn't. I just turned with my chin on my chest and my shoulders slumped, to continue what I now believed to be the last walk of my life. My mind was taking a hammering; I didn't know how much longer I could keep it all together.

We made it into the thicket of mango trees and along a thin path that forced us to walk in single file. Noor was out in front with Plooy at the back, Bob and I in between. We continued down the path with thick jungle on either side of us, until we came to another small clearing. There we were confronted with the remains of a burnt-out fire and lots of empty beer bottles, which had been discarded here and there along with other refuse. A rather rickety-looking bench was fixed to the ground on one side, with a sheet of corrugated tin lying on the floor next to it. In the middle of all this was a badly-made A-frame which to my mind could only have one purpose – to have people tied to it before they were shot.

I was standing in the clearing now with my back to the militants, up to my ankles in filth and rubbish. I had my friends close by, which gave me some comfort. I wish I could say I was strong enough not to want my friends with me, but I was unashamedly glad they were there. I didn't want to die alone, not in this backwater third-world shit-hole, but what sort of mate did that make me, taking comfort that I wouldn't die alone?

The whole charade seemed to be just another game, however, another exercise to break our spirits and wear us down. I breathed again, although my heart was still racing well above the speed limit, as did my friends when we realised there were to be no executions at this point. The General wanted us to sit, which we did, squatting amid all the debris from past gatherings. The General pulled out his phone and showed it to us. It was one of those flashy new flip phones that had a colour screen and showed music videos, and the first thing the General wanted to know was whether we liked 50 Cent or not; we all agreed that we did even though we didn't. He then proceeded to play one of his music videos for us. I found myself nodding along with the rest of my new gangster-rapping mates.

There was a fairly large group surrounding us now: the entire assault team, the General and all his bodyguards, about fifteen men in all. While they all laughed and chattered amongst themselves, passing bottles of spirits and joints of strong-smelling weed to each other, we all huddled in the middle looking very washed-out and sorry for ourselves. The General spoke to us again in his broken

34

Pidgin English, not even bothering to look in our direction as his attention was still firmly fixed on the 50 Cent video.

'You are prisoners of MEND. We keep you here for very long time. Months, years before ask for money for you, or if we like, will just kill you.' He and his gang all laughed at us as we bowed our heads and looked at the filth. My stomach lurched and I thought I was going to be sick as my aching head spun with the words: a long time, death even. A long fucking time with these people, I couldn't cope with that. Death wasn't a good option either, but maybe better than hanging out with this crowd for months or years. The survival instinct once again reared its pretty little head, though. A long time was going to be hard in this environment, but I would cope. I told myself that I was not alone, and if my mates could survive then I would cope with them.

That was when Mr Crazy got up and staggered over, a bottle of kai-kai in one hand and a big fat joint in the other. He was short, so he only had to bend his head a little to get eye contact with us. With one hand he pointed back towards the General and then screamed in our faces with unfocused yellowy eyes and spit flying from his mouth. 'Respect the General! You respect the General or we kill you all!' He drew his finger across his throat to enforce his message and jabbed us all with it, and then staggered backwards clumsily and fell on his arse next to his laughing war buddies. Oh yes, we were going to serve some very hard time at Camp Horrid.

For the rest of the gang it was now party time. All they wanted to do was get stoned and celebrate their latest victory and capture. All we could do was sit and contemplate our fate. I was wondering what the hell this MEND gang was. We sat on amidst the contamination while the party around us started to take shape. Someone brought over a ghetto-blaster and jammed it up with some more gangster rap. Bags of drugs were distributed and a new drink

35

was brought out and passed round, one I had never seen or heard of before. It went by the name of 'Monkey Tail'. It was kai-kai with a twist – a stick of marijuana bud was stuffed down the neck of the bottle to blend with the clear spirit, turning it pea green. These guys didn't just like to get tiddly, they liked to get completely bombed.

The sun started to go down and small campfires were lit; they threw sinister dancing shadows against the impenetrable jungle walls. The General and his merry men had all returned down the river by gunboat, using the fading light to guide them through the maze of swamps. We had time now to talk to each other and to tend Bob's wounded face, while the rest of Camp Horrid descended into a drunken shambles. I saw Mr Crazy being carried by two men as he was too wasted to walk. Some men were just sitting nodding to the music, while others were dancing round fires. Shots were occasionally fired into the air and across the river, causing us to jump.

Bob's nose wasn't too bad, just a flesh wound, and the rest of us were physically without complaint, just a couple of scrapes here and there. Mentally we were exhausted, all four of us grousing about terrible headaches and the strange emotions we were feeling. We chatted among ourselves while keeping an eye on the party. They had moved us from the small clearing in the jungle and sat us down by the rubbish pile. The camp fell into darkness, but my eyes had adjusted and with the small fires dotted here and there, I could make out most of what was going on. Mr Crazy had been put to sleep, thanks to large spliffs and copious amounts of Monkey Tail. I couldn't see the Secretary.

Most of the original assault team were still partying, with one man in particular who was worrying us – Prada. He kept swinging his assault rifle toward us, cocking it and either firing it above our heads or mouthing the word 'bang'. The small group that he was with found it very funny and laughed along with him, whilst drawing their fingers across their throats. The finger thing across the throat had happened quite a lot today but I was still finding it a little creepy, and as for the gunshots, I had well and truly reached my limit with them.

No one seemed to be in charge. Everyone was simply left to do as he pleased. It was a young lad's paradise, as much booze and drugs as they could handle, and they got to play with guns and explosives. There were boys and men passing out, sleeping and pissing where they lay.

I kept one eye on Prada and an ear on our conversation. Plooy asked if any of us had kept track of our direction on the way up-river. Bob hadn't, he'd been nursing his nose, and Noor, well, he'd been too damn angry. I told Plooy all the twists and turns I could remember and the distance I thought we had travelled. I put us about twenty to twenty-five miles up-river from the ocean running just a bit west of north, and, as the crow flies, about ten to fifteen miles from the beach. Plooy agreed with me. The only thing we could not agree on was whether we first took a left or a right when we entered the river mouth, which wasn't bad considering the stress we were under.

As we were debating this, a short, stocky man with a slightly bow-legged walk came over and sat with us. He introduced himself, but I didn't catch the name. He looked much older than the others, in his late thirties, perhaps even as old as forty. It was hard to tell with some of the river men; most looked as if life had constantly beaten hard upon their leathery faces. His eyes were friendly enough and we all soon warmed to him. We tried to prise some information out of him, such as when we would be released and would we be killed, but he avoided the questions and stuck to telling us about the general running of the camp. As he was so willing to school us in the ways of the camp we later called him 'The Teacher'.

His laugh was quick and infectious, leaving us all feeling a little bit more comfortable. The rest of the camp seemed to respect this man, as the death threats all but disappeared. After a while the Teacher took us to our cell, which was in the main hut at the opposite end to the rec room. It was a couple of metres square, with a cracked and grubby hard concrete floor; the walls were timber-clad but bare and shabby, and an open-beamed ceiling made a perfect home for all manner of creepy-crawlies. There was one hole for a window and one for a door. They obviously felt there was no need for lockable doors or bars on the windows here. The furniture in our cell was sparse, and consisted of a single foam mattress a few centimetres deep.

The Teacher wished us a good night, told us to feel free and then left us to it. We pushed the mattress into the corner farthest from the door, and all sat down with our backs against the wall and our legs stretched out, leaning against the man next to us. I was the last man in the row, leaning into the corner. We sat in silence. Not much needed to be said.

I can't say what was going through the others' minds at that time, but I'm sure their thoughts were running depressingly parallel with my own. We could, however, draw two positives from the day's events, and I do like to finish the day on a positive. Number one was that we had some idea of where we were, and number two was that we seemed to have found a friend in the camp – the Teacher.

I closed my eyes and turned the two positives over in my head, willing sleep to come. Our cell felt so humid, hot and sticky, and without much air. I perspired constantly, so that my coveralls were clinging like a second skin to my body. I had worked in Nigeria for three months so I was acclimatised, but it's a lot cooler at sea than it feels in the jungle. All manner of nocturnal insects came alive and started hunting us down, attracted by the smell of fear we were giving off and the musky sweat our bodies were generating.

To begin with we brushed them off with fast panicky swipes and hard slaps, but we soon tired of this as it was exhausting us and there was no way we could keep it up all night; in the end we just left them to explore and feast on our bodies. Hot, sweaty and itchy with bugs crawling all over me and a banging headache, I was no longer thinking of the two positives. I thought of home, my girlfriend and my family, wondering whether or not they knew what had happened to me.

When the human mind and body are put under extreme stress we all end up dealing with it in different ways. I looked across at my friends and wondered how they were dealing with it. In the dim flickering light I saw three battle-weary men, broken and fatigued, bloodied and bruised, shadows of the tough, happy, laughing, oil men I had worked with just the day before. I closed my mind to what was going on around me, the party and noises outside the cell, and began to think back to certain times and places in my past and recall episodes in as much detail as I could. It didn't really matter what those times and places were, as long as they would steal me away even for a while from the terrors of Camp Horrid. This was the way I would deal with it.

LIFE OR DEATH

Right from the off, even before I set foot on earth, I had found myself in a live-or-die struggle for life. I was waiting to be born in a hospital in Pembury, Kent. It was the crack of sparrows on 23rd October, 1973. The Yom Kippur war, the biggest battle in the Arab-Israeli conflict, had just three days to run; the last US soldiers had withdrawn from Vietnam; Sunderland had just won the FA cup, beating the once mighty Leeds United 1–0. Ted Heath was in his third year as Prime Minister, the ha'penny bit was worth about a hundred pounds in today's money, and Pink Floyd had just released 'The Dark Side of the Moon'.

For most new-borns-to-be, getting out is just a straightforward passage from the dark side to light: a quick cry, a warm blanket and then a nice cuddle, and hopefully straight on to the breast for warm milk followed by a well-earned snooze… But not in my case.

Somehow during that passage, a few things went belly-up. The worst thing for me was that I had managed to get myself in a right tangle with the umbilical cord taking a couple of turns around my pencil neck, blocking off my source of precious oxygen. The worst thing for my mother was that I was attempting this slick manoeuvre sideways. And the worst thing for my old man was having to listen to my mother screaming, blaspheming and cursing me through gritted teeth, while managing to save most of her obscenities for him. I'm told I died at least half a dozen times during my birth. The medical term is 'nuchal cord', and the hospital I was in was one of very few in the country at that time with the technology needed to save my life. I would like to say that my early brush with the Grim Reaper directed me forever to the side of caution and kept my moral compass pointing true, but it wasn't to be. From that day onwards I always chose the path of most resistance.

I was born into a fairly normal, run-of-the-mill family, the third child of four. My father was a fireman. He stayed at the same station, on the same watch and at the same rank for twenty-five years, got his long service medal and then baled out with bad knees. Like any fireman worth his salt he had a second job, a 'fiddle' job. He managed his fiddle job from the garage at home, where he hand-carved high-quality reproduction furniture. This second job was worked in between his fire duties, family life and enjoying the odd pint or two with his mates down the Nag's Head. Like most sons, I idolised him; he is a strong and dependable man.

My mother is a true lady and also totally dependable, with strong values of what is right and what is not, and she laboured incessantly to instil these views into us kids – with limited success where I was concerned. Our house was kept neat and clean, and food was always on the table just a couple of minutes before we were expected. Our clothes, although sometimes a little thin in the knees and elbows, never wore completely through and were always clean. Mum juggled the kids, the house and the old man with different part-time jobs and an Open University course. When the course had been completed and we were a little older she taught at a primary school, and worked tirelessly to become headmistress.

My sister Julie was the oldest and has moved away; she carried on our tradition of marrying young and having a large family, five lovely kids. Then there was Brother John who pops up later in the book, then me, and Dave, who was the youngest. We all got along marvellously, with never a cross word said.

As I grew and the years passed, my parents became increasingly concerned about my hearing. The incident that finally made my mother take me to the local nurse for a hearing test happened on a Sunday. Like most Sundays it started out with a trip to the park, then a short walk, crossing one of the busiest roads in town, to the ex-servicemen's club where my old man would be enjoying a couple of pints before the Sunday roast.

The year was 1980, and Robin Cousins had won gold in the Winter Olympics. Radio Caroline was forced to cease transmission when the ship it was based on sank; also sinking was the Alexander North Sea platform, along with another one hundred and twenty three souls, after a massive wave caused it to collapse. The Iranian Embassy siege in London was brought to a sudden climax after the Iron Lady authorised an SAS unit to storm the building, killing five terrorists and freeing all hostages. West Ham beat Arsenal 1-0 to take the FA cup, while unemployment reached two million, the highest figure since 1935. And John Lennon was shot dead in New York, leaving an army of female fans bereft.

As my family and I waited patiently at the kerb for the red man to turn green, a woman on the other side of the street was walking towards us pushing a pram with a very squeaky wheel. Not exactly how the little green man is supposed to express himself when he changes from red, but with hearing like mine any noise would do. It was on hearing that noise that I took my cue and stepped straight out into the oncoming traffic.

All around me were the sounds of grinding brakes and screeching tyres, and the dreadful smell of burning rubber. But my eyes were focused dead ahead and safety was just yards away – all I could hear was beep, beep, beep – the squeaky wheel.

I reached the other side leaving a scene of destruction behind me at the crossing. Cars were at funny angles, lorries had mounted the pavement and everyone was wiping sweaty foreheads with their sleeves. Except for my mother, that is, who was in hot pursuit of her child. I had only one thing on my mind: a glass of coke and a packet of Golden Wonder cheese 'n' onion crisps.

The very next day, operation 'Mutt and Jeff' was cleared and authorisation was given. I was marched up to the local clinic and the wheels were set in motion for another right royal fuck-up. The nurse was a big intimidating woman with a slight moustache and a mono-brow, who held on to me far too tightly for my liking. She put headphones on me and made all the right noises into them. She prodded and poked me. I looked back at her and tried to respond at the correct moment. When she had completed all her tests she stamped a big red 'F' on my forehead, and sent me back out to the waiting room and to my mother.

Arrangements were made for me to have grommets fitted into my ears at the local hospital. When the time came I was frogmarched with my overnight bag and a brand new pair of pyjamas to where this fiasco was scheduled to happen. Arriving at the place wasn't that scary, even though hospitals thirty-odd years ago weren't very appealing. They were big, old, run-down places, with thin, cast-iron window frames and tall, imposing chimneys belching black smoke. No, I wasn't scared, because everyone had told me there was nothing to worry about, and me being me, naïve and only six, I trusted them. I was to spend the day before the op in hospital for pre-jabs, checks and other such nasties and the day after for recovery, so that was three days, easy bird... I could do that standing on my head.

Time to put me under. I was lying on my front I think, in one of those white hospital gowns with the split up the back that shows off your arse to the rest of the world. The bright white lights were glaring down at me, along with a bunch of aliens wearing green hats, masks, coats and wellies. One of them told me in a calming voice that I might feel a slight sting on my right hand and then to count to ten. I felt the sting and started counting; it was all over for me by the time I got to four.

I woke up in intensive care on Shrove Tuesday with nurses running up and down the corridor flipping pancakes, quite a surreal experience, but I was told that the operation was a success, and not to worry about being in intensive care, as it was just a precaution. The operation was a complete success in as much as I woke up from the procedure and there were no complications from the surgery they had carried out. That was where the successes finished and the doctors could stop patting themselves on the back. I had my grommets, but where I once had a lovely wrinkly foreskin was now just a bright shiny helmet, and I was sure to be called 'Jew Boy' for the rest of my days; they had scalped me. I was never told the reason for this or who was responsible for this botched op, but I suspected that it was down to that large intimidating nurse with the face from Outer Mongolia and her box-ticking skills – probably putting a tick in the wrong place. This was one of those situations where you have no choice; you just have to smile and roll with the punches, and then keep rolling. The Health Authority did have me back in again the following year, whipping out my adenoids as well, by way of an apology, I think.

CHAPTER FIVE

NEXT OF KIN

The phone had rung half a dozen times before my mum put down her crossword, walked into the next room and picked it up from its cradle. There was a man's voice at the end of the line. The voice was tense, serious, but very much in control.

'Is a Mr Michael Durdey there, father of Philip Durdey?' asked the man.

'No, he's out for the day. Can I help? I'm Philip's mother, Michael's wife.'

'No, I'm sorry but I must speak to Mr Durdey, it's very important. It's regarding Philip. Can you get hold of your husband at all?' continued the man.

'Listen, if it's important and it's regarding Philip then you can just tell me; I am his mother after all.'

'I'm sorry, Mrs Durdey, but this is a serious matter and I can only speak to your husband, Philip's next of kin. Can you please get hold of him and get him to contact me on this number.' With that the line was disconnected, leaving my mum a little frightened and wondering just what the heck I had managed to get myself into now.

My mum grabbed her keys and left the house. She jumped into her car and raced to the pond just two miles down the road, where she knew my old man was spending the day doing a bit of roach fishing with a couple of his old mates. Seeing Mother in a bit of a panicky fluster, the old man quickly rewrote the rules of communication and actually listened to what she had to say, then hurriedly packed up all his gear and followed her home.

45

About fifteen minutes after the original call, my old man was nervously waiting to be connected after dialling the number my mum had given him.

'Hello, Mr Durdey here. I understand you have some information regarding my son, Philip.'

'Yes, Mr Durdey, that's correct. The news isn't good, I'm afraid. At about six-thirty this morning the vessel your son was working on was attacked just off the coast of Nigeria, and he's been taken hostage.'

'Oh… Thank God!' replied the old man.

'I beg your pardon; did you hear what I just said?'

'Yes, sorry, but I thought you were going to tell me he was dead. That's the norm isn't it, when you want to talk to the next of kin?'

'Yes, sorry, I suppose it is.' The caller then went into more detail.

It didn't take the company I was working for very long to put all the necessary protocols in place. The Foreign Office and all other agencies – home and Nigerian – had been given the heads up. The man took time to take my dad through the predicted scenarios and likely outcomes. He then asked my dad to pass on his apologies to my mum for being so abrupt with her, and put the phone down.

The police were not far behind. The local constabulary had been alerted. They sent round one of their Family Liaison Officers and a couple of techies. They brought with them listening devices to connect to the phones in case I got in touch or, worse, my captors did. Although they had plenty of information about me already on file, they milked my parents for more, trying to get a feel as to how I might cope with the stresses involved with such a scenario. They left all their equipment, saying they would return if there were any new developments.

The Foreign Office was also in touch that day. They promised to make contact every day at about the same time to give my parents daily updates and reports, and to keep them abreast of any statements or demands as soon as they were released. They also told my parents to try not to worry as these things normally played out all right.

With all the official business concluded, my parents put the kettle on to make a cup of tea. They now had to decide how to break the news to my girlfriend Sophie. Sophie had just the day before finished her degree, and was at home nursing a hangover from the previous night's celebrations. She watched my mum and dad pull up outside and thought, 'Ah, that's nice, Mick and Sue are coming round to congratulate me.' She opened the door to let them in, not quite clocking their serious faces. Sophie closed the front door and turned to face them, only then sensing that something was not quite right.

'Mick, Sue, is everything OK?' she asked.

'Sit down will you, love, we've got something to tell you.' Sophie sat down as Dad continued.

'The barge Phil was on, it's been hijacked. Phil's been taken hostage. There's nothing to worry about as everything will work out okay, we just wanted to let you know.' Now whenever someone tells you you've got nothing to worry about, that's normally the time to start worrying, and Sophie was flapping big time.

It was a small, tight-knit, fairly remote place I lived in, and news travelled fast, well, bad news anyway. At my local pub, the Torcross Tavern, the news was bubbling away quite nicely and the Tavern soon became the official Kidnap HQ for all concerned. My brother and some of the locals had taken a vow of drunkenness until they received news of my release. My parents and Sophie would be the ones sitting by the phone, relaying updated information and sending food parcels down to the vigil at the pub; only now and again did Sophie weaken and join that vigil for a drink. I'm not sure how true this is, but it was said that my brother John wept by the sea wall that night. I had left for Africa still owing him fifty pounds and he was convinced that he was never going to see me or his money again.

47

CHAPTER SIX

LEARNING THE ROPES

I must have dozed off for a bit, for I was startled back to the present when the steely cold barrel of a gun was pressed firmly against my forehead. My eyes shot open to see a grinning gunman, with a smoking joint clamped between his teeth, looking straight back at me.

The gunman was not alone. He and his comrades were full of drink and high on drugs, and they were ready to torment us. After sticking a gun in my face, they started off the night's entertainment by getting us to check the barrels of their assault rifles for bullets. Then they either slapped us about with the pretence of getting rid of the mosquitoes that were feasting on us, or they kept moving us from one side of the cell to the other. After that they took away our mattress altogether, saying they needed to wipe their arses with it, and making us all sleep on the hard concrete slab. Four grown men reduced to pathetic wrecks, broken and quivering on a piss-stained floor.

They kept these shenanigans going well into the next morning until about four-thirty, when they finally tired of the bullying and let us be, giving us back our precious mattress and leaving us to the mosquitoes and other creepy-crawlies of the night. Sleep was sporadic after that. I kept jumping awake just after dozing off, madly brushing away the insects that had just bitten me, forgetting where I was for a second; and then the full horror would come flooding back to me.

Emotionally I felt very low and beaten, but physically I was still in pretty good shape. I had a pounding head, my body ached, and my mouth and throat felt like a junkie's carpet. I wondered if my mates were feeling as bad as I was, and struggling like me to accept the reality of our situation. Then I heard the sound of a drumbeat out in the yard. Voices and laughter floated in through the window. Plooy was lying next to me and I nudged him with my elbow until he stirred.

'You awake?' I whispered to him.

'Goeie more,' he grumbled. Which was 'good morning' in Afrikaans.

'Yes, morning, mate. God, man, you look like crap,' I said.

'Believe me, Philip, you don't look so good yourself.'

Plooy was a good bloke to have on your team, one of the best. After working with him for the best part of three months I had got to know him well. He was five foot ten, of medium build and strong with it. A ready smile was constantly slapped across a handsome face that would often dissolve into fits of laughter. A dedicated family man with a wife and two kids, he had served in the South African military as a youngster and then in a steel works before becoming a diver. Plooy was well adapted to building sub-sea oil fields for companies that supplied you with little more than a roll of duct tape, a handful of zip ties and a hastily scribbled set of procedures, so he was extremely resourceful and could adjust easily to any situation. He was a calm, confident character who was always positive and would certainly keep our morale from sinking to unknown depths. Like most South Africans I had met, his passions were barbecuing (they call it braaing), good red wine and grotty spirits.

He was halfway through telling me how he felt and that he had known better nights' sleep when his kids were babies, when the Secretary entered our cell with a couple of guards. We both instinctively lay back down 'asleep'; I think I even heard Plooy give a little snore. He stood silently over us for a moment before he delivered a 'good morning' kick to the legs and a quick berating for being a 'fucking white man', before he ordered us all outside for roll-call.

The Secretary stood taller than most, and looked taller still with his trousers always looked freshly laundered resting two inches short of his ankles, and a purple polo shirt forever neatly tucked in. His smug, arrogant face could stir the most placid of men to fits of violence; you just wanted to punch him on the nose as soon as look at him. His hands and feet were large and clumsy, which hinted at the reason for the large chip on his shoulder and the role he played of paper-pusher.

We slowly stretched ourselves to full height. We were all very groggy and stiff, and ached like a scrum of ninety-year-old arthritic rugby players. Bob grunted and took the longest to pull himself up. I didn't know Bob at all well and had only seen him in passing on the vessel, but I guessed he was knocking on the door of retirement or maybe just past it. He was a slow, heavy man and not in the best of health. If an English doctor were to plot him on the body mass index he would come out on the positive side of jolly. He was from the Southern part of America, Louisiana, and sounded like it; at times he could be hard to understand. Bob had been working around West Africa in the oil industry all his adult life. The short periods he was back in the States were spent in Vegas. Bob just loved to gamble.

We said 'good morning' to each other, trying to look and sound brighter than we actually felt, and then, like a chain gang on its way to break rocks, we shuffled our way outside in single file, squinting into the Delta's bright morning sunshine.

It had just gone six but the sun was already high enough in the sky to shed some warmth, which was going some way to ease out the aches and pains we had gathered from the previous night. The two

50

guards escorted us over to the other side of the clearing, shoving us lightly in the back with the stocks of their weapons, to where a small tree stump had been fashioned into a make-do seat. We let Bob sit there while Plooy, Noor and I squatted down on our heels. Next to us was the rubbish dump, which would increase in size and smell as the days went by.

'Eyes right...' said Noor, keeping his voice to a low whisper.

Now Noor was in his late thirties and had served in both the armed forces and the police. He was UK-born but had been living in numerous places in Asia and West Africa for a number of years. A shade over six feet tall and of stocky build, he had a mass of shaggy dark hair and a strong, square chin. Noor was highly intelligent and, once he had consumed copious amounts of coffee, unflappable: another good egg to have on your side. Again, I had worked closely with the man for the last ninety days and now considered him a close friend. Surfing was his passion, which suited his shaggy long-haired look, and he was always harping on about point brakes and hunting for the perfect wave. Also, as a dive supervisor, it went without saying that he was calm, confident and resourceful.

We all turned to the sight of two bedraggled, sorry-looking Asian men, dressed in old and worn Nigerian military uniforms, heading towards us. One was tall, old and frail-looking, the other much younger and slightly thicker set; both had that pale, drawn, scared look and the dispirited slump to their shoulders. Yes, they were definitely hostages and therefore friendly to us.

The younger of the two was called Sachin and the other Aditya; both were from India, but had been working shore-based in Port Harcourt for some time. Port Harcourt was a fairly dangerous place, but also unavoidable as it was the main port for us oil workers. They had been kidnapped the week before, after a two-hour gun battle between MEND and the security forces employed to protect the compound they were living in. They were both robbed and then snatched from their terrified families after MEND had outgunned and overrun the compound. Thankfully they were the only two who were taken. They were then thrown into the back of a waiting getaway van and driven for an hour through the congested back roads, before being transferred to a gunboat and sped here through the mango swamps. Another five hours of terror followed before they finally arrived here at Camp Horrid.

While we were listening to Aditya and Sachin's story, what I can only describe as a ritual had begun in the yard, one which we would have to endure every morning that was to follow, with only ever a slight variation from the main script. There were four men on the bongos, all sitting in a row together on a horizontal log, drumming away to a near-rhythm of some sort. Two rows of about ten to fifteen hung-over militants were doing a toi-toi, an African shuffle a bit like our conga. Back and forth they went in different stages of undress, stamping in the dust with bare feet, as the Secretary chanted some sacramental passage at the top of his voice.

They all looked to be taking this very seriously and it went on for the best part of an hour. They still appeared to be pumped up, not wanting to end the celebrations of the night before. Another man then took the place of the Secretary. We were still seated on the side-lines, watching. He was a gnarly little fella who shared a similar physique to Gollum, and he led the praying to the 'Lord Almighty Jesus Christ'. Oh yes, we seemed to have been kidnapped by a bunch of God-fearing Christians, not exactly your born-again, happy-clapping type, but Christians all the same.

In between the shuffles and chants that were going on during the ritual, we prised as much information out of the Indians as we could, about how they had been treated and how long they expected their stay to be. Aditya and Sachin said they had been expecting us, not because they had a crystal ball but because the night before our barge was attacked the militants had thrown a big party with lots of toi-toiing, drugs and booze, and because they bragged to them that they could expect some company very soon. Sachin did most of the talking and he went on to say that negotiations were already well under way between their company and the General, an amount of money was nearly agreed and that they only expected to be here for another week at the most. This seemed to me to be a little optimistic, considering they had only been in the jungle for a week, but I took the information as a great comfort and used it to lift my spirits. We quickly learnt to hold on to anything that might give us some hope; even the tiniest glimmer could make a difference between holding your head high or being near-suicidal.

We also learned that Mr Crazy was actually Mr Boss-man; he led this dishevelled ragtag army and answered to the General only. The name he went by, and what we were now expected to call him, was Commander Jackson, and apparently when he was not completely pissed on Monkey Tail and kidnapping people, he was one of the calmest, nicest men here. I would keep my own counsel and believe that last piece of intelligence when I saw it for myself.

The Secretary brought this morning's show to an end and they all clapped passionately, hugging each other and shouting 'Isowanna! Isowanna!' with voices and faces full of sincere emotion. We later learnt that these were magic words that when roughly translated meant, 'If you do something to me, nothing will happen', i.e. 'if you shoot me with a gun I will not die because I am bulletproof,' and they believed it fiercely. Their juju, black magic, voodoo, whatever you want to call it, wasn't something to be sniffed at or mocked by us. It was serious stuff and every one of them believed in it wholeheartedly. Their warriors had all been blessed by the witch and were now considered to be invincible. You add some kai-kai or Monkey Tail and some hard drugs to this warrior and you've got yourself a problem child.

The militants disbanded after the ritual and went about their daily business of getting drunk or high or both, and the two Indians returned to their cell; two guards were left to watch over us, relaxing against a tree, sharing a joint and paying us little attention. There wasn't much for us to do other than sit down, try to relax, and stay out of the way. It was a good time for me to find out about this gang called MEND. I asked Noor, our walking encyclopaedia.

'MEND,' he went on to say, 'stands for 'Movement for the Emancipation of the Niger Delta'. They are without doubt the number one players in this part of Nigeria. There's a never-ending number of armed gangs popping up and operating in and around the Delta region, all born out of the high number of disgruntled people living here. Many have grown tired of watching the oil being pumped from their fishing grounds and through their villages, and not seeing any revenues from it finding their way back into the communities for schools, roads or clinics. All they are left with are highly polluted and toxic waterways. You can't blame them, really.' I didn't even know what the word 'Emancipation' meant, so I was pretty sure most of this lot didn't either, and yet they were fighting for it.

Plooy also had some information. 'MEND haven't been around long, only arriving on the scene a couple of years ago in 2005; but make no mistake, they are a very serious bunch, responsible for the rigging of elections, murders, bombings, attacks on oil infrastructure and bunkering (theft of crude oil from live pipe lines), which causes most of the pollution out here, and of course kidnappings.' He went on to add, 'I read a MEND statement before I came out here and the message was loud and clear. No oil worker is safe, they want all production stopped and the Nigerian Government incapable of exporting a single barrel of crude. Nigeria has already dropped from

54

number one oil producer in Africa, losing at least a quarter of all production, and they're still falling down the rankings. Thanks to MEND, the waters in and around the Delta are now classed as a war zone.'

'Oh, terrific! It might have been handy if I had got to read this report before I left,' I said.

'Would you still have come?' Plooy asked.

'Maybe, more than likely I s'pose; you never think it's going to happen to you, do you?'

A cooking smell wafted over from the lean-to, which was right next door to the main hut. The smell was neither pleasant nor offensive; it just made me realise it had been a while since we had last had anything to eat. The Secretary came over.

'Food soon,' he spat, before turning and stomping back the way he had come, kicking up dust as he went with his big feet. Charm the birds out the trees could the Secretary. While we waited for our food we chatted about our other main concerns, and they were mosquito bites and the headaches that we were all still suffering from. Noor thought our headaches were due to the fight-or-flight theory. He explained that in most cases when you're faced with a danger your body gives you a powerful surge of adrenaline. You either use this to fight head-on, or turn and run yourself the hell out of whatever danger you're faced with. In our case, though, we could neither fight nor fly, and our adrenaline couldn't burn off in the way it was supposed to; hence the incredibly bad headache. Sounded plausible, but whatever the reason it was causing us a great deal of discomfort.

As for the insects, I must have had nearly five hundred big red angry mosquito bites all over me, many more than the others. I think they must have been climbing over them just to get to me. Malaria is one of the single biggest killers in Africa. It's passed to us via the female mosquito only, which needs to feed on blood to help with the development of her eggs. I felt as if I was playing a game of Russian roulette with the Delta's most efficient killer. Who knows, I could have caught the disease already.

The mosquitoes came out at dusk and would bombard us with wave after wave of fire-power until early morning. We called them the Nigerian Air Force, the 'NAFy' for short, and believe me when I say that they earned this most prestigious of titles. I was checking out the bites on the back of Plooy's legs when Commander Jackson made his way over, shadowed by some of the assault group that attacked the barge: we called them his Lieutenants.

Commander Jackson looked physically unimpressive, especially when flanked by some of the beefier members of his gang. Now that the craziness had gone and the man was sober you could see that his strength came from within - his eyes were cold and without compassion, and hid an intelligence that was beyond the understanding of most people in this camp.

We shuffled in closer to each other and I postponed inspecting Plooy's bites. My level of fear was creeping up a couple of notches as I stood waiting for them to reach us, still playing the grey man and trying not to make any eye contact. Commander Jackson showed no sign of over-indulgence from the day before; he looked fresh and in control. Dressed in camouflage combat trousers, black military high-top boots and a dark T-shirt, he oozed competence and walked with confidence. The rest of the militants eyed us with a cold arrogance from a distance, enjoying our discomfort whilst sharing joints of cannabis and kai-kai with each other.

Jackson noticed our insect bites and laughed like a villain from James Bond. 'I see you have all made friends with the Delta mosquitoes. They are brutal, no?' There was no malice in his voice when he said this; it was just matter-of-fact, almost welcoming us to the hardship. He then went on to say that we would get to know the mosquitoes well and we should all feel free while we were guests of MEND, and that during our stay no harm would come to us... Unless the General dictated otherwise. It was the second time since being snatched at gunpoint that the conspirators had told me to feel free. Were they taking the piss?

I didn't know whether we should draw comfort from these words or not, and decided to sit on the fence for a bit. Commander Jackson was a different character altogether from the unhinged professional psychopath of the day before; he was Mr Level-Headed now and I just hoped it was going to continue. He then went on to announce in his best clipped English that our food was ready to eat before they turned and let us be.

'Bloody hell,' I said, 'that was a different man completely from yesterday.'

'Son of a bitch, the two Indian fellas was right,' Bob mumbled in his deep southern drawl.

We fetched our food from the chef at the hideously unclean cook-house and returned to our spot on the edge of the yard. This was our first meal in nearly two days; no-one had much of an appetite, but we ate as much as we could and then forced down some more, struggling through every disgusting mouthful, scratching at our mosquito bites as we did so. You could probably put wallpaper up with this stuff; it was just like a sticky paste. We washed down the *à la carte* cuisine of rice and a couple of beans with a vintage bag of water, which tasted as though it had just been dug up. It had a very earthy aftertaste. It makes you think a country has maybe gone a little mad when they serve up water in bags and peanuts in bottles, as they do here in Nigeria.

We spent the rest of the day sitting in the yard trying to blend into our surroundings, as the camp descended into a drunken madness once again. I lost count of the number of death threats we

57

received that afternoon. The preferred technique was the drawing of a grubby black finger across the throat, while silently mouthing 'You die', or pointing a rifle at us with the words, 'Bang, you're dead'.

The Lieutenants have stayed close by all day. There was Prada, the biggest and cruellest of the bunch. He seemed to influence the large number of guards and other members of the gang when it came to tormenting and threatening us; his eyes and his smile resembled those of a Great White Shark. There was also Commander Jackson, Frog Face and another two we had named BA and Denzel: BA because he had a 'bad attitude' and looked a bit like the stocky, muscular character of the same name from The A-Team, and Denzel because he had the smouldering good looks and air of arrogant calm of the Hollywood superstar Denzel Washington.

As the sun began to set, campfires were lit, music was turned up and the party began to get started. Frog Face seemed to be in charge of the sounds and spent most of his day listening to Nigerian pop music, drinking and smoking.

'These all-night jungle parties are going to take some getting used to,' Noor said, as he slapped his ankles to beat away another wave of the NAFy.

'I'm finding it easier to ignore the party than I am these bastard mosquitoes,' replied Plooy as he fought off some more. They were everywhere, great clouds of them hovering all about us. I drove another wave away from inside my coveralls.

'Goon squad are on the move, heading our way.' I said.

We had taken to calling the members of the gang that were lower down in the pecking order the goon squad, due to their retarded behaviour. Next up the chain of command came the guards, then the Lieutenants who answered to Commander Jackson and sometimes seemed to be in charge of different pockets of goons, and right at the top of the pyramid was the General with all his bodyguards. Our two

58

personal guards, whom we had named 'Eagle Eye' and 'Gastro Pod', were at this moment leaning back against one of the palm trees smoking cigarettes and watching the goon squad approach us with interest.

Eagle Eye got his name for his serious demeanour while on guard and his uncanny resemblance to the Action Man figure. He was always on the ball and would be a hard man to outwit. Promotion was a certainty for this character, and I was sure he would be fast-tracked to a raiding party soon. He was like a superguard, with no sense of humour or personality to go with it; he was fully capable of watching us twenty-four-seven without so much as a lunch break or a snooze.

Gastro Pod in comparison was one of life's unfortunate characters, the sort of man anyone being held captive would want as a guard. He was of low intelligence and very slow-witted; we would often catch him drifting off into a world of his own, paying us little or no attention. He was tall and broad but slow and clumsy, and the reason he received the unflattering name of Gastro Pod was the mangled stump of a foot that hung uselessly from the end of his leg. It comes from the scientific name given to slugs, snails and their relatives, and loosely means 'one-footed stomach thing'.

The drink and drugs these militants had been consuming all day were giving them all the bravado and justification they needed to start getting stuck into us. We were now all being jostled and pushed on to each other by the encircling mob, and we tensed up for the beating we were sure would follow as they continued to heckle us.

On the feet of one of the guards we were yet to award a pet name to were my diving booties. During the raid on the barge one of the gang must have swiped them from where they were hanging out to dry, and they were now being shared about from one grotty pair of feet to another. Over the past couple of days I had been shot at, rifle-

59

butted and been on the receiving end of a bit of slap and tickle. Now it would seem I was to get the snot kicked out of me by my own booties. The Teacher casually strolled over with his wide smile, clutching a bottle of Monkey Tail and instantly defusing the situation before the first kick was delivered. We were all very grateful and exchanged some relieved-looking smiles with our saviour. He smiled back sympathetically.

The goon squad slithered back into the shadows under the mango trees, and Prada and his friends went back to getting high. Our two guards looked a bit disappointed. The Teacher sat down and leant back against a tree stump, and it was enough for us just to sit and enjoy the protection he offered, watch him drink his beloved green stuff and listen to the stories he shared about life in the Delta, and a little about himself. We had no idea where he spent his days; he used to pop up from nowhere and then, when he had had enough of our company, he just disappeared again.

We learnt that the Teacher answered to no-one in the camp, and was working directly for MEND to make sure the camp was run in the proper manner. MEND seemed to be structured like a franchise, with lots of independent networks acting under one umbrella, and he was acting like a sort of company rep, making sure MEND's interests were catered for. The Teacher was also very proud of the fact that he could strip and rebuild any outboard engine using no more than a couple of blunt screwdrivers and a rusty spoon. We sat listening to the Teacher for as long as we could, knowing that he was all that stood in the way of yet more hostile treatment, but after a while he just stood and stretched, said 'Good night, feel free,' and then wobbled off into the jungle, tossing his empty bottle on the rubbish pile as he went.

With the Teacher gone we also decided it was best to disappear, so trying not to draw too much attention we all stood up as one and made our way back to our cell, fending off drunken militants as we went. Before I could cuddle up with my three bed companions, though, I needed to empty my bladder. I didn't feel like running the gauntlet during the late hours of the night when the militants were at their most playful, so I had to get it over with now.

'Please boss,' I said, 'I need to go toilet.'

Eagle Eye escorted me to the toilet area where everyone 'eased' themselves. Eagle Eye had the sense of humour of a murky puddle and I was yet to see him laugh, smile or even utter a single word to another fellow man, so the walk to the toilet began with a nod of his head and was made in complete silence.

The toilet area was at the river bank where the rise and fall of the water would clean away all the waste: nature's sewer system. Hundreds of tiny land crabs lived in holes buried in the river bank between low and high tide. They had black and red shiny armour-plating, one small claw and another much larger one that was constantly held aloft to ward off any trespassers. Quick to react to the new threat they scurried back below ground with lightning speed; perfectly synchronised, they looked just like a retreating army of Samarian warriors. I wished I could have been one of those crabs; I would have much preferred one of those dark damp holes to being forced to live up here.

Going to the toilet with a man of Eagle Eye's serious calibre sticking a gun in your back was, to put it mildly, pretty unnerving. I tried to compose myself and get on with the task in hand, and although it wasn't easy I managed to empty my bladder, enough I hoped to last me through to the next morning. If I could help it I didn't want to have to go again until the sun was up. Even the simple act of relieving oneself was a logistical nightmare in Camp Horrid and seemed to stretch my nerves to breaking point.

On the way back to the cell I was stopped by three men from the goon squad who were smoking cigarettes and blocking my path. One of the three held out a packet of Marlboro Red and offered me one. As he fired up the cigarette for me he asked, 'Do you like pussy?' in a husky tone. 'What?' I replied, slightly puzzled at the strange question.

'You heard, white man; do like pussy?' It was at that moment I knew I should have just pushed right past them and pressed on to my cell...

'Yes of course, doesn't everyone?' I replied, somewhat naïvely.

'No, not everyone, white boy,' he replied, whilst seductively blowing smoke in my face. He looked like a black macabre Joker from the hit Batman series from the seventies, and his two side-kicks looked like a couple of scary pantomime villains, their faces covered in small traditional tattoos and self-inflicted scars.

My fear had just found a new level: of all the things I had been worrying about since I had been kidnapped, being sodomised wasn't one of them. I bit down hard on my cigarette, dropped my eyes and pushed past the three men who were blocking my path. Looking nervously over my shoulder, I walked at a near-jog back to our cell. I rushed in, barged right past Noor, Plooy and Bob and threw myself down into the corner on the mattress and hugged my knees.

'We've gotta get out of here,' I said.

'What's up with you?' they asked. 'You all right?'

'Nothing, I'm OK,' I replied. Camp Horrid for me had just got worse. I could hear the party going on outside our cell as waves of hopeless depression swept over me. I'd always prided myself on being able to stay positive and to make the best out of a bad situation, as over the years I had been in enough. Since we arrived I'd been trying to come up with a plan for getting through this, but with no training how do you plan to get through a kidnapping? I decided then

62

and there that you can't plan; not really, you just have to take whatever they throw at you, whatever that may be, and then act accordingly, with only one objective in mind, survival.

Once my three companions had sorted themselves out and had settled down next to me for another grim night, I leant up against my corner and shut my eyes. My mind was racing out of control, running away with all sorts of horrible potential outcomes that could befall me in this morally bankrupt camp. I had to calm myself down and try to block out all the bad thoughts before they turned me into a useless, blubbering mess.

CHAPTER SEVEN

ZERO TO HERO

The Tanker War had just started, with Iraq attacking Iranian oil tankers; Maggie Thatcher was stamping her authority on her fifth year and second term as Prime Minister; Man United had won the FA cup in a replay, beating Tottenham Hotspur 4–0. The plight of millions of Ethiopians was brought to the attention of the world's media with the birth of Band Aid; Glam rock was big in the charts and burgundy tank tops and legwarmers were all the rage. It was 1984 and not the best decade for being trendy.

I had had my first brush with the law the year before and my school reports were atrocious, filled with comments like 'Should be doing better', 'Has a short attention span' and 'Has to be constantly asked to leave the classroom'. It was not all doom and gloom though; I had taken up cross-country running and winning races was proving easy. I could run like the very wind blew.

Not fast enough to outrun the police, though. My brush with the law happened in the company of my older brother John and a mate of his. This kid was trouble, born with tattoos, a ring through his ear and a fag in his mouth – although he was barely ten he was already on a twenty-a-day habit. We used to go into the town centre on a Saturday and get up to all sorts of skulduggery. Our little firm had taken to stealing football stickers and bouncy balls. The football stickers we would lovingly stick into our Pannani sticker albums or swap with other kids in the school playground, but the bouncy balls we would have some fun with.

We used to chuck the balls off a notorious local bridge, known as Suicide Bridge due to its height and the number of people who had thrown themselves off it. We would then try to catch the balls on their way back up. The only problem with this entertainment was that the traffic using the road underneath the bridge was usually as thick as grass, and it was only a matter of time before we were apprehended by the boys in blue, bringing our criminal empire crashing down around us. Of course, as we were all juveniles and under the age of criminal responsibility, our parents were summoned to the local nick to collect us.

I will never, ever, be able to shake away the image of utter disappointment on my parents' faces, or my own feelings of utter shame. Problem was, it got easier after the first time. With subsequent transgressions their look of disappointment was still there, but my utter shame was replaced with, well, just shame, and then with just a mild guilty feeling. The dark side was winning. While my brother seemed to have learned his lesson, I just got myself into more and more trouble, causing my parents a right load of misery that they didn't need or deserve. What I needed was an incident that would overshadow all my past wrongdoings, something that would make my parents forgive me and once again look at me with pride.

That opportunity came along one Saturday in the summer of 1984. We were on a family walk, Mum, Dad, me and my younger brother Dave. The plan was to have a nice stroll through the countryside, and on the way round hook up with John, who was out fishing with some new friends who were much better behaved and had kept him out of trouble.

Well, the walk was pretty uneventful although very pleasant. Dave was only five so he was dragging his heels and slowing the group down. I was a young, fit ten-year-old setting a blistering pace up ahead. My parents were dilly-dallying somewhere in between, holding hands and thinking that nothing could spoil such a lovely peaceful day. I knew exactly where John and his new chums would be fishing, so I quickened my pace and was almost jogging, keen to get there ahead of the rest.

I reached the pond, which was hidden from view by a wooded area, a good five to ten minutes before the rest of the party. That was my first mistake. I was pushing through the trees heading to where I knew they would be, but something about the screams and shouting I could hear was telling me that all was not quite right. Anglers as a rule are supposed to stay patient and quiet, so as not to scare the fish, and John was with his new square friends who should abide by these unwritten rules. My alarm bells started ringing and my mind was on high alert.

I covered the last thirty yards at a run, and as I reached the bank I came across a sight that I just wasn't prepared for. I was expecting a fight over the best fishing patch between rival groups of anglers. But all I could see were three panic-stricken people screaming and shouting, waving their arms around and jumping up and down, all of them looking quite demented.

As I started to take in the scene and make sense of the noise, I realised all the fuss was focused in one direction. I scanned the surface of the pond following the direction of the mayhem, and there it was: an upturned rubber dinghy. Just by the dinghy, in a violent, foamy mass of water, was a young lad of about fifteen. I looked back to the bank where the distraught lads were crying, 'He's drowning, and he can't swim, save him!'

My head swung back to the drowning boy, then over to my brother doing the dance of death on the bank with his two friends, then again to matey blowing bubbles just under the surface of the murky water.

Decision time. Only I didn't decide, I didn't even really think, I just turned and started wading straight into the stinking, stagnant water, (it wasn't the cleanest of ponds,) stopping only to slip off my new Nike trainers. That was my second mistake.

The thing with doing the hero bit is that before the medals are handed out and you get your picture in the paper with your award-winning smile, you first have to chuck yourself into the middle of a nasty situation and do the dirty work. Without the power of foresight you just don't know which way the pendulum will swing.

Arm over arm, I front-crawled, bearing down on the stricken angler. As I reached Flipper I stretched out my arm and grabbed hold of his shoulder. That was mistake number three. As I grabbed hold of him he clamped down on me, the way a limpet locks on to a rock when you nudge it with your foot. He then started climbing me like a ladder, trying to get his head out of the water. This guy was five years older than me, a lot bigger and heavier, and he was also very, very desperate. People who think they're about to die can become incredibly strong and resourceful, and I had just thrown him a lifeline.

Flipper was thrashing around so violently that he was in danger of knocking me out. All I could do was hold on and try to dodge the blows, then wait for a chance to break surface and suck in another mouthful of air. I was not getting much air in, but what I was getting would have to do. Every time I broke the surface I could hear the lads on the bank screaming, especially my brother. He was shouting for Flipper to let go of me, but Flipper was not having any of it. He started gripping me even tighter as his energy faded and he couldn't tread water any more. All his efforts were concentrated on keeping his head above water, and in the process he was pushing me down deeper. I couldn't do a thing. As I went under again, my lungs were searing. Every muscle I had was working to get my head above the water, but it was not enough.

I couldn't compete with this guy; he was just too strong and desperate. I was not liking this hero thing one bit, it sucked. Something funny happened then. Just as I was about to give up, when my lungs felt as if they were going to burst, my life flashed before my eyes, and it was very, very depressing. I gave myself a big shake, told myself I couldn't die in this horrible pond, it just wasn't right; and I managed to find a little extra bit of strength and was given the chance to try and get another lungful of air. I took it, and started clawing my way up him the way he had climbed me before.

I broke the surface with just my nose and lips for the briefest of moments, only to be knocked straight back below. I probably only had a split second of sky, a quick gulp of air and pond-weed and water, but it was just enough to keep me going for a few more seconds.

The pain was unbearable. My energy levels were falling fast. He was going down and not letting go of me, so I was going down with him. But just as my whole world was shutting down and turning black, I felt a strong hand grabbing me by the scruff of my neck and starting to pull me back to the surface. It must have been my father, he saves people all the time. It's his job, dashing into burning buildings and carrying people out, one on each shoulder, cutting people out of wrecked cars. He doesn't even question his motives before putting his life on the line. Only one problem with this train of thought, though – my old man can't swim, not a stroke.

As my head broke the surface I realised it wasn't my dad – it was my mum. As our eyes met I knew I was safe. There was the sort of determination in her face that you only ever get to see once or twice in a lifetime. She looked skyward and started doing the frog thing with her legs, swimming on her back. She was keeping hold of each of us by our shirt collars, and all three of us started for the bank. As I took in air and got a bit of strength back I tried to help by also doing the frog thing and the rowing motion with my arms. But Flipper to my left was just a dead weight in the water.

We reached the bank and my old man was already in the water up to his waist, dragging Flipper clear. Fortunately Flipper started being sick and coughing water up straightaway, which with any near-drowning is a good sign. My father then turned to help my tired mother and steadied her on the bank. I was standing in the shallows, water up to my ankles, limp arms by my side, looking half drowned and feeling a little unsure about myself, when I got a ruffle of my wet hair.

As my old man looked down at me I knew I'd done enough to redeem myself. There was both relief and pride. He said only a few words but they were enough: 'Well done, son.' Everyone was in high spirits now and slapping each other on the back for a job well done. Ambulances were called, and we all ended up in hospital to be checked over.

It emerged that Flipper had ended up in the pond after trying to collect fishing floats stuck in the overhanging branches of trees. He went out in the dinghy whilst the boys on the bank tried to dislodge the floats by throwing large sticks at them. With the law of averages working against them, one of the sticks came down and knocked Flipper out of his dinghy and into the pond.

I did get that photo in the paper with my award-winning smile though, along with the word 'hero' directly below my mother who was standing beside me.

CHAPTER EIGHT

JUNGLE COMFORTS

It was growing light outside as the sun edged its way up over the trees on our third day in captivity. Again during the night we were visited by militants and the NAFy, and tormented until the small hours. I was sitting squashed into my corner on the edge of our mattress with my head hard up against the wall, with Plooy resting his head on my left shoulder. He in turn had Noor using his shoulder, whilst Noor was being leant on by Bob. It was the only way we could maximise the size of the mattress and retain a small amount of comfort. We were making the most of the last of the quiet time before being forced outside to watch the drums, and then to endure another day of whatever hostilities they decided to toss our way.

Things always seem worse at night. It doesn't matter whether there's an outstanding bill that you can't afford to pay or whether you are having a bad time in a relationship; the problem is always magnified tenfold during those nocturnal hours. It was the same here.

After thinking all night about the way I had been collared and then propositioned on my way to the toilet, I was convinced that those three intended to 'gang-bang' me and leave my arse looking like downtown Baghdad. I didn't want to be part of anyone's gang-bang, not because I was concerned about the psychological baggage that goes with it or catching Aids; no, those were long-term problems and I had already learned to think in the now, just survive the morning and then the afternoon. I just didn't want to go through the humiliation of being overpowered and having a cock forced into my bum, which I think is a fair one. I shared my concerns with Noor,

Plooy and Bob, who took the threat to me seriously and suggested that I should never be left on my own for any reason. Bob joked that I shouldn't provoke them by swaying my hips in a camp manner when I walked; he followed it up with a wink and a smile. It was good advice, but I was going to go one better. At the next opportunity I would find myself a small sharp stick and secrete it on my person, and then if one of the three sisters wanted to have his wicked way with me, he was going to get the sharp end of that stick straight in his eye.

Quiet time was over. The Secretary marched into our cell and ordered us outside for roll-call. We all struggled and fumbled to our feet, leaning on each other for support, and made our way outside. Our late nights of torment were starting to take their toll. The hapless Gastro Pod escorted us down to the river's edge so that we could ease ourselves. The drums behind us started up an accompaniment to the sound of our urine splashing into the dirty brown river, and I allowed myself a little smile of relief as I emptied my bladder.

Last night's bombardment by the NAFy had left my arms and legs covered in small angry bites, and I couldn't stop the itching. Already I had scratched the tops off several bumps and now they were weeping.

'Stop scratching, they'll just get worse,' commanded Noor.

'I can't, they're driving me nuts,' I said as I went from scratching them with my nails to rubbing them frantically with the flat of my hand. We had moved to the area by the rubbish heap that seemed to be reserved for us, and watched the drums. Sachin and Aditya stayed in their cell as Aditya was not up to coming out today. Gastro Pod sat on a tree stump and picked his teeth as Eagle Eye sauntered across and joined him. Just then, through a gap in the jungle canopy, a Bristol helicopter flew slowly overhead. These are the workhorses that they use to ferry us oil workers back and forth between the off-shore installations and the beach. I stopped rubbing my bites.

'Didn't a chopper fly over yesterday?' I asked.

'Twice I think, once about this time in the morning and then again late afternoon,' replied Plooy.

'Don't tell me they've built their hideout under Bristol's flight path.' Noor said this with a mocking chuckle and we all joined in.

'Seriously, though, when we get out of here we can let the authorities know what time we spotted them, they can check with the flight paths and then voila! No more camp.' Plooy looked like the cat that got the cream when he said this.

'Well, I saw a prisoner-of-war film once where the inmates wrote messages on the ground so that the pilots wouldn't bomb them. We could write SOS or HELP in the yard; a pilot's bound to spot it and report back. They must be on the lookout, who knows? He might be flying over for that exact reason,' I said.

' No, I don't like it, Phil: one, they will see us writing it, two, the only bit of ground to write it on everyone walks over and last, they can read, you know, they're not stupid,' suggested Noor.

'You think?' I said this as a question as we all turned to survey our hosts. Noor was unperturbed.

'Treat everyone like a genius until he acts like a fool; never underestimate your adversary.'

The morning ritual was being brought to a close and everyone was dispersing. One militant had his finger jammed down the end of his AK, another was play-shooting imaginary somethings out of the trees and a third was actually looking down the barrel of his. I kid you not, and it was a sight I was to see often. We all looked back at each other with bewildered shakes of the head.

'Let's stick a pin in it,' said Plooy.

I waved a hand as though to dismiss the whole idea. 'I'd like to stick a pin in these bloody bites and save them for later,' I said. But Noor was right; the main players in Camp Horrid were not stupid.

'We need to get clean,' said Plooy. 'Bob needs to wash his nose, you've got to keep those bites from going septic and I'm starting to stink. We saw some of the militants washing in the river yesterday, let's ask if we can too.' We all pulled ourselves up and Eagle Eye was instantly blocking us off, while Gastro Pod was balancing precariously on a tree stump sleeping off last night's over-indulgence. We asked Eagle Eye if we could wash in the river. He eyed us suspiciously for a moment before heading off across the yard, beckoning with his rifle for us to follow. We did.

Eagle Eye ducked into the rec room and a minute later came back out with the Secretary.

'What you want?' he spat with an angry face. This wasn't what we expected and suddenly a wash didn't seem so important.

'Could we all have a bath in the river? We need to get clean,' Noor asked. Well, you would have thought Noor had just asked for a ride on his wife. The Secretary exploded in a fit of rage, shouting and balling his fists; the rest of the camp had all stopped to watch, some of the guards levelling their weapons in our direction. We backed away, keeping our hands up, and kept going all the way across the yard to the rubbish area and sat down. The Secretary, fully vented, ducked away into the rec room, with the rest of the camp going back to whatever they were up to before.

'What the fuck just happened then?' I asked.

'Sonova bitch,' said Bob.

'No idea,' said Plooy. Noor was quiet. We later found out that the Secretary and his gang were especially suspicious of us as we were divers. They thought that we had magic powers and that we could stay under the water for hours; they were right of course, but

73

not without our equipment. They weren't going to let us in the river to have a wash for fear of us swimming to freedom.

The rest of the day was spent sitting by the rubbish pile and watching the ebb and flow of the river, none of us having much left to say. I think it was starting to sink into everybody just how much control these guys had over us. We couldn't wash, eat, drink, walk, sleep or do anything without the express say-so from the Secretary, and that control included life or death; it was a sobering thought.

The rest of the day passed in near-total silence, as the mood among us was very sombre. Three long shadows cast over us, and we looked up. The cook was displaying his proud smile; I don't know what was smiling more, his eyes or his mouth, but it was nice to see a happy face. He had two of his goons with him carrying four plates of food. We thanked him and settled back down to eat. We studied the food as we let out a collective sigh.

'You know it's Sunday, don't you?' Noor asked.

'Yes, we know,' came the reply.

'What I wouldn't do for a roast beef dinner, Yorkshire puds and a couple of pints,' I said. That was it; the flood gates were open, we all sat talking about our favourite food and what we missed the most, getting hungrier and hungrier with every revelation. Plooy fancied himself a full rack of marinated spare ribs cooked on the braai with a side order of fries and buttered corn on the cob, washed down with a large brandy and coke. Noor was quick to put in his order for a coq au vin with tiramisu for dessert and Irish coffee. Bob, well, he would be happy with a bucket of fried chicken, some corn bread and a cup full of quarters for the slot machines. I popped in the first mouthful.

'Mmmmmm, nice,' I said.

CHAPTER NINE

POLITICS

In the same time zone some three thousand miles away my family was also preparing to have something to eat. Mum had just dished up one of her famous lamb roast dinners with mint sauce and all the trimmings.

My brother John had left his vigil at the bar of the Tavern and made the journey, a brisk walk up the hill, for some much-needed sustenance. George, his son who was nine at the time going on ten, was already waiting for him up there.

The table was set and my old man was carving the leg of lamb, slicing through the crispy skin into the juicy meat within, while my mother stacked the plates with piping hot roast teddies and steaming fresh vegetables. The carved meat was served and lush thick gravy poured generously over. My parents, brother and nephew were all ready to tuck in when the telephone rang.

'Bloody hell, who's that? Why do people always wait until ruddy dinner time before they phone?' grumbled my old man.

'Quick, pick up the phone, it may be someone about Philip,' shouted Mum.

'Oh, I'll get it then, shall I?' He put down his knife and fork and went to the phone on the sideboard.

'Hello, who is it?' There was a short pause and then my old man cupped the phone with his hand and turned to the dinner party. 'It's the Foreign Office, they have some news on Philip. I'll stick it on speaker phone so we can all hear.' Dad pushed the button for the speaker option and replaced the phone. 'Yes, go ahead,' he shouted, not realising that you could still speak at the same volume as when you had the receiver by your mouth.

'We've just received some information that you may find upsetting. MEND have issued a statement. It says that if their demands for the release of Alhaji Dokubo-Asari, who is being held in custody by the Nigerian authorities, are not met by 29th May, they will start executing all foreign hostages. The Foreign Office is still actively doing all it can to secure the safe release of your son.'

With that the conversation was over, along with the dinner party. All plates were pushed into the centre of the table, as the thought of any food was now quite obscene.

'The 29th is the day after tomorrow,' said my quick-thinking old man. Panic swept through the dining room and an argument ensued; only George was left with the good sense to pop a piece of lamb in his mouth.

'What did you put it on speaker phone for? George heard all that,' John demanded.

'I thought it was going to be good news, that they were going to release him,' the old man flapped. Dad and my brother continued to shout at each other until Mum stepped in.

'Stop your bickering, you two, you're upsetting George.' George had just swallowed yet another piece of juicy lamb. 'We need to decide what we're going to tell Sophie.'

They debated what to do for an hour or so; the ruined dinners were scraped into the bin. The old man was against telling Sophie, but John was adamant that they should. George was tucking into a bowl of apple and blackberry crumble and custard, so the final vote was left to Mother. 'We tell her, she's got a right to know, and if the press get hold of it, well, the news is better coming from us.' The decision was made. Mum and Dad jumped into the Volvo and drove round to see Sophie, who was having dinner at her parents' place.

76

Sophie had just finished her roast when she answered the door to my concerned-looking parents. It's not an easy job passing on bad news, and I can only guess at what was going through my mum and dad's minds at the time.

'Hello Mick, Sue, what are you doing here?' asked Sophie, having a hunch that some bad news was going to follow. Mum delivered the news with as much sensitivity as humanly possible; Sophie stood, head spinning, for a minute or two, then rushed to the bathroom and hurled up her dinner. It would appear that Plooy, Noor, Bob and I weren't the only ones today not to receive our recommended daily amount of calories.

Sophie was quick to turn detective; she had studied to become a forensic scientist so she slipped into the role with ease. As soon as my parents had left and she had recovered sufficiently from the shock, she raced upstairs to the computer to go online. She put the name she had been given into Google, and after a little digging Sophie was able to put together a thumbnail sketch of one Alhaji Dokubo-Asari.

Born in 1964, he was christened Melford Dokubo Goodhead Jr, and was raised in a middle-class Christian household. He belonged to the ethnic group Ijaw, into which most Niger Delta residents would fall. In 2003 he formed the Niger Delta People's Volunteer Force, (NDPVF). Originally a youth group, it became involved in oil siphoning, kidnap, extortion and war with other militant factions. NDPVF struggled for fairer distribution of wealth in oil-rich areas. He was arrested in September 2005 (the same year MEND became active) for treason, after declaring 'all-out war' against the government. At the time he was currently being held on remand.

CHAPTER TEN

ESCAPE

We were all still bitching about the quality of the food as we rounded up the last of the stray grains of rice with our fingers. With the plates clean we took them back to the cookhouse, where I guess they washed them ready for tomorrow, and thanked the chef.

Although the food here was falling well short of what is considered healthy we still needed to stay active and alert, so we had decided to do laps of the yard as the sun began to go down on another day. It was not a large yard, and at a slow walking pace it only took around fifty seconds to complete a full lap. The ground was hard and barren, with very sparse greenery and just the odd outcrop of dead tree roots and stumps. Round and round we would walk, always in a clockwise direction; Eagle Eye and Gastro Pod must have thought we were mad. Bob never joined us either, preferring to stay resting by the rubbish pile. We were already lapping into double figures when Plooy quietly started singing. At work he would often come out with an old classic that would suit any situation; he was a good singer and always managed to infect those around him.

'We've gotta get outa this place... if it's the last thing we ever do.'

As we continued round Noor joined in and then I did too, all three of us singing along to that old classic by the Animals. And then it struck me like a golf ball to the forehead.

'Let's plan an escape,' I exclaimed.

'Sshh! Keep it down,' said Plooy.

'Well, listen,' I continued in a hushed tone as we walked, 'we form an escape committee, just the three of us. We put our heads together and come up with a plan, what we got to lose?'

'I'm in,' said Noor. 'Sounds better than your earlier idea of writing love letters to the Bristol pilots.'

'Lekka (nice) idea,' added Plooy; 'if nothing else it will give us something to do, keep us busy and keep up morale. You never know, we might even find a way out of this shit-hole.' We carried on lapping with a new spring in our step and our spirits already lifted. I hoped the militants didn't notice.

Sachin and Aditya were already in their cell as they were venturing out less and less, and it was time we went back to ours. The nights were long what with our midnight visitors, but we still felt safer in our cell during the wild parties. Eagle Eye and Gastro Pod took us all to the toilet, and I enjoyed a cigarette before bed; it was my last one. I scrunched up the empty packet, tossed it on top of the mounting pile of rubbish and turned to join the others in the cell. I was thinking of quitting anyway.

CHAPTER ELEVEN

TOM, DICK & HARRY

The following morning, after yet another night of torment, we had gathered again on the edge of the yard and settled down on the baked earth as the drums picked up their rhythm. Last night was nowhere near as bad as the ones that had gone before. The music had remained at full volume, as was Blood Diamond that was still showing on the telly, but the attacks aimed at us were far fewer, and when they did come they lacked conviction; only twice did they come into the cell and half-heartedly slap us about the heads and stick guns in our faces. Prada was nowhere to be seen last night and we think that perhaps this was the reason; he does seem to be the head and the venom of this particular snake. Of course we had absolutely no idea where he had gone, but the longer he was away the better for us. Sachin and Aditya had told us that Prada and his gang left them alone and never so much as looked at them in a threatening manner all the time they'd been here. This information left me wondering whether we had 'victim' written on our foreheads, or whether we were antagonising them in some way.

While keeping one eye on the morning ritual that was going on in the centre, we focused our energy on more pressing matters. Plooy, Noor and I were still on a bit of a high from our newly formed escape committee. We still knew that the best chance we had of getting home safely to our families was if MEND's demands, whenever they made them, were met quickly and they then released us into the care of the correct authorities. We also appreciated that if you were going to get kidnapped anywhere in the world, Nigeria was probably one of the better places. We suspected that even an outfit like MEND, which supposedly operated under a blanket of political motives, was still basically a business and wanted one thing and one thing only, a big pay day. But there was still every chance that the milk could turn sour. I have since learnt, after reading 'Ross Kemp on Pirates' that more people have died due to piracy in Nigeria than anywhere else in the world. So that milk had not only every chance of turning sour but of turning to cheese.

Our escape committee would not only boost morale, it would also keep the mind on its toes and help pass the time. We wanted to take back some sort of control over our lives and maybe get the hell out of here, so Operation Tom, Dick and Harry was now under way.

The operation involved each of us over the next couple of days coming up with an escape plan. When we had each dreamed up our plan, we would get together and decide which one was most likely to succeed. Then all three of us would work on the chosen plan and fine-tune it. Then, on an agreed date, we would go 'over the wire' as one.

It had boosted my morale already just thinking about it; I felt a bit more positive. We were even beginning to crack jokes with each other and have a bit of a laugh, in between scratching our mosquito bites. In an environment like this you could really notice every second of every minute, every minute of every hour – time took on a new meaning. The days would drag on at a sloth's pace if we just sat around feeling sorry for ourselves.

Noor's plan was called 'Tom', Plooy's was called 'Dick' and my plan, when I came up with it, would be called 'Harry'. My competitive streak was beginning to ooze to the surface and I really wanted my plan to be chosen, so I had to make it sound brilliant and as simple as shortcake. The challenge had been set and looking at my friends' faces I could tell that like me, they were up for it.

81

The first drops of rain cut short the drums and everyone scurried inside the huts to take shelter. Although very hot, West Africa and especially Nigeria is notoriously wet. With its tropical climate, even outside the rainy season you can pretty much rely on a short deluge most days. It doesn't just rain here, it hammers down. Noor and Bob were sitting on the mattress with me and Plooy standing, looking out of the window, watching the downpour. It was running off the corrugated roof in torrents and we leaned out, cupping our hands to catch some, and then drinking heavily; we were also using it to hand-wash ourselves. The whole camp changed during a rain storm; the only noise you could hear was the thundering of rain on the tin roof as if a heavy metal drummer was up there. All it took was a bolt of forked lightning to split the sky and a clap of thunder, and the militants would huddle together in the rec room filled with superstitious dread, not daring to venture out until the storm had passed, and leaving us to relax a little.

'Noor, Bob, do you want to swap places so you can drink some more?' Plooy asked.

'Na, I'm full,' Bob replied.

'Me an' all,' said Noor.

Looking through the window at the green foliage against the heavy rain suddenly reminded me of home: walking the Jack Russells across the fields with Sophie and being caught out in a storm, getting soaked through and running back to the house to sit by the fire and enjoy a nice cup of tea. When everything is stripped away from you it's just your family and your loved ones you miss, and the very basics in life, like walking the dogs, a cup of tea, lying in a nice safe warm bed intertwined and snuggling up with your loved one; nothing materialistic comes into it.

'Do you think our families back home have been informed?' said Bob in his deep southern drawl. I wasn't the only one thinking of home; whenever we had a quiet spell I think we all went there.

'I reckon so,' answered Plooy.

'Bet they're all worried sick,' Noor said.

'Mmmmm,' I agreed. I was still walking the dogs in the field and getting wet, when a sudden thought hit me. 'Shit!' I said. 'About two weeks ago Sophie booked up for us to go away for a holiday on the 18th June, three weeks away. Was supposed to be a treat after me getting my first proper diving job.'

'Where to?' asked Plooy. We were still leaning out of the window, watching the rain.

'Maldives. Nice, hey? I can forget that now, though – extended jungle holiday for us four in the Delta, sharing the honeymoon suite.' We all laughed at this as the storm clouds moved over and away, and the sun came back out. In ten minutes the camp would be bone-dry again, as though it hadn't rained for weeks.

'Now it's stopped I'm off to the little boys' room,' announced Noor. 'Where's that Gastro Pod got to?' I turned to see Noor's back leaving the cell. Eagle Eye was just outside the door and escorted Noor to the river bank; I think Gastro Pod was still glued to Blood Diamond. Bob was still enjoying a bit of room on the mattress, and I was chatting to Plooy about our families back home.

'Come to think of it mate, my mum and dad are due to go on holiday around the same time; hope I haven't ruined their plans,' I said to Plooy.

Plooy was then halfway through telling me how he thought his wife and his immediate family would be coping with all this, when a panicked Noor came running back into the cell shouting, waving his hands up and down and indicating for us to hit the deck.

'Get down, dynam...' he didn't get to finish as a massive boom shook the cell. We all dropped to the ground, grabbing each other as we landed on Bob in a heap. Struggling to work out what had happened, I rolled away from the group and tried to stand up as another shock wave ripped through the cell, *boom*. Back on my knees, I just concentrated on getting air back in my lungs; I shook my head and stared at Noor.

'What did you say?' I shouted as my ears were still ringing.

'It's Prada, he's back, he's outside with some of the goon squad and some sticks of dynamite.'

'Lekka!' shouted Plooy.

'On my way back from having a piss I saw him setting up the sticks outside. I only just made it back in to warn you.'

'That sonova bitch Prada is gonna kill one of us soon,' said Bob, sitting back against the cell wall.

'I blew up my nephew once,' I shouted as my ears were still ringing. Plooy and Noor also sat down against the wall before asking me to repeat myself.

'I said, I blew up my nephew once.'

'I know, I heard, just thought I hadn't,' said Plooy. So I told them the story to take our minds off of Camp Horrid for a bit.

The year was 2004, the year of the Madrid bombings, when 191 people were blown up by four separate blasts on Spanish trains. Dr. Harold Shipman was found hanged in Wakefield Prison; he had been convicted of killing fifteen people but authorities feared the true number could be as high as two hundred and fifty. Ireland called an outright ban on smoking in pubs and clubs, setting an international trend. The underdogs Greece beat Portugal to win the European Cup. George W. Bush was re-elected to run another term, while his nemesis Saddam Hussein went on trial for the murder of one hundred and forty-eight people in the village of Dujail. In the same year I was

84

sharing a house with my girlfriend Sophie, my brother and his son and a dog called Alfie that my boss had given me instead of a cash bonus.

The nephew I blew up was called George; he was a terrific little chap, totally fearless, with a good sense of humour. He was just how a seven-year-old should be. I hadn't known him long as he had spent his first seven years over the other side of the world. He was a little Kiwi and we needed to bond; I also needed to show him just what was expected of him if he was to mix with lads from England. We got along great, and I took him under my wing to pass on all my knowledge of how to make a young boy's world complete. The Master Jedi schooling his young apprentice, if you will. I taught him how to load, aim and fire an airgun. We took Alfie, my Jack Russell, for walks and selected good branches from which to fashion bows and arrows, and then spent time honing George's archery skills. He was a good pupil. In the fields behind our house in Devon I taught him how to make and set off small and inoffensive incendiary devices, another skill essential to a young lad's upbringing. On one such occasion I made a couple of miscalculations, one being the size of the device, and the other the extent of the blast zone. We should have been standing about a hundred feet away, but were only standing off about fifty. When the bomb went off there was a much bigger bang than I had anticipated, and debris and shrapnel shot a hundred feet into the air. The neighbouring horses galloped for their lives and George dropped like a sack of manure at my feet, clutching his head in his hands and screaming, 'My face, my face, my face!'

Holy shit, I'd really done it this time. I picked him up by his shoulders and pulled his hands away. I couldn't see his face; it was covered in blood. I'd just blown up my brother's son.

I picked him up and started up the field towards the house to get George some medical attention. Sophie had heard the big bang from

85

the kitchen and was already running down the back garden to investigate, with a look of panic on her pretty face. When she saw the state of George her face turned to thunder; veins were popping out of her forehead as she spat, 'You bloody fool... you... you...' She snatched away the bloody mess that was once my nephew, and headed back towards the house.

As my eyes followed her I saw my brother standing at the back doorstep, hands on his hips, waiting to see what all the fuss was about. I smiled ruefully and shrugged my shoulders. Sophie and John took the little man inside, leaving me in the garden. Alfie sat by my feet looking up at me with an expression on his face that said, 'I still love you', so I took him for a walk. It was best I stayed away for a bit, and gave everyone time to calm down.

After a couple of hours hunting rabbits with Alfie, I started making my way home. I couldn't stay out of the way forever, but I wasn't looking forward to finding out what had happened to George. If he had lost his sight, or was permanently scarred, I would never forgive myself. When I made it home and went inside I was pleased to find that no-one was throwing stuff at me or hurling insults; that would have been no more than I deserved, but it was a good start. John and Sophie had cleaned up his face to find only superficial wounds. A piece of shrapnel had hit his top lip and gum and then shot up his nose, making a mess but leaving no lasting damage as it was easily pulled out with a pair of tweezers. I was off the hook for now but had to promise no more bomb-making, which I did, whilst crossing my fingers and giving George a wink.

The next day I went some way in making it up to George by giving him some shooting practice with the air rifle. John wasn't keen but I told him I'd be careful, and that we would only shoot targets from the safety of my bedroom window.

'Come on bruv,' I pleaded. 'What's the worst that could happen? I need to make it up to the little fella.' John caved in.

George's aim was improving with nearly every shot; I couldn't work out whether he was a natural or I was a brilliant teacher. During one of George's many trips out to the garden to check his progress on the target, I shot him. It was one of those one-in-a-million shots. George had just passed the steps at the back where his dad was making some repairs to the door frame, and was heading towards the target. John called out for him to be careful and reminded him that playing with his uncle could be dangerous, to which George replied over his shoulder, 'No worries Dad,' in his little Kiwi accent.

I shouted down, 'I resent that, bruv.'

George checked his shots and gave me the thumbs up. We had a pair of binoculars in the bedroom for checking the target, but George liked to check it up close and personal. He then made his way back to his dad and was asking what he was up to and whether he needed any help. I made my shot just as John told George that he didn't, and that he could go back upstairs and carry on his schooling. My shot hit smack in the middle of the target – it would have been a bull's-eye – and ricocheted off the MDF board that the target was made from; it never happened before. It flew back up towards the house and embedded itself in the soft flesh of George's left buttock. George grabbed his backside and let out a high-pitched scream as only a seven-year-old could: 'I'm hit!' For the second time in just over twenty-four hours I shouted out, 'Medic!' as I ran down the stairs to check out the damage I had once again caused to my nephew.

It didn't look good, so I checked my options. Alfie was already sitting at the front door with his 'I still love you' look across his face. I bolted out of the front door with Alfie at my heels to chase rabbits for an hour or so, until the heat had died down.

That was it for me and George though; I was officially banned from playing with him unless properly supervised by a responsible adult, by order of George's dad and grandma.

'Goddam sonova bitch,' Bob whispered.

'Not lekka Phil, poor little lighty,' said Plooy.

'Well fuck me, if we need to blast our way out, you can be the bang man,' said a rather bemused Noor, still shaking his head.

'You were listening to the story weren't you, Noor? The part where I got it all wrong and blew up the good guy. I am certainly no Uni-bomber.'

'Yes mate, I was listening, but these are extreme times and we may need a Uni-bomber to go with them. Besides, in case you hadn't noticed, health and safety is no longer our biggest concern.' So it was settled there and then: I was to be in charge of explosives. Not that we had any.

Prada pointed his AK47 through the window and slowly pointed it at each of us while mouthing '*bang*', several goons crowding round him with wicked faces. The four of us backed up further against the cell wall and held our breath. Prada flashed us his shark smile and was gone. We let go of the breath we were holding and our light mood with it, and just sat for a while.

After another horrible meal we took to walking the yard. It was just the three of us, as Bob, Sachin and Aditya were sitting by the rubbish with Gastro Pod and Eagle Eye close by. Frog Face sat on a fuel drum which was stacked with the rest near the moorings. He was smoking and drinking from a bottle of beer while playing music on his stereo; Frog Face spent most of his time like this. Last night after I smoked my last cigarette I told myself I was going to quit, but watching old Frog Face pull on that smoke got my cravings all in a caper and I just knew I had to have one.

'Back in a minute,' I announced as I peeled away from Plooy and Noor and headed over to Frog Face to beg for a smoke. As I got to within a few paces he sensed me and reached for his AK. 'Fuck me', I thought, 'all this for a cigarette. It's amazing what lengths us smokers will go to for a fix.' I was about to try and ponce a smoke from the armed getaway driver of a snatch squad. I put one hand up, palm out in a placating gesture, while I mimicked a smoking action with the other, and then went on to speak to him as though he was from Mars.

'Please boss, cigarette, I beg you.' Frog Face didn't speak a word of English but he got the message. He leaned his rifle back against the fuel drum and looked at me for a minute, tilting his big ugly head to one side.

'Please,' I pleaded, putting even more desperation into my voice. Noor and Plooy had stopped walking and were watching from the yard. Frog Face grunted something and then reached into the pockets of his tatty jeans before pulling out a packet of Marlboro Reds. He banged the packet against his thigh twice and popped one in his wide mouth, lighting it from the one he had finished smoking, and then offered me one. I pulled one out and put it between my lips and said thank you, but he kept the packet there. I hesitated for a few seconds, so he pulled out two more himself and gave them to me. I quickly smuggled them to my coverall pocket and took a light from him; then I nodded a silent 'thank you' before turning back to catch up with Noor and Plooy, who had continued lapping. My heart racing, I pulled up alongside them.

'Enjoying that smoke are you?' asked Plooy.

'It's bloody fantastic,' I said as I exhaled a big cloud. Plooy chuckled and patted me on the back and we started lapping the yard again. I wasn't going to be able to give up in here, that was for sure. Bob had gone back to the cell, no doubt to take advantage and stretch out on the whole mattress. Sachin and Aditya had gone back to theirs as well. The rec room was bursting tonight as a new DVD called Air Force One was playing. It was the story of a mid-air hi-jacking involving the President of the United States of America. Gastro Pod had quickly forgotten us and was sitting among the rag-tag audience, but Eagle Eye was pacing his perimeters and watching us closely.

We hummed Plooy's song 'We gotta get out of here', and then we started singing. We kept that up for a few more laps before the conversation turned to escaping. Plooy hit us with a question.

'What do you think is our biggest danger if we escape?'

'Getting caught,' I answered quickly, as though it were some kind of pop quiz.

'No,' said Noor, 'we get caught, we simply get caught and we're no worse off. Like anywhere you're incarcerated, escaping is frowned upon and punishment severe. I'm not sure what this lot would do if we were caught escaping, I'm sure it would be harsh but certainly not death. At some time they'll still want a ransom for us. If we get found by some other outfit it may be a case of out of the frying pan into the fire, but again I think we'll survive. I think our biggest danger will be getting lost in the jungle and just perishing; it's a very harsh place.'

'Noor's right. I think our biggest threat comes from stumbling about in the jungle.' This was from Plooy. 'There will be poisonous snakes, spiders and God knows what else, and we will have to find food as we go. It's not going to be, how do you English say? A walk in the park.'

'No, it will definitely be no walk in the park, mate, but this is no picnic either; we'll adapt and we will make it.' This last bit I said with utter conviction.

'I don't doubt it, Phil, but it's best to plan from all angles; we must try and think of everything,' said Plooy.

'If a snake bit me, would you suck the poison out?' I asked.

'Fuck off, you've got no chance,' said Noor. 'What about Bob, do we bring him with us?'

'No, he's too unfit, he'll never make it, and nor will we if he's with us,' I said. 'Besides, he'll be happy with the mattress to himself.'

'I agree, just the three of us,' said Plooy.

'Me too,' nodded Noor, 'still just the three of us then.' We finished a few more laps and then turned in to kick an already-snoozing Bob off the mattress. We re-arranged ourselves so that we all had an equal share. I was back in the corner leaning my head against the wall and listening to the noise outside; the party was just beginning to start.

A cigarette was flicked through the window and hit the opposite wall, showering the floor in bright red-hot embers, and then the window was filled with faces and guns. Tonight the party was going to be right outside the window. We all moved, shuffling in closer to each other, and dropped our chins on to our chests; it looked like another long night. The three sisters were out there with Prada, I could just make out their ugly faces with some of his gang, and they all seemed in high spirits. Another cigarette was flicked through the window followed by a sprayed mouthful of kai-kai.

These were overwhelmingly miserable times for us and very frightening. We were totally at their mercy, they knew it and so did we. Very quietly, almost in a whisper, I heard Plooy humming 'We've gotta get out of this place, if it's the last thing we ever do'. I heard Noor start up next to him and join in. And then we all chorused together, as quiet as mice:

'Cause girl, there's a better life for me and you.'

CHAPTER TWELVE

DRESS CODE

It was a carbon copy of the drumming session from the first few mornings, and the ritual was brought to an end with the usual enthusiasm and shouts of 'Isowanna, Isowanna'. As the militants dissolved from the yard to go about their daily business of getting stoned, the Secretary, BA and Denzel marched purposefully over, all with cruel, lop-sided smiles and a fake gangster strut. The Secretary looked at us each in turn with mild contempt, almost as though it was too much effort for him to deal with us this morning. 'It's time for your wash,' was all that he said.

Now I should have welcomed a good wash, for I hadn't had one for a while now and probably stank like a dead polecat. Especially as we had asked him for one the other day and he had rebuked us; he had obviously gone away and given it some thought, but I had a bad feeling about 'our wash.' It was very important to keep ourselves as clean as we possibly could, to try to stave off any infection. Even the smallest of cuts out here could get infected and turn nasty fast if we neglected them. Some of my mosquito bites were already looking a little anti-social, so I was just going to have to get on with it.

BA and Denzel led us to the pit behind Hut Two. The water pit was exactly that, a hole in the ground some ten feet deep with about a foot of dirty, muddy water at the bottom. The pit took some getting into and out of as its walls were steep and very slippery, but some of the goon squad were already in there, baling water out into buckets for us to wash with. When all the bags of drinking water ran out these guys actually drank the stuff; one teaspoon of this would probably be enough to have us bent over the toilet for a week, if we were lucky. However, BA had conjured up a bottle of disinfectant from where I don't know, but once he had added a glug of this to the bucket it was just about good enough for washing in. I just hoped we would never have to drink it.

The goons handed us a bucket of silty water with the added capful of disinfectant, which we were very grateful for, and a cup for pouring the water over our heads. We walked past the third and last hut to the wash area. Many of the camp members had turned out to watch the white men have their first wash; they were sitting about in their social groups, smoking and drinking and getting ready to mock and poke fun.

We let Bob go first, as he was the eldest. The rest of us waited in line for our turn, and I for one was dreading it. Just over the other side of the clearing, sitting in the shade of some mangrove trees, were the three sisters who had propositioned me the other night. I could only guess why the sisters had singled me out for a bit of sexual harassment and not the others. Bob finished his wash with as much dignity as he could muster, and he did himself proud.

It was Noor's turn next, and when he pulled off his coveralls and the militants spotted his tattoo they all got very excited. Noor had a large mermaid on his shoulder blade and they didn't like it one little bit. In their world Noor's tattoo was an evil spirit called a Mummy Water, and they were very wary of it. A couple of men even walked off in disgust, but most just got angry. Poor Noor was in danger of getting lynched. He kept his head down and carried on with his washing, trying to ignore all the commotion that was going on around him. He did well, setting a very fast time in the process.

Plooy was next up to the ocky and got on with it like a true professional. He was defrocked, washed, rinsed and back in line smelling like a piece of hospital furniture in what must have been a record time, and all done I might add in a very respectable manner. Must have been all those safari holidays in the bush he'd taken.

It was now my turn. I stripped off my filthy coveralls and stood naked where my friends had been washing just before me. The ground had turned a little soft and slippery where the water had worked into the hard-baked earth, causing cool mud to squelch up between my toes. I felt a little self-conscious and more than a little vulnerable, and as I emptied the first cup from the bucket over my head, I realised that the coldness of the dirty water, combined with my nervousness at being on display, was having a direct effect on my body. My ball-sack tightened into a leathery pouch and my bollocks began to constrict, retreating back inside my stomach. My penis then started to wither away. I thought I could hear the sounds of hoots and jeers from the crowd, and I was very conscious of the number of eyes on me, especially from the three sisters under the trees.

In their leisure time quite a few of the militants chose to walk around naked, which is fair enough considering the stifling heat and lack of good clothes boutiques in the area. But right now wherever I looked I seemed to be confronted by a super-sized penis; they seemed to be everywhere. I was feeling very inadequate. In an attempt to stop my pecker shrinking any further I tried to think of anything other than big black cocks, the cold water and numerous sets of eyes looking down upon my naked form. It's strange how the human brain functions. With all that we were going through, and being surrounded by trigger-happy, big-peckered gunmen, all I could worry about at that moment was the size of my manhood. I have no idea why I looked over at the three sisters at this moment, but the split second that I did I caught them laughing to each other and blowing me a kiss. I looked away fast, but the damage had already been done.

I washed as quickly and as thoroughly as I could, paying special attention to my sore weeping bites, rinsed and then handed the cracked bucket and chipped cup back to a beaming BA. I turned and stood with the others to dry off, trying to look as nonchalant as possible, as if I always stood naked in public drip-drying in the sun.

A laughing Denzel and BA walked over with a very slight lad of no more than fourteen, who had some clothes and flip-flops for us. The young lad then disappeared with our old dirty clothes, with the promise of cleaning and returning them, but that would be the last time we would see them. I had to wrestle back my work boots, though, as I couldn't afford to lose them. If we ever had to walk out of here, flip-flops just weren't going to cut it. BA and Denzel gave up and let me keep my boots; it was only a small victory but a very important one for me. In an environment like this my boots were priceless. Bob gave his up, but Noor and Plooy only had flip-flops to start with.

The new clothes we'd been given were comical to say the least; I was convinced that they were straight out of an Oxfam charity box. Someone here had a sense of humour for sure. Bob was given a pair of three-quarter-length stripy pyjama bottoms and matching top that were a size and a bit too small. Noor was slam-dunked in an American basketball strip, a bright purple Knicks vest top and green shorts. It was a good fit but didn't offer much in the way of protection from the NAFy. Plooy was dressed in what I called a holiday outfit: a smart denim shirt with a patch of chequered material across the shoulders, and a pair of Tom Jones tight-fitting jeans. I definitely came off best for once. I was handed a pair of green combat trousers and a shirt to match; apart from the Nigerian military insignia on one of the arms I could have been an officer of the British Army. I felt like an extra from the Great Escape. BA came up to me to boast that he had personally butchered the Nigerian soldier who once wore it, little scamp!

We looked like something out of the Village People as we all made our way over to the other side of the camp. When we got there we were already sweaty again and caked in dust, with the freshness we had felt after our pit-water-and-disinfectant shower now just a distant memory. On entering the cell we noticed that an extra mattress had been dumped on the floor with a couple of mosquito nets rolled up on top. The Secretary snuck up behind us. 'Feel free, they are yours, make yourselves welcome.' We felt about as welcome as a turd floating in a fruit salad, but we turned and thanked him all the same and then started re-arranging the cell. Plooy and I took the new mattress and set it up against the far wall, on the opposite side to Noor's and Bob's. We stretched out our new mosquito net and tied it so it hung down covering the mattress, using bits of old string and twine that were lying around the yard. The net had a few tears here and there and a couple of holes, so we set about mending them as well.

We came to the conclusion that the wash we were allowed earlier and this latest act of kindness were a very good sign, and meant that none of us would be killed just yet. We busied ourselves making the cell as comfy as possible. Our good mood was short-lived, though, when Bob pointed out that the only reason they had provided us with all these home comforts was that we were going to stay for a very long time. Yeah, thanks for poisoning the well, Bob, but he did have a point.

Aditya and Sachin came through to our cell from theirs which was next door; they already had nets and even a mattress each, they were living like royalty. Sachin was standing up quite well to the hardships, but Aditya, the older man, was starting to look quite ill. I got a sudden movement in my bowels and my net-darning duties were hastily put aside. When you've gotta go, you've gotta go. I hadn't had a crap since I was captured, perhaps due to nerves from being in a strange place with strange people, or the very questionable diet we were on, or even because for the last few days I had had all the shit scared right out of me; whatever the reason I now needed to go, and quickly.

I left Plooy finishing up with the net and shot out of the cell, squeezing past the two Indians who were chatting to Bob and Noor, to find Eagle Eye standing alert and ready for anything. He needed to get out a bit more, did Eagle Eye, he took all this militancy stuff far too seriously. I quickly explained my needs to him and he nodded towards the river bank, as he was still on his vow of silence. He followed me as I headed that way.

As I neared the river's edge I spied a perfect spot for doing my business, as the mud crabs all darted as one down their holes. There was a tree growing out from the river, with high roots that sat just above the water, and just enough room for my feet to get a good purchase; so I perched on that and squatted. Now, having a piss under armed guard was not much fun, but having a crap, well, that was just downright uncomfortable. However, I lost all my inhibitions as I strained, and Eagle Eye didn't so much as blink during the process. I started to evacuate my bowels neatly between my feet into the river. I thought to myself that I was not exactly doing things in the correct order; I should have had a crap first and then showered, as there wasn't any toilet paper to wipe myself with. This was going to have to be a scoop with the fingers job, left hand of course with some river water.

As I squatted there the branch I was holding for balance snapped, causing me to stumble backwards. If I hadn't managed to grab hold of the main trunk I would have splash-landed in my mess; it was slack water, so the flow of the river was still leaving my mess right where it landed. I now had crap on my buttock and down my thigh, with splashes on my calf and ankle. This was going to take some getting used to.

I finished my business and scooped with three cupped fingers. It was a weird sensation. From the day you get out of nappies you're told not to touch your own crap, or anybody else's come to that, and here I was going against all my instincts, scooping the stuff right out from between my buttocks and washing it off my leg. It was horrific, and as I caught a whiff of it in the back of my throat I started to retch. I have a pretty hardy stomach but one thing has always got me, and that's the smell of shit.

I flicked the crap from my fingers out towards the river and frantically washed my hands and arse. When I had finished and had stopped retching I stood to pull up my trousers, wipe my streaming eyes and runny nose and then inspect my business. Lying on the surface of the river was a neon-yellow liquid mess that resembled radioactive waste. I turned and rushed as fast as Eagle Eye would allow back to the cell, to warn the others that things weren't quite as they should be with my constitution.

The others eased my worry and put my mind at rest, as we all reported the same bright neon-yellow colour. They wrongly thought that they were the only ones suffering from strange-coloured crap, and were too embarrassed to mention it, so were as pleased as me to find out that it was a joint effort. We put it down to the complex diet of rice, beans and fear.

As we were admiring our homely new cell, we heard an outboard engine heading our way up the river. Commander Jackson called us and the two Indians outside, and told us to stand and wait together on the edge of the yard. Everyone in the camp was rushing about and seemed to be on edge; the mood of the camp was changing fast, and we were getting very adept at detecting the slightest change in the atmosphere.

The gunboat banked around the corner into view. The General was standing tall in the middle of the boat, surrounded by his bodyguards, who were displaying an awesome amount of fire-power. The tension in camp was there to taste. We instinctively closed in together for safety as the gunboat was tied up and the General and his gang entered the camp. 'Isowanna, Isowanna,' he cried.

'Wonna' the rest of the camp chorused.

The General was handed a bottle of Monkey Tail and a spliff that had already been lit by one of his underlings, and he marched straight past us without so much as a nod. He was dressed in the same outfit as the other day, and his facial expression was cold and business-like. Commander Jackson, BA and Denzel followed him, dragging Sachin and Aditya out of our view and into the jungle where that horrible A-frame stood, leaving us surrounded by the General's bodyguards.

We tried to relax as the bodyguards engaged us in conversation but the whole situation was quite tense. They were the same bodyguards that had always accompanied the General, but they had never spoken to us before; they spoke good English and were freakishly polite. One of the bodyguards wanted to know where we all came from. I replied that I was from England, and he immediately went on to tell us how many times he had been to England and how much he enjoyed it there; he was studying at a drama school in London to become an actor. That's excellent news, I thought to myself, as I watched him chewing a match and repositioning his pump-action shotgun over his shoulder; these people are breezing in and out of England whenever the fancy takes them. He even boasted a genuine UK passport.

His mate on the other side of us wanted to know how Plooy had such plump, fit-looking calf muscles, and bent down to squeeze one.

99

This guy was a bit of a worry; he looked and behaved like a total psycho. We had already got the impression that he was quite intimate with the General, who was certainly from a similar mould. They both shared that East African bone structure: high cheek bones and elegantly tall, quite different from your typical Nigerian physique, which in comparison is solid and stocky. They had an almost Somalian or Ethiopian look about them, so we called this bodyguard the Somali.

Plooy looked down at the Somali, still holding onto his leg, and told him he used to play a lot of tennis. The Somali seemed satisfied with this explanation and went on to inform Plooy that he would like to eat him. This was said very seriously and was even backed up with a hand motion to his mouth, like a third-world beggar would make to put across the point that he's hungry. The Somali brought to our attention the fact that both he and the General enjoyed the delights of human flesh from time to time. All four of us were very concerned about this new piece of information and were not too pleased about being left in such company.

Every day the camp just seemed to get more and more hazardous. The budding actor leant his shotgun against a tree and pulled up his T-shirt to show me a wound he'd incurred during the gun battle to kidnap the Indians. A bullet had cut cleanly across his shoulder; the bone was not damaged but now there were signs of infection. I was just about to give him some medical advice about patching up and keeping the wound clean when the shotgun fell on its side, with the business end landing right behind Plooy's foot.

Two shots came in quick succession, followed by a flight of bird life to the sky, and then silence. First I thought Plooy's foot had been blown off, and then when we realised the shots had come from the bush the colour drained from each of our faces. We had just listened to the murder of our fellow hostages, Sachin and Aditya. I looked to the ground, not wanting to believe what had just happened, and breathed deeply, trying to calm myself. I felt sick and was trying hard to fight the vomit back down to my stomach. All I could picture was the A-frame and a dead Sachin and Aditya hanging from it.

The Somali said something to the actor and the rest of the bodyguards, and they all began to pick up their weapons and make their way across the yard to the jungle. The General walked smartly out of the jungle and headed to his boat, stuffing his pistol back into the waistband of his trousers as he went, followed by Commander Jackson, BA and Denzel. The bodyguards changed direction to follow. The General shouted something and they all casually climbed back in his boat as though nothing had happened, and raced down the river the way they had come.

We were in shock and all visibly shaken. A depressing weight was trying to crush me into the very soil I was standing on. 'Fucking hell,' I said. We looked at each other, still not believing what had just happened, when Sachin and Aditya emerged from the jungle.

'Thank fuck,' exclaimed Noor. 'They're alive.'

'Jesus Christ, I thought they'd been whacked,' I said.

'So did I,' replied Plooy. We all gave a collective sigh.

The relief was all-consuming; we had thought that this was the start of something horrible. Sachin and Aditya looked close to tears and very shaky and we were still feeling a little wobbly too, but also extremely thankful to see that the two of them were very much alive.

'What the fuck just happened in there?' we asked quietly, so Gastro Pod and Eagle Eye, who had moved back in to replace the General's bodyguards, couldn't hear. 'We heard shots, we all thought you two had just been killed.'

Sachin did the talking as Aditya was getting sicker all the time and finding it hard to hold it together; he was a diabetic and the lack of medication was starting to cause him some problems.

101

'The General now wants more money from our company and got quite impatient with them; he made us kneel for the shots.' Sachin was struggling to tell us what happened but we all got the idea; it must have been horrendous for them. We looked at each other and said the same thing; 'Can't wait till our negotiations begin.'

With all our appetites well and truly dampened, the cook and his two goons brought over the evening's main course. It was everybody's favourite time of the day again, rice and beans seasoned with bodily fluids. We all took a plate, thanked him and made our way over to the rubbish dump. Sitting down in the dirt, we put our plates on the ground and just stared at the food for a minute. This was going to be hard work.

The rice just clogged up in the throat even when we had a bag of water to wash it down with, but tonight there wasn't any water. I swallowed hard to clear the dust from my palate and then rolled up a small ball of rice and beans with the fingers of my right hand – remembering I had not so long ago wiped my arse with the left – and popped it in my mouth. Mmmm.

'Chef's on form, this is worse than yesterday's; if it gets any worse I'm gonna down tools and go on strike,' said Plooy, forcing in another mouthful.

'You may have to then,' said Noor. 'Sachin was saying that they were running low on supplies, and that's the reason the General's getting his balls all in a twist over their ransom.'

'What, he can't be skint, surely?' asked Plooy.

'Running low? We only started off with rice and beans, how much lower can you get?' I asked, and then went on to add the obvious. 'If they open their eyes a tad they'll see mangoes and all sorts in the trees, and a big fat river full of fish.'

'That's just it though, Phil, these guys are only interested in robbing and getting high; they'll all starve long before anyone suggests a spot of fruit picking or fishing. I mean, just take a look at them,' suggested Plooy. Noor and I turned to look across the yard, still chewing on a mouthful, to see one militant passed out and another two well on the way, already struggling to drink from the bottle of kai-kai without spilling it down their chests. Eagle Eye was OK though, fully alert and watching us battle through every mouthful. Gastro Pod was struggling through his drunken haze. He looked all fingers and mangled stump as he tried in vain to roll another spliff. Noor and I looked back at Plooy and nodded in agreement.

The food did taste foul, but we desperately needed to keep our strength up. So we forced down as much of the slop as possible, as wasting any was tantamount to a crime punishable by fierce hunger later on. We then took the empty plates back to the cook and thanked him for another lovely meal. He would knowingly smile back, just like any chef who was at the top of his game.

Thankfully the sun was setting to put an end to another sorry day in this mosquito-infested hellhole. During the early evening, we huddled around a small tin of oil that was burning off smoke to try and keep the NAFy at bay. I had at last found a suitably sharp stick and pocketed it. It would remain on me at all times and be used only for emergencies, e.g. any funny business from the sisters.

Apart from Bob, who for now had managed to stay under the radar, the rest of us had all attracted some unwanted attention from various factions of the camp. Noor was in danger of having his tattoo ripped from his back and being turned into a lampshade; they were threatening to make a roast dinner out of Plooy; and I was about to be dragged, kicking and screaming, from the closet I was never in.

'I really need to get home and decompress,' I mumbled.

The camp was livening up again; it was that time when the drink and drugs kicked in and worked their magic. Sachin and Aditya had slipped back to their cell, still reeling from their earlier 'board' meeting with the General, and as there was no sign of the Teacher tonight we decided to turn in as well. At least it was only two to a mattress tonight, and we had the added security of the mosquito nets. After we had eased ourselves and said good night to our two guards, I climbed in under the net and lay down next to Plooy, propping myself up on one elbow in that classic catalogue pose. It felt kind of special to be under the net and not have to worry about the NAFy for a while, and to be able to stretch out on the mattress. I also hoped the net would repel other nasties, such as militants.

We talked for a while, continuing the discussion we had had outside about the pros and cons of being made into a lampshade, eaten or sodomised, and which one would be best. My arm began to ache so I went to lay my head down, and as soon as it was a couple of inches from our new mattress I caught a whiff of the most disgusting smell ever. It smelled as though I was about to lay my head on a week-old dead tramp with an onion stuffed in his rectum.

'Fucking hell,' I said, dry-heaving, 'that smells a bit psychedelic.'

Plooy laughed and replied, 'I was waiting for that; it's a bit funky isn't it? I dread to think what action this thing's seen.' It took our minds off being eaten and buggered for a while, so that was no bad thing.

'Good night,' whispered Plooy.

'Yeah, good night, don't let the bedbugs bite,' I said back, and that was when the rain started and the wind picked up; a squall was on its way. The tin roofs rattled in an attempt to hold to their fixings as the rain beat a ferocious rhythm. This storm would do several good things – clear the camp of bad smells and mosquitoes and quieten down the party people. Let it blow.

CHAPTER THIRTEEN

PERFECT STORM

It was still the swinging eighties and a fun time and place to be growing up. By my side were my best mate from school and wingman Alfie, who later gave his name to my Jack Russell, and together we had cornered the market for hired help. Between us we were earning a shed-load of cash, and with plenty of money on the hip we were starting to learn the joys of fast push-bikes and faster food.

Since my experience with Flipper I'd managed to keep my nose fairly clean and had got my life back on track. The straight path I was now trekking down in the direction of righteousness was enough to make any parent happy. I was a model son. I was still running like the wind, and the trophy cabinet at home was bursting at the seams. Taking centre stage were the trophies I'd won at the 1987 Sussex Championships. I'd breezed home first in the 1500 metres, the 800 metres and the cross-country, breaking records and cleaning up in all three categories.

I needed results like those though, and lots of them. I needed them to draw attention away from my school work. But it was money I craved, and lots of it, and to earn money you've got to work, and I wasn't shy of that.

My working day would start at five on the dot, just after the alarm clock had shattered one of my saucy dreams. Like all self-made men I was quick to realise that if you're due in at the office at five-thirty it's best to be there at twenty-five past. I cycled to the paper shop and started my morning chores. The rest of the paperboys weren't due in until six, by which time I'd marked up all the rounds and got them ready for collection. I then left the shop for the start of my own round at just past six, and after delivering to the thirty-odd addresses on my list I went back home for a well-deserved breakfast at around quarter to seven.

After a quick wash and change into my school uniform, I was back out of the door at twenty minutes past seven for the two-mile hike to school, arriving just after eight and picking Alfie up on the way. We'd both been grafting since the crack of dawn, so we took the school day as a chance to get some rest. School had finished at half past two since the teachers' strike, when the school day was shortened from four o'clock. We both met up outside the gates and headed to another school on the other side of town to clean it, stopping on the way for a burger and chips at the Wimpy bar. We arrived for our cleaning job at half past three, and it took us a little over an hour and a half to complete the cleaning of the classrooms and corridors.

Tea was on the table for about half past five, and I joined the rest of my family there – sometimes minus my old man if he was on night duty. Evenings were taken up with either athletics club or football on the playing fields at the end of the garden. At the weekend there was still no time to have a lie-in, but I didn't need one as I'd had all the rest I needed at school. On Saturday the alarm clock buzzed me awake at five again, but this time I was off to market. I met Alfie on the way and we arrived at market at six o'clock, where we would start setting up the stalls for the traders. We had a couple of hours off in the middle of the day before taking down the stalls at the end, and we were ready for a night on the town by about half past five with roughly forty-five pounds in the pocket. Not bad for a week's work; we were young, flush with cash and getting up to all sorts.

It was midweek, 15th October 1987, I had just finished my tea, and my parents and I were sitting in the lounge watching the weather after the Six O'clock News. In those days there was only ever one TV in the house and whatever your parents watched, you watched too. The weatherman was Michael Fish and he had just uttered the most famous weather quote of all time: 'Earlier on today, apparently, a woman rang the BBC and said she heard there was a hurricane on the way... well, if you're watching, don't worry, there isn't.'

That night the wind blew like never before. My brother Dave, with whom I shared a bedroom in the loft, and I were woken up at about three in the morning by sounds that you thought you would only hear in hell itself. It sounded as if the space shuttle Challenger was crash-landing in our back garden over and over again. The bedroom window and roof were shaking with such force that we expected them to implode at any moment. We lay there for hours, pulling our duvets tighter up under our chins and listening to Armageddon just outside the window. It was relentless, on and on it blew. We had a sixty-foot willow tree in the garden, and the wind snapped it like a stick about six feet from the base.

Five on the dot – my alarm clock buzzed my already alert brain. It was time to get up for my paper round. But money didn't seem that important this morning, so I headed straight to Mum and Dad's room. I told them that I was not well, that it was far too windy out there for us mere mortals, and asked if mum could phone in sick for me. 'No', came the answer, followed by the 'loyalty and commitment' speech. Back up the stairs I went and got changed. I couldn't believe it. They hadn't heard a thing all night, there was a war going on out there, and nature was winning. Their bedroom window faced in the same direction as mine; how the hell did they get a peaceful night's sleep?

Still grumbling I went out through the kitchen, tripping over my old man's home-made beer brewing kit which was giving off a really bad smell. As I opened the back door the weather hit me straight away. It was as wicked as a cut snake. I went to the garage, got my BMX and started pedalling up the back garden, past the felled willow and out through the garden gate. On the other side of the gate the whole world had changed, and I was about the only one out in it. There was complete devastation. Nothing looked the same, trees were down everywhere, not a single one left standing. It looked as if an atom bomb had been dropped.

At the top of our garden was the old primary school we used to go to. The two main halls of the school had copper-sheathed roofs about thirty metres long by twenty wide. The wind had just ripped them off, screwed them up and chucked them back down to earth as though they were old discarded Ribena cartons.

Once I'd left the house, my mum put on her bedside radio. As soon as she had switched it on she heard a very serious voice telling her that under no circumstances was anyone allowed to leave the safety of their home, unless it was for an extreme emergency. The voice went on to explain that the winds now battering the south-east were the worst on record, and that there had already been several fatalities. After rousing the old man from his sleep, Ma spent the next couple of hours pacing the carpet, wondering how she could have sent her little boy out into such a hostile environment, and what course of action was open to them. My old man made a cup of tea, did yesterday's crossword and checked on his home brew.

As soon as I started pedalling my bike towards 'dog-shit alley', I realised that this journey was going to be tough. It was like being in a washing machine out there, absolute madness. I had never known a night like it and I didn't think I was going to enjoy the journey home either. I covered about thirty metres and discovered that the alley was blocked by tree after tree, lying like sardines.

I was pretty good on my BMX, but to get over this lot I would have to ride it like Elliot did at the end of ET, so I had to carry it. I slung my bike over my shoulder so that the pedals were digging into my side and the crossbar was running over my shoulder. Then I started climbing. The trees were conifers, so they were nice and soft, no prickly branches or thorns. Climbing one or two with a BMX on your shoulder would have been easy enough, but there were nearly two hundred metres of obstacle course in front of me. After only managing twenty metres in as many minutes, I admitted defeat and turned back.

I was not about to give up, so I started heading in the opposite direction. With my mother's 'loyalty and commitment' speech still ringing in my ears, quitting was not an option. I was now faced with a different set of hurdles and started weighing up the hazards. Not only was it going to take me twenty minutes longer this way, it was less sheltered, so the wind was giving me a right thrashing. There were not as many trees down but many of the telegraph poles had been floored, and the cables were whipping around like a cat-o'-nine-tails.

I pressed on, debris flying around everywhere. A dustbin lid flew dangerously close at about head height, followed by a cat. All I could do was keep my head down to make myself as small a target as possible, and ride like the devil. It was taking a tremendous effort just to stay on my bike. Every time I got blown off I picked myself up out of someone's garden, retrieved my bike from a bush, mounted up and headed off again. I was pedalling as hard as I could down a hill that I would normally have freewheeled down, ducking and dodging as I went. The force of the wind in my face was making me look like a skydiver. When I reached the bottom of the hill and turned the corner, I had the wind to my rear and it was now pushing me up the hill with ease. I took my feet off the pedals – this was cosmic.

As I reached the main road my job got easier. There were no trees down here, and not much debris. I started making more progress and finally arrived at the paper shop forty-five minutes late.

Puffing like an old smoker attempting to climb stairs, I entered the shop. The owner of the shop was behind the counter with the phone stuck in the crook of his neck. He was ringing round the rest of the boys, making sure none of them had left for the shop. He raised an eyebrow at me and put down the phone as I closed the door behind me; the wind outside was starting to ease now.

'All right, boy', he said with a knowing tone. 'Your mother rang about an hour ago, in a right flap she was. Said I'd send you home as soon as you got here.' I surveyed the shop and noticed the lack of papers on the racks. 'No papers this morning then, boss?'

'No', he replied. 'Wasted journey for you my son, at least you showed willing. I've phoned round the rest of the lads and none of them were that keen; see you tomorrow.' With that I turned for the door and he stopped me.

'Help yourself to a Sherbet Dip Dab,' he said, so I did and then headed for home.

Later that day we all went for a walk to the milk depot; no milk had got through either, and the whole of the south-east was at a standstill. In daylight the world that we lived in looked ruined. Where great trees had once stood there were just big craters, up-ended roots were everywhere. Fifteen million trees were said to have been felled that night, and eighteen people lost their lives. The Met Office recorded southerly wind speeds of up to a hundred knots and, combined with the saturated ground from prior heavy rainfall, the trees that were in heavy leaf fell like dominoes. If the storm had arrived an hour or two later it would have been a different story for me; I was just catching the tail end of it when I ventured out. To my knowledge I was one of the very few civilians out that morning, and probably the only paper-boy. It was, and still is, the most thrilling morning of my life.

CHAPTER FOURTEEN

THE FOURTH OPTION

The next morning my body felt a lot better thanks to our new sleeping arrangements: being able to stretch out and lie flat, and the protection that the mosquito nets afforded. Not only did they stop all but a few of the NAFy getting to us, they also shielded us from the mob. The militants couldn't see in through the nets so they left us all alone. The nets behaved in the same way that your Grandma's old net curtains did: you could see from the front room on to the street, but people passing by couldn't see in. We didn't get one visit throughout the whole night, so we were all feeling a little more chipper than normal. That was soon cut short, however, when we felt the atmosphere in and around the yard.

It felt like a hot zone, charged to a dangerous level of high voltage; with the mob milling about in tight groups, they seemed to be as unpredictable as a swarm of drunken wasps at a picnic. We all stood together by the rubbish until Sachin and Aditya, sensing another squall was about to hit the camp, split back to their cell, their survival taking precedence. The angry wasps swarmed around us, feeding off each other's hatred; Noor seemed to be their jam sandwich. We were knocked to the ground, and a young guard who was wearing my dive booties ran in and kicked Noor hard before darting away. Noor reacted on impulse, momentarily seeing red. He launched himself from the ground, Plooy and I just managing to grab him in time to restrain him. Noor is big, strong and very fit and could have quite easily crushed the small guard with one hand, but this was no time for macho heroics. The red mist had passed and Noor was rational again, but we were all still very worried and confused. What the hell was going on?

It went dark as the swarm engulfed us, blocking out the sun, bodies all wanting to deliver stamps and kicks whilst we were sat in the dirt. I thought we were going to be torn apart in a moment of jungle passion; I was beginning to wish we had let Noor loose on them. In my pocket I still had my pointy stick, but it was never intended for riot control, only as a small discreet anti-rape device; I couldn't get to it anyway as I was too busy fending off incoming feet.

Commander Jackson was all of a sudden in the middle, pushing them apart and away from us with some of his Lieutenants. There was a lot of confusion and shouting of commands while the bodies were dragged away from us and we continued cowering in the dirt. The mob scattered, backing away a few metres to different parts of the yard, and everyone simmered down a degree. Commander Jackson offered his hand to help us up; the Secretary, standing next to him, did not.

Although the mob had quietened a little it was quite obvious that they were still angry about something, and that their anger was wholly directed at Noor. We asked what the problem was.

Commander Jackson barked an order and one of the goons peeled off and ran away. Commander Jackson turned on us; pointing at Noor, he simply stated: 'No one happy with mummy water on back.' Noor was in a bit of a conundrum. No one liked his tattoo; in actual fact they hated his ink so much they were quite prepared to kick us all to death, but what could Noor do? Short of finding a clinic that specialised in laser removal he was pretty much stuck with it, and they with him.

We were halfway through babbling out explanations and half-cocked remedies when the goon Commander Jackson had sent away came running back and handed him a T-shirt. Commander Jackson threw the T-shirt underarm at Noor and said, 'Cover up mummy water.' He then turned to address the mob. 'No one harm prisoners until the General says so.' Which I think was lost in translation; what he really meant to say was, the only time the prisoners are to be harmed is IF the General says so. Commander Jackson turned and stormed off with his Lieutenants on each flank, Frog Face, Denzel, BA and Prada, and they all followed him into the rec room.

Noor pulled off his purple Knicks vest top and tossed it to the Secretary, and then slipped the T-shirt over his head to cover up the offending tattoo. The Secretary went to leave, clutching the vest top, before turning back to us.

'So-called colonial masters, look at you now, you are nothing here and you all die.' This was said with a generous sprinkling of disdain and a large pinch of hatred, not only in his voice but shining in his eyes.

The drums were played out with a renewed vigour as though they had a point to prove or a bad spirit to quash. We sat in silence, all deep in thought; Bob aside, I knew Plooy and Noor would be thinking of escape and fine-tuning their plan if they had come up with one. Mine was starting to take shape and I was keener than ever to take it to the next level.

The drums and accompanying procession were over, and the angry wasps dispersed after a grand finale of 'Isowanna, Isowanna'. Eagle Eye and Gastro Pod stayed close while managing to keep a respectful distance, but the rest of the mob moved away, not wanting to be around Noor or his tattoo. Ignoring the open hostility towards us we went back to our cell to collect our mattresses; we wanted to bring them outside to air in an effort to rid them of that dreadful smell. Next to the rubbish heap was a small tree, so we leaned the mattresses up against the trunk and settled ourselves down in its shade.

'Noor, what the fuck was the Secretary on about when he called us so-called colonial masters?' I asked.

'It's got nothing to do with me and Bob. Trust us to get caught up in your sordid history, hey Bob,' said Plooy.

'Plooy's right, mate, this one falls at us Brits' feet. We'd colonised Nigeria for about seventy years, only granting them independence in the early sixties; that's why they can blame us for all their ills. You know, up until the year 2000 the military ran the country.'

'Oh terrific, it just gets better and better don't it,' I grumbled.

'Fucking Brits,' chuckled Bob as he closed his eyes, leaning back against one of the mattresses; 'always getting yourselves into trouble and expecting your cousins across the pond to come and bail you out.'

'Well, I wish you lot would shake a leg and come and bail us out of this mess,' I said, leaning across and punching him playfully on the leg. Sachin had come out to see if we were OK, but Aditya had opted to stay in their cell. He joined us under the shade and we just sat for a while swapping stories about each other's families.

It was quite late in the afternoon before our food was brought over, and the whole camp still seemed keen to give us some space. Commander Jackson and his Lieutenants were sitting around the cheap plastic table in the rec room chatting, smoking dope and drinking Monkey Tail. Air Force One was playing on the telly and a bit of a party was brewing down at the other end of the camp by Hut Three, next to where we had washed the day before. I just hoped they kept it down that end, but I doubted it.

We heaped much praise on the cook and his two helpers when we took back our empty plates, and they basked shamelessly in their glory. Sachin rejoined Aditya in their cell and Bob went to have a lie-down, taking both the mattresses back into our cell. Plooy, Noor and I started lapping the yard to walk off our food. The conversation soon turned to our escape plans, and it was good to hear that no-one was shirking the duty of putting one together. We discussed all manner of dangers, from short-term ones like crocodile-infested rivers and bumping into flesh-eating cannibals, to long-term dangers like catching unknown exotic diseases, and the possibility of still walking around in circles fifty years from now. It would appear that venturing out into unexplored jungle is just fraught with peril.

I don't know when the conversation shifted from escaping into the jungle to mass murder, but it did, and I can't remember who instigated it; it could well have been me but I honestly don't recall. When you find yourself plotting murder on a large scale it should be time to worry, but as I looked into my friends' eyes I could tell that they were as excited by the prospect of a little ethnic cleansing as I was. We discussed taking over the camp by force as our last resort, 'Operation Overkill', but it was mainly a time-killing exercise. We got so carried away with it that we could fantasise for hours about the different ways in which we would do it. If we felt that we had no other option and that there was a very real threat to our lives, and if we had time to put it into action, this was going to be our fourth option.

We would start our assault at around three to four in the morning, when it's reported that the human mind is at its lowest ebb, and when hopefully everyone was crashed out after partying hard. Moving as one, we would slip out of our cell and pick up a rock each from outside. We would then creep back in past our and the Indians' cell to the next room, where two or three guards were on rotation, fast asleep. Again moving as one, we would strike them on the head hard enough to immobilise or kill them. Once we were sure they were incapacitated came the next and hardest part of the plan, the taking of the rec room. Because of the constant high volume of the TV, we were banking on the few guards still awake being totally unaware of what was unfolding. We would stroll casually into the room as though we couldn't sleep and wanted to watch the telly, each standing near to a guard, hopefully without making him feel uncomfortable. Plooy had needed the toilet during the early morning, and had noted the slack and sorry state of the guards left watching the telly at that time. When Plooy gave the signal we would overpower the guards with rocks or machetes, if we had been lucky enough to find some in the guards' quarters. The next room to secure would be the armoury, and now totally unguarded it would be ours for the taking. Arming ourselves with an AK47 and sticks of dynamite, Plooy and I would take Huts Two and Three simultaneously. Noor would stay back in cover and man that big belt-fed machine gun. Again on Plooy's signal, we would toss the dynamite into the huts where the militants were sleeping soundly and blow them all to hell, with Noor picking off any loose stragglers. This is where we got a little carried away. All three of us would stroll around the camp, spraying down any militants that dared to stay alive with hot lead, and putting extra rounds into those already dead just to make sure. When we were sure no one had survived, we would grab as many guns and as much ammo as we could carry, jump into a boat, hot-tail it out of there and be home before last orders.

We played it out in our minds many times with always the same outcome: us being victorious and escaping to freedom. The sun was down and the NAFy were back with a vengeance; after being forced to abandon last night's sorties due to bad weather, they were reminding us just who was capable of massacring whom. It was time to duck under the mosquito nets and dream of genocide.

CHAPTER FIFTEEN

DIRTY GAMES

It was early and we were all washing our faces in the river, crouching on the balls of our toes in the soft mud with the cool water gently lapping over our feet. We had taken to keeping in a tight group whenever possible, so as not to leave ourselves open to attack. The last couple of days had scared us all into taking Operation Tom, Dick and Harry very seriously, and Plooy, Noor and I had all come up with a hasty plan. We finished washing and went and stood on the bare parade ground to watch the parade and listen to the drums. Eagle Eye and Gastro Pod seemed relaxed this morning, so we figured the curse of the mummy water was postponed for now. Sachin was out doing stretching exercises, and even Aditya had shown his face.

We waited until the drumming had climaxed and the yard was clearing before retrieving our mattresses from the cell to take them outside to air. It was making no difference to the awful smell, but we hoped a few hours in the fresh air would put some extra life back into them. If nothing else it made us feel a bit better. Bob laid one mattress straight down on the dirt floor and assumed his position. Sachin and Aditya went back to their cell, leaving us co-conspirators to lap the yard and reveal to each other our well-laid plans.

All three plans were very simple because there weren't a great many options open to us, and we all believed wholeheartedly that the simpler the plan, the greater the chance we had of success. We had all pinpointed the same area of the camp to exit from, which from my point of view was good – three great minds couldn't all be wrong. But that was where the similarities ended. We had each come up with

117

a different direction in which we thought we should travel, and now all we had to do was figure out which one we thought had the best chance of leading us to freedom. There was no room for failure.

The area from which we had all chosen to go over the wire was between the rubbish dump and the lean-to, where the cook prepared the food and where the river met the jungle. This small area was out of view from the rest of the camp and was normally unguarded. We would break out any time between the early morning hours of two and four; when most of the guards should be busy snoring and scratching their balls; this would give us a better chance of slipping by unnoticed and leave us at least three hours to make good our escape before the camp came awake and raised the alarm. We would have to do a recce at around those times, but we were pretty sure that the whole camp was completely comatose by then; even Eagle Eye had to sleep some time.

Noor's plan, Tom, was to move under cover of darkness back down the river, exactly the same way we remembered being brought in. We were to swim or walk in the river and cover as much distance as we could before the sun came up, then hole up in good cover on the bank for the day and wait until dark again. Once we had made it back to where the river met the ocean we would run along the beach until we came level with the production platform we were originally working by, and then Noor, being the strongest swimmer, would swim out and get help.

If we were to use Dick, Plooy's brainchild, we would exit the camp in the same place but travel up the river, in the opposite direction to Tom, for about two hundred metres. We would then head in a westerly direction and try and keep in a straight line on that bearing, which would bring us on to the beach, which we estimated to be no more than twenty miles away. Once we had made sure the coast was clear we would again make for the platform or hike on to

Cameroon, which we estimated to be some two hundred kilometres away, trying on the way to find a friendly person to assist us.

My plan, Harry, was different again. After escaping from the camp we would cross the river and then hike, keeping a little bit East of North and head to Port Harcourt. We would get as far from the camp as we could on the first morning and then travel in daylight hours only; I had concluded that travelling at night in the jungle with our non-existent navigational equipment would be near to impossible. Once we had cleared the jungle or reached some form of civilisation, we would either hijack a car by any means to get ourselves to safety or find a phone to contact the office for help, or both.

All three plans we thought had strong and weak points, but there were still lots of details we needed to iron out before we decided on whose plan we would run with. Drinking water would not be a problem, as there was a heavy rainfall every other day hereabouts and it was fast approaching the rainy season, but food would be a different matter. None of us were experts in the art of jungle survival, and we weren't sure what was and what was not safe to eat. There would have to be a bit of trial and error, death being nature's way of saying we failed.

We would also need to brush up on our navigational skills, as we didn't have a compass to hand. There are many methods of steering yourself without a compass, but we knew little of these techniques. Boots and suitable clothing would also have to be found. I already had boots to wear, and the military uniform given to me would serve me well, but Plooy had no boots and neither did Noor; he was also dressed only in shorts and T-shirt. None of us would last long out in the harsh jungle without boots or some better clothes. From now on we would have to keep our eyes skinned for anything that could prove useful in the aiding of our escape: boots, clothes and any other odds and sods we could squirrel away.

119

The main problem we faced, though, was what we were going to do about Bob. None of us felt good at the prospect of leaving him behind, potentially at the mercy of a very pissed-off General, but if we wanted to give ourselves half a chance of making it to safety we would have to leave him. He was just too old and unfit to attempt such a perilous journey; it would prove challenging enough for us young guns. For now anyway we would have to exclude him. All our planning and fine-tuning would be strictly between the three of us, no Indians and no Bob.

Today would be spent lazing around in the dirt, keeping out of the way of the militants, trying to stay invisible and willing the time away. Noor suggested we play Hangman to help with the passing of time and to keep our minds active. We used a stick to scratch out the game in the dirt, the only rule being that the words we had to guess were something to do with the camp, like 'rubbish heap' or 'A frame'. After several games of this we decided to switch to draughts. The board we could again scratch out in the dirt, but we needed to find from somewhere twelve counters for each player; we used this as good cover for us to look about for anything useful to aid in our escape.

So one at a time we wandered off for a scavenge in and around the area where we were sitting, though never straying too far or exposing ourselves to attack. We didn't want to make our guards jumpy either. Gastro Pod wouldn't notice if we started to dig a tunnel under him, he was too busy dozing with his chin resting on the end that went bang of his AK47; but Eagle Eye was alert, watching us warily from his perch, forever switched-on and taking his responsibilities very seriously.

We were looking for beer-bottle tops; there were hundreds scattered about and it would only have taken a few minutes to collect the twenty-four we needed, but we made out that we wanted twelve of one colour and twelve of another, discarding all but the very finest examples, which was going to take us a little longer. The best place I found to rummage was the rubbish dump. I've always found it amazing what people throw away; one man's rubbish is another man's treasure. But not here – this rubbish dump was filled with just that, rubbish. I wasn't going to be deterred, though; I was in my element now and conducted my fingertip search with the patience of a forensic scientist looking for clues to a murder.

My patience paid off, for as well as finding four beer-bottle tops that were in mint condition, I also found some three metres of frayed baler twine and a broken plastic comb that I was going to turn into a shank (a crude stabbing device) by breaking off all the teeth on one side, and then wrapping the baler twine around to make a handle. The handle was already honed to a sharp point. The shank would replace my current weapon, the stick. The last item I found that I thought might be of use was a clean, empty plastic bottle with screw lid; we could use this for storing fresh rainwater which would see us through the sunnier parts of the day.

Noor chose to go looking around the other side of the cell block and came back with a bounty of treasures: half a dozen bottle tops, some more baler twine and an old rusty machete blade minus the handle, which was a superb find. All it needed was a new handle, which we could make from a fallen branch, and after a quick sharpen from a stone it would be as good as new. Noor's other find was like winning the lottery for him. Round the back of our hut, half buried in the dirt, was a pair of tatty old boots. The boots had no laces but baler twine would work, and they were full of holes but would be incomparable next to flip-flops. Noor left them where they were for now, in case someone had left them there for a reason.

We needed just one more pair of boots, for Plooy, and I knew where to get two of them, the only problem being that most of the time one of the pairs was laced up tightly on Commander Jackson's feet. Although Jackson was very small his boots looked at least two sizes too big; either that or he had massive feet, so Plooy should slip in to them. The others that I had my eye on for Plooy were my stolen dive booties, which had been worn by a different militant every day so far, so they might be a bit trickier to pin down. All we had to do was find out where either pair of boots was kept when the occupier went to sleep – as no one sleeps in his boots – and then swipe them just before we went over the wire. I just wouldn't like to be in Plooy's shoes if we got caught. Footwear in the third world was a highly-prized possession and guarded most fiercely.

When it was Plooy's turn to go hunter-gathering, he came back with enough bottle tops to start our game of draughts. He went scouting along the other river bank towards Hut Two and found a long piece of thin rope, a pair of old scissors and the best find of the day, a Frisbee; it was absolutely no help in anyone's escape plan but would prove a winner at killing time on the yard. The 'Frisbee' came in the guise of an old unloved custard-tin lid, about nine inches in diameter, perfectly flat and round. Plooy looked very pleased indeed with this find.

We buried all the items we had found in a couple of different locations, so if one should be discovered it would not only protect the rest but shouldn't raise much suspicion either. One place was under a log behind the hut on the opposite side of the wall to Sachin and Aditya's cell; we hid the rusty machete blade here. Another hidey-hole was in the deep roots of the tree that we rested our mattresses against to air, which was an ideal place for the old scissors and twine. And the last location was on the edge of the rubbish tip itself, where we put the plastic bottles and the rest of the twine, blending in with all the other rubbish. All locations were very close to each other, so we could round up the kit at a moment's notice. The items may not have sounded like much, but if Eagle Eye had stumbled across them all hidden together they would have looked like just what they were, tools for an escape. It took a while to complete this task as we had to choose our moments carefully. One at a time at different intervals we would ask Eagle Eye to take us to the toilet as a diversion and then quickly hide away our gear – all very cloak-and-dagger. Once we were satisfied that the goods were well enough hidden from prying eyes and that none of the guards had noticed us hiding them, we set about sorting out a game of Frisbee. The rules were simple: throw the Frisbee to your chum, who would hopefully catch it and then throw it back.

The yard was perfect for this. We would normally just walk around it to stretch our legs, but now it had become our playground. Plooy, Noor and I formed a triangle and threw the custard lid to and fro, and for a while I almost forgot where I was. It was quite a high-profile activity, though, and it soon caught the attention of some of the mob, who gathered around the edge of the yard to watch the three stupid white men wasting their energy. Prada especially took an interest in the game; he had the sort of look on his face that suggested he wasn't at all happy to see us relaxing and looking comfortable, his shark eyes following the Frisbee's every move. I was half expecting him to shoot it out of the sky like a clay pigeon.

After the game we sat back down by our mattresses that were still airing and waited for something to eat. The chef didn't disappoint, and after about three hours of waiting in the shade and playing draughts he brought over yet another plate of rice and beans that looked as if they had been cooked to death.

There were no complaints from any of us, though, as we tucked into our food that night. We were still in fairly high spirits, and just to top off a very good day the Teacher turned up with a bottle of Monkey Tail. We finished off the food and asked him for some of the green stuff to wash it down. He wasn't sure at first – he deemed it far too powerful a drink for a mere white man to handle. He took some persuading, but we finally managed to talk him into sharing some of his precious green stuff with us. The Teacher arranged some cups from the camp boss - three cut-down coke tins - and poured generous measures into each. We clinked cups, said cheers and poured a good mouthful down our throats. It was the perfect companion to an honestly dreadful meal; Monkey Tail simply tasted awful. It was very similar to a vintage bottle of turpentine, but like many awful drinks it only took a couple of mouthfuls before your taste buds got used to it. It kicked in fast too; it didn't take long before the brain started to fuzz with the potent mix of marijuana and cheap, strong gin.

A few of the guards also came over and started to sit nearby, moving in a little closer as time went on to join in with what we and the Teacher were talking about, which was the constant struggle most people from the Delta faced each day. One by one more militants came by, making up a fair amount of chatter with several conversations now bouncing back and forth. Gastro Pod was in amongst the circle and was now wide awake, smoking joints of weed and consuming large quantities of Monkey Tail himself. He interrupted the conversation to tell us that he was planning a trip to the UK to kidnap a white woman and make her his bride. He was deadly serious about this, and assumed everything in life was as simple as just going out and taking what you wanted. This caused us all great amusement, though, and the rest of the guards who were sitting around us soon backed us up.

Another of the guards, whom we had come to call the Preacher for his outstanding ability to whip the mob into a frenzy during Morning Prayer, butted in to tell us that he was organising a raiding party to kidnap the President of the United States of America. He was a short guy, standing only a shade over five feet, and impossibly puny;

his limbs were wasted and he danced about bow-legged, sores, scars and discoloured patches covering his spindly pins. His face was always happy enough, though, for one born so unfortunate. He looked like old Frog Face's mutant love child. He shared all the same facial features – impossibly wide mouth, squashed nose and big bug eyes; but one attribute he didn't share with Frog Face was the smile that was always turned up as bright as it would go. Perhaps that was how he understood and passed on God's word to the rest so well.

At the time the President was a certain George W. Bush. The Preacher's plan was utterly foolproof and we were all ears. He had personally hand-picked a few foot soldiers to accompany him on this mission impossible, and they all proudly stepped forward and started egging him on.

As I said before, it's always the simple plans that have the greatest chance of success. They were going to jump into one of their fast boats and speed all the way across the Atlantic Ocean to George's house – the white one, I guessed. They would then kill all the Secret Service officers protecting the President and bundle George into the boat, then speed all the way back again, dodging the might of the American Navy on the way. We were all in agreement that if he could pull it off the rewards would be significant. As far as I know from watching CNN or any other news network, no such attack on the President of the United States has yet taken place.

Today was the first day that we hadn't been or felt physically threatened; we still felt the fear, which was always present but a little more manageable at times like these. However, as we mixed a little with the mob a new, deadlier danger arose. The friendlier and chattier these guys got, the more animated and excited they became, acting out in full the storming of the White House and the taking of George W. Bush. Full of drink and high on drugs they started waving their guns about, half-cocking them and dry-firing. It was very worrying as they swung the barrel past your face and snatched at the trigger, not fully aware whether or not they had a round in the chamber. We spent most of the evening ducking and diving as they swung their rifles this way and that, fully expecting a bullet to slam into our faces every time someone pulled the trigger. We wouldn't be the first to be killed by accidental fire or negligent discharge. Accident or not, the result would still be the same: lying in a shallow grave with my chin on my chest and a hole in my head. We were beginning to regret the new rapport we were building with some of the guards.

Prada put an end to the festivities just as they were bringing George back across the Atlantic, battling big waves and sea serpents. (Not a mention of the American Navy; they were obviously not seen as much of a challenge compared with the ocean and the monsters of the deep.) Prada sauntered over with BA and Frog Face and barked at the guards, who all scattered to their various posts. I had noticed Prada standing off in the shadows with some of his cronies, all of them looking more and more disgruntled as the goons played out their plan. That was the problem here. Just when you thought you were making progress and building bridges there was always something or someone waiting to knock you back down and put you in your place – and our place was at the very bottom of the food chain. In this small clearing the law of the jungle applied, and Prada and his merry men were the ones with all the teeth and claws.

Prada had chased everyone away, apart from the Teacher who was now so trashed we couldn't understand a word he said anyway, his normally good pidgin English long since replaced with a drunken ramble. Prada sat close to us with his pals, using all his techniques in domestic abuse, flicking cigarette butts at us and talking with his cronies about the many ways in which we would die. He was a cruel man and only seemed happy when we were not. The only thing left in our arsenal was retreat, so that's exactly what we did. We said goodnight to the Teacher, who couldn't even focus on us, and headed to our cell.

An early night was needed as we three had work to do. Each of us was to go out on a midnight recce between the hours of twelve and four o'clock. Normally if we needed to relieve ourselves during the night we had to grab one of our guards who were supposed to be stationed outside the cell, but never were. If they hadn't passed out already or gone to bed they could be found sitting at the other end of the hut with all the TV addicts, watching the latest war movie. Even Eagle Eye was partial to a bit of war on the telly, and tonight's recce was to see what sort of manpower was still around and alert during the wee morning hours.

At staggered intervals we were to go to the toilet while trying not to be noticed by any of the goons, guards or foot lieutenants. Once we had successfully left the hut we would make for the river bank, where we had chosen to make our escape. If we made it to the exit point without being noticed we would stand there for about ten minutes and observe any enemy troop movements in the camp, with the pretence of going to the toilet. If at any stage we were rumbled by Eagle Eye or any other sharp-sighted guard, we would cross our legs and plead ignorance.

Plooy went first at about zero-one hundred. He made it to the exit point but didn't stay out long; he reported a lot of traffic at that time and came straight back after a quick wee, as there was no point staying out and getting spotted. Plooy set the alarm on his watch for zero-two-thirty for my turn, but there was no need; I awoke naturally at around two-thirty genuinely needing the toilet. I crept out and headed straight for the river bank, head down and using purposeful movements.

I figured if anyone was out and spotted my shadow moving confidently through the camp, it would raise a lot less suspicion than

127

if I was spotted creeping about unsure of myself. Making it to the exit point unchallenged, I squatted on my haunches with my pants pulled down and relieved myself like a girl. I don't know how long I stayed there, it seemed longer than ten minutes, but was probably a tad shorter. In that time I only saw three people. All three of them walked from the TV room in our hut across to Hut Two, nowhere near where I was standing; one of them was the Preacher, weaving drunk and bow-legged from side to side. A lot of guys seemed to share this bow-legged cowboy strut. I couldn't make out who the other two were, but they were in a similar state.

I stayed a few moments more, listening to the breathing in my ears that sounded much louder than it could possibly have been, and then made my way back to the cell and slipped under the mosquito net, silently wishing luck to Noor who had the four o'clock slot, our deadline. If we couldn't make it out by then, it would be abort, abort, abort.

CHAPTER SIXTEEN

TIME PIECE

An explosive shock ricocheted around our cell, blasting us all awake. Delta's own alarm clock. I was looking Plooy straight in his big saucer-like eyes, as we'd both shot bolt upright from our top-and-tail sleeping positions. Prada and his cronies had just set off some dynamite right outside our cell. I had no proof it was Prada, but it was the sort of vindictive prank he would pull. The shock wave caused by the explosion sucked the air right out of our lungs, leaving us both breathless and shaking. I grinned at Plooy and said, 'Morning.' We both laughed nervously and fell backwards, breathing deeply to recover our oxygen levels and composure.

'Fucking charming, what's all the noise about, are we under attack again?' I heard Noor say from beneath his mosquito net on the other side of the cell.

'Goddam sonova bitch!' No prizes for guessing who said that. Yesterday evening before bed we had asked the Secretary for some water to wash with, and he grunted that tomorrow we would be allowed one bucket of pit water each, so after all the fuss of the TNT explosions, drums and prayers was finished we went to the pit to collect some. A couple of the goons helped us bale some water out of the pit, but most of them were still sitting about smoking and laughing at the earlier explosion. When we had our allocated bucket of water, we set about getting ourselves clean. We didn't go over to the wash area this time, choosing instead our usual spot next to the yard; we felt a bit more comfortable here and a bit safer too.

As we began to wash away the sweat and grime from our bodies, I asked Noor and Plooy to check the soles of my feet as they were very painful. I sat down and leaned back on my hands, offering them up for inspection. The reaction I got from those two told me all I needed to know; both of them gave a sharp intake of breath through gritted teeth and screwed up their faces in mock pain.

'What the fuck have you done?' they asked. 'They're black.' I explained the theory for my mashed-up feet. The mosquito net didn't fit, there wasn't enough room for both my head and my feet inside the net. I was a couple of inches taller than Plooy so part of me had to come into contact with the net. I wrongly figured that the soles of my feet, being hard and leathery, would be able to withstand any onslaught dished out by the NAFy. So I used my feet to stretch out the net to keep my head from touching it, and the end result was mashed-up feet. The bottom of each toe and the balls of both feet were extremely sore from being sucked on all through the night – those mosquitoes were more like vampire bats than insects – and it was so painful I was having trouble walking.

After checking that Bob was out of earshot, (he was drip-drying in the sun), Noor began to tell us in a hushed tone about what he had seen last night during his ten-minute recce. He left his mattress at about quarter past three, Bob didn't stir, so he made his way to the exit point, listening and keeping an eye out for any movement. At that time in the morning the exit point was totally unguarded and there was little or no camp traffic in that area. This was good news and confirmed what we all thought. Over the coming nights we would continue checking at various times during the early morning, but as far as we were concerned, the place at which we had decided to leave the camp was the safest bet.

I had finished washing myself and sat in the sun to rest my feet and dry off. Plooy washed my clothes, Bob's and Noor's all in one bucket and hung them out to dry, which wouldn't take long in the fierce Delta sun. As we waited for our clothes to dry we chatted about whose plan we should run with. We all felt comfortable with Plooy's, although I was disappointed my plan wasn't chosen. We figured plan Dick had the best chance of our making it to safety. The main reason for choosing Dick was that we estimated we only had about twenty miles to navigate from the camp to the beach as the crow flies. Once we hit the beach, all we had to do was turn left and follow the coastline until we found help, or until we reached Cameroon if we had to, which would be one hell of a hike but still better than sitting here.

We brought the board meeting to a close as Bob came over to collect his clothes. I grabbed mine and covered up as the three sisters had just wandered over, probably to ogle at my naked form. My clothes still needed some time in the sun, but they could finish drying on me while I took some exercise around the yard. Plooy and Noor also dressed and joined me, while Bob remained resting. I found walking terribly painful and hobbled as best I could around the yard; I just didn't want to sit still and make myself an easy target for my new bum chums.

Most of our escape plan was coming together. We had plan Dick, a time window and a point where we were going to exit the camp. We also had useful items that would aid in our escape hidden in different caches. We still needed to find Plooy a pair of boots, as well as some decent clothing for Noor. Our other priority now was to take the time we had left to learn how to navigate without a compass. It would be the one thing that could let us down; we knew we had a high chance of making it out of the camp, and that we then had about twenty miles to travel through the jungle to the beach; but twenty miles was a long way even with a compass in that terrain, and could easily turn into a hundred miles if we spent the whole time walking around in circles.

The three sisters blocked our way as we walked around the yard and they offered me another cigarette. The ones Frog Face had given me were all gone and I was dying for a smoke, but I refused to prostitute myself so cheaply and declined the offer. But Plooy, who had read the situation well, accepted one for me, before all three of us pushed past the sisters and carried on with our exercise. Plooy didn't smoke so he handed the cigarette over to me. I took it gratefully.

'If you think for one minute I'm going to step in when the General and his Somali lover come to get their McPlooy happy meal, you've got another think coming,' I said.

Plooy flashed me a halogen smile and replied, 'Just smoke the damn thing before I give it back to your sweethearts.'

'Cheers mate,' I said as I peeled off to find a light from one of the guards who didn't want to sodomise me. When I re-joined the walk at a hobble Noor had remembered a navigation technique involving a watch, and explained.

'You point the hour hand of the watch towards the sun, and then take the mid-point between the hour hand and noon, and that hopefully will give you south.'

'Brilliant,' I said, 'who's got a watch?' Noor and I looked at Plooy who was the only one of us with a watch, but it was digital. For a minute we all paused, had a think and then looked towards the old man sitting next to the rubbish dump. 'Bob!' we all said in unison.

Bob was totally unaware that he held the final piece of our jigsaw puzzle. 'What are you lot staring at?' he asked.

'Your nose has healed up nicely, Bob, hasn't it?' I asked, and it had. All Bob had left to show for his rough-and-tumble on the day of the kidnapping was a yellowing around the eyes and a lumpy dark scab still attached to the bridge of his nose. I didn't like the thought of mugging Bob, so I came up with a plan. Noor and I would mug Plooy for his digital watch and then give that to Bob in exchange for his.

The rest of the day and into the evening was spent studying other ways in which we could guide ourselves through the jungle. We looked at the sun and logged its progress through the sky, but we found this method a little tricky and weren't even sure if it worked. I knew you could tell the time by the sun, but could you navigate? I remembered at Cub Scouts we would turn to the trees and look to see which side the moss grew on. In a perfect world the moss would grow on the shadier, damper side of the tree, and in the northern hemisphere that was the north side of the tree as our sun shines from the south. In the southern hemisphere the sun is in the north, so it would be the south side of the tree. But where was Nigeria, southern or northern hemisphere? Fuck, things would be a lot easier if we just had a compass.

By the time the stars came out and we looked skyward we knew we were in trouble. Every star in the galaxy was twinkling down at us saying, 'Follow me, follow me'. It just looked like one big mess up there. We were all competent seamen, but navigating by the stars was well out of our league. We came to the conclusion that we would just have to use a little of all the techniques, but on the whole just go with our instincts, Bob's watch and hopefully a lot of luck. I made a note to myself that if we ever made it out of here I would never leave the house again without a compass, and would even go as far as backing it up with a bit of star-gazing knowledge.

It was getting late, I couldn't walk any more because of the bites to my feet, and the NAFy were yet again out in force, so I turned in. I placed my rigger boots in between the net and my feet, which made a barrier against the vampires. I even thought about wearing them but no one sleeps in his boots, so I made myself as comfy as I could. Lying on my mattress, I suddenly felt a little more confident that we could make it out of this alive. There was a very high chance that the militants would simply release us to the authorities. We still had to believe this, but now we also had a plan to work on and use if the opportunity presented itself.

CHAPTER SEVENTEEN

SLIPPERY SLOPE

My paper delivery bag had been hung up now for three years. I had delivered my first paper at the age of nine, my very last when I was fifteen, and after six years I felt it was time for fresh challenges. I had also hung up my running spikes. An injury to the tendons in my foot had forced an early retirement, much to the delight of my fellow competitors. And then when Fifth Form came to its conclusion my headmaster didn't exactly throw me out, he just told me that when my exams were finished I wouldn't be welcomed back.

I left with very poor results. When we chose our subjects I opted for pottery over computer studies. Back then we were using BBC computers and I really didn't think that computers would catch on. Also, my Gran was always harping on about how the world was always going to need pots, so the choice seemed easy at the time. I left school with a 'C' grade in pottery. I flunked all the others by taking a cocktail of magic mushrooms and a large dose of 'I don't give a fuck'. After eleven years at school, I only just knew the difference between a thesaurus and a diplodocus.

Times were changing for us, drugs were becoming trendy again with the rise of the acid house scene, and I didn't have anything going on to focus my attention away from them. Neither had I the will to resist them. Besides, they were a laugh. At school there was a little group of us into smoking a bit of pot, harmless enough stuff, but we would take anything else that we could find, and I mean anything. Drugs were becoming a bit of a menace in some schools and they were threatening to bring in random testing, but we had our own testing programme in place. If one of us found a bottle of pills at the old folks' home while visiting the grandparents, or at home in our parents' secret bedside stash, we would bring them to school and give them to a lad called Jeremy. Half an hour after he'd swallowed a handful we'd see what he was doing. If he was rolling around in agony clutching his guts we'd leave well alone, but if he was smiling like a Cheshire cat and telling everyone that he loved them then we'd start popping them like Skittles.

When the last day of school finally came I couldn't wait to get out on the other side of those gates. Best days of your life they say; well, I'd had a bit of a giggle but I would never go that far. I now needed a full-time job and I needed to find one fast, as the rule of thumb in our house was that if you weren't staying on to sixth form then you had to pay your own way. I fancied myself as one of those dapper, sharp-suited, car-sales types, so the best place to start looking would be in a car showroom, and that was where I headed.

Alfie, my wingman, was staying on at school to do his A levels, and after taking the piss and telling me I had no chance, he waited outside on the forecourt while I went in feeling a little nervous. After a ten-minute chat with the manager I walked back out onto the forecourt, looking like Captain Cocksure, not as a future car salesman, but as a grease monkey. Alfie didn't need to know that for a day or so, though. That night we celebrated the only way we knew how at the time, by getting off our chops.

The first week in my new job was not what I had imagined. I washed about sixty cars, scraped a cat off an exhaust box and helped change the windscreen and bonnet of a car that somebody had fallen on – Suicide Bridge had claimed another victim. All of that I could handle, but when I picked up my wage packet at the end of the week and found out I'd been earning just as much when I was at school

136

doing my part-time jobs, it was a little too much to bear. This wasn't how it was supposed to be.

I was feeling more and more disillusioned with life, stuck in a rut. I could graft, work as hard as the next man if not harder, but I wanted to get paid well for it. A little short-sighted, I know, but I couldn't quite see the big picture at that time. I stuck at the job for six months and then told them to stick it. It was also at this time that I parted company from Alfie and hooked up with another gang. I was starting to take drugs a little seriously and Alfie was concentrating on his studies. There was no falling out, we simply went our separate ways; but I would come to regret this later.

The time for making crap decisions was upon me and that was one of my first. It was the first year of a new decade, the 1990s. Margaret Thatcher had been forced to resign and John Major had filled her high-heeled shoes. Smoking on all commercial airliners had been banned, just a small taste of the persecution that was to follow for smokers. Nelson Mandela enjoyed his first taste of freedom for twenty-seven years. Man U beat Crystal Palace 1–0 in a Wembley replay to claim the FA Cup. The first Desert Storm was authorised by George Bush Senior after Saddam Hussein sent 100,000 troops into neighbouring Kuwait. The rapper Vanilla Ice released 'Ice, Ice Baby', which went straight to the number one spot, and open-air all-night rave parties were going off all over the country every weekend.

It was an exciting time for someone who was disenchanted with all he saw around him. We were young and managing to find money from places other than work, and we had drugs and energy to burn. I ended up following a well-trodden career path to hard drugs and self-destruction, but I preferred to call it the scenic route, one that has been used by so many before me and many more since. I stopped off at all the main points of interest: warehouse parties, open-air parties, all-night parties, parties that started in the mornings and ones that wouldn't end. And I sampled all the local delicacies while I was sightseeing: LSD, MDMA, ecstasy, ketamine, amphetamine, cocaine and free base to mention just a few. All the parties and all the drugs and all the fun were just grooming me for my final destination, and I remember it so well.

One day, with a few friends, I was resting in some dark and dingy sitting-room after another long weekend of partying. The curtains were drawn and the sun was coming up; we were smoking dope and drinking brandy on yet another long come-down. There was a knock at the door. It might as well have been the Grim Reaper knocking, but I don't think even he could have handed out as much destruction as what was behind that front door. It was another friend of ours who had brought a friend, and he had a little bag of brown powder on his person. Nobody wanted to call it heroin because that made it sound dirty, so we called it magic powder, and it was magic. It was also the beginning of the end of the carefree, flower-power years. We were now two snorts and a burn away from a whole new world of shit. As if my life wasn't already zigzagging down a slippery slope to bum-fuck-somewhere, the very last thing I needed to get involved with was smack.

I could try to come up with a hundred and one excuses for getting into smack, but there really aren't any good ones. At the time we thought we knew best, we were just teetering on the wrong side of curious, and the rave scene and the Es which were our bread and butter were now getting a little stale. There were hundreds like us up and down the country, fed up with Es and the party scene and now dabbling in a little recreational brown. Anyway, we were just going to try it, maybe do it three, four times, and then bin the stuff just before addiction set in.

For the first few months using the brown took me to a completely different level of getting high, completely out of this world; it was like nothing I had known before or even since. But then, very quickly and without my even realising it, it was just shite, a never-ending cycle of running around after your next hit just to keep yourself from getting sick.

Within four to five months of first trying the magic powder, we were all hopelessly addicted and travelling down our own separate pathways to disaster. Heroin had us all by the balls. It's one of the strongest painkillers known to man, and highly addictive. It's extracted from the opium poppy, mainly grown and refined in Afghanistan. It is then shipped here to the streets and sold to muppets like us.

There are two main ways of getting heroin into your system. One, you burn a small amount on a piece of kitchen foil and inhale the smoke through a tube, also rolled out of foil. This is known as 'chasing the dragon', and is the way most people are introduced to the drug, me included. Two, you can inject, or 'mainline', heroin straight into your bloodstream. First you have to break the powder down and turn it into a liquid. To achieve this you mix the powder with vitamin C or citric acid, and a little water. You then heat the mix, normally in a spoon over a lighter or candle, until it boils and the powder liquefies. This is called 'cooking up'.

Once you have your clear brown liquid in the spoon it's time to draw it into the syringe. This is done through a filter, normally broken from the end of a cigarette, which stops any foreign bodies contaminating the mix. When the liquefied heroin is safely inside the syringe it's time to take your hit. Then you sit back and enjoy the ride.

You could take heroin every day and still live a very normal life, hold down a job, start a family and see your friends. So why is heroin so anti-social and why does it cause so many problems? The answer is quite simple – it is just not possible to get hold of heroin every day, and if for some reason you can't have your daily fix then your normal day has just been gazumped.

There are two things that stop addicts feeding their addiction. Number one is money, and anyone who's into smack will run out of money on a regular basis; number two is your supplier's failure to restock on time. This is called a 'dry spell', and they hurt the most. The difference between the two is this: if you run out of money you can always go and get some more via the art of beg, borrow or steal (which is also not without its problems). But if your suppliers have run out and they can't get any more for a few days (or weeks), then you're fucked. You're not going to work, sleep, eat, or even wash until the drought is over and your bloodstream is once again flowing with smack. You can forget about family, friends, work or play. This may seem a tad dramatic but it's just the way it is. Heroin is some very serious tackle.

Desperate men do desperate things and a man who is addicted to heroin and can't get hold of any can be a very desperate man indeed. That's not an excuse for the way he behaves, it's just a fact. I'm not proud of any of the stuff I got up to during this time, and neither am I all that ashamed either. I rarely think about it at all any more, just the occasional dream or nightmare.

Most of the heroin addicts I met were never nasty people; most were just normal like me, and hadn't thought much about what they were getting themselves into. Heroin has the potential to turn anyone into a bit of a nuisance; the person you ended up hurting the most was yourself, and I paid for it with some very heavy coin. I hurt my family a lot too. You try and keep it secret from them; addicts are accomplished liars and can be very economical with the truth, but it's only a matter of time before you bring some form of trouble to the doorstep.

After a few years on the brown I started getting my collar felt on a fairly regular basis, and my name ended up in the papers. My parents were disappointed with me for sure, and it wasn't a nice way for them to find out, but they were there for me, and they wanted to help. Step one on that road to recovery was to admit I had a problem and seek help. I had already sought help at the substance misuse centre, having been forced to admit I had a problem by the courts after an earlier knuckle-rap, so with that the doorway was open.

My parents and I went along together to see my substance misuse counsellor. The more they heard from him the more they realised that the road to recovery was neither short nor straight. We all decided that I should move back home into a stable environment, and for the next twelve weeks my old man wouldn't leave my side. Only during my baths and bed-time would he have time out.

Every morning I would urinate into a sample jar, with my old man standing behind me watching, and I would then hand it to him and he would give me my daily fix of methadone, a heroin substitute. Over the next twelve weeks we would come down on the dosage until I was down to zero. That was the plan, anyway. We would then have breakfast and drive to the workshop, dropping off the sample jar at the clinic on the way. The sample would be tested to see if I was sticking to the programme, and more often than not it would come back with 'Yes'. I was making an effort, and we would continue as we were. My dad and I would then spend the day in the workshop carving furniture – four-poster beds, tables, chairs, all top-quality stuff.

Even though we were in each other's face twenty-four/seven, we got along fine and we would often share a good laugh whilst completing all the orders, stopping only occasionally for a well-earned pint and a pie. If we hadn't stopped for a pint during the day we would stop off on the way home. It was during one of these pit-stops that the road to recovery started coming apart at the seams. I needed some cigarettes, so the old man handed me some change (I wasn't allowed my own money for obvious reasons). I then walked the fifty yards down the street to the corner shop, on my own for the first time; I'd be away just a few minutes while my old man waited and supped his pint back at the bar. No-one can get himself into trouble in that amount of time.

On my way back from buying the cigarettes a police car pulled up alongside me; they bundled me in the back and away we went to the station for a bit of a shakedown. Two hours later they released me with no charge, but told me they would soon have enough evidence to put me away forever – the normal spiel, simply trying to blow smoke up my arse. Oh, and they also kept hold of the mobile phone I was carrying, which was the works phone and the size of a house brick, as they all were back in those days. They told me that if I wanted it back then my old man would have to go in and pick it up. Fair enough.

Dad had given up waiting and I met him at home, after convincing him that I hadn't been off to score and that I really was picked up by the police. He calmed down and drove to the station to claim his phone. The constable behind the counter at the police station wasn't a normal copper, he was a Special. He not only gave my old man the phone but handed him a separate bag. My old man thanked him and left.

When I saw him at home later he explained and showed me the bag. Inside was the evidence that they no longer had against me. My old man didn't know the significance of this, and he handed the bag over to me. I made a snap decision. I took a walk to the end of the garden to have a smoke, and dropped the bag of evidence in with the rubbish for the bin men who were due in the morning. And that was the end of that, or so I would have hoped.

The next day we went through the same routine. Piss in a pot, breakfast, drive to work and drop off the sample at the clinic, do the day's graft, drive home. We stopped off at the Nag's Head on the way; the fags I bought the day before were gone so I nipped to the shop again to buy some more. Same script. As I left the shop on my way back to the pub, there was a screech of tyres and I got bundled into the back of the same police car. Neither the police officer nor his deputy was looking happy. Good cop/bad cop had gone out of the window, along with any hope of my getting away with this with as little fuss as I would have liked.

They pulled into an empty car park to give me another shakedown, demanding back their bag. Now was not the time to tell them that the bag was gone and buried in a landfill site, so instead I told them that I had no idea what they were talking about. Not very smart, but what else could I say? They let me out of the car with the threat of further action ringing in my ears. Yeah, whatever, what could they do? It was their fuck-up.

By the time I made it back to the pub my old man was sweating big time, but I managed to smooth things over and convince him yet again that I hadn't scored any brown. We both came to the conclusion that perhaps I shouldn't go off on my own any more to buy cigarettes. We finished our beer and went home.

It was day three since I was first picked up by the police, and I woke with a bad feeling that I couldn't quite put my finger on. Nothing went wrong, though, and after putting in a productive day in the workshop I was beginning to think my earlier bad feeling was just me being paranoid. We stopped off again at the Nag's Head; it was quite a busy afternoon at the pub, being a Friday, and all the tradesmen had finished early, looking forward to the weekend. It was POETS day, 'Piss Off Early, Tomorrow's Saturday'. The bar was busy and everyone had congregated around the normal corner by the window.

Someone noticed a police car pull up outside, and it was brought to the attention of my old man. He turned to one of his mates and said with a chuckle, 'Oh, someone's in trouble.' My body immediately went limp and I got that sinking feeling. This couldn't be good; it was the police officer, heading inside with his deputy in tow. They walked in through the crowd straight up to my dad, put a hand on his shoulder and read him his rights.

If there was ever a time I wanted the world to open up and swallow me whole, this was it. Everyone in the bar was watching open-mouthed as my father was led out, shoulders slumped and a copper on either side. The police officer turned and gave me a wink. It was now my turn to sweat and be left on my Jack Jones nursing my pint, wondering what in all the fuck to do. My old man hadn't even had a parking ticket in his life and I had just got him a capture by the Old Bill.

Several sweaty pints later on – on the tab because I was still not allowed my own money – my old man returned, looking like Charles Bronson just after his wife was murdered by those thugs in Death Wish. Before I knew it I was out the back, through the fire escape, up against the chicken-wire fence. He told me that he had just been arrested for stealing off the Crown, a hanging offence back in the old days, and that if they didn't get their stuff back they were going to throw the book at him. You can't talk your way out of a situation like that; it was just a case of damage limitation.

So I told my dad straight that I would put my hands up, come clean and take it on the chin: anything that would come close to taking the heat off him and making some sort of amends. Parents are funny things; you never know which way they're going to go. He cuffed me one on the ear and told me to stop being a prat, to keep mum and see how it panned out. He was, and always has been, an upstanding and hard-working, law-abiding citizen. My old man's only crime was hanging around with his son, but you know what they say, 'guilty by association.' I was in a tight corner. He didn't want to see me in any more trouble, so the plan was that we would both say nothing and do nothing. Together we walked casually back inside for a quick sherry and many a raised eyebrow.

Over the next few days I sweated like a hippo in a cat suit. My old man was still seriously pissed off with me and rightly so, but was keeping up a pretence for my mother's sake. We were going through the motions, but I'd put too much of a strain on our normal light-hearted relationship. It was then that I got the worst phone call of my life. It was a Saturday, and I was at home watching Mr Blobby molest the general public on national telly. Mother called through that the phone was for me. I picked up the receiver; 'Hello,' I said and then listened.

They were the kind of words that ricochet around the skull, playing over and over like a scratched record; my old wingman Alfie was dead. In a head-spinning few moments I was told he had been in a road traffic accident and was killed instantly. I replaced the receiver and stood for a few moments motionless in the kitchen. At a time like this you ask yourself how the fuck a great guy like Alfie, who was doing everything right in life, was dead, and a complete muppet like me was still bumbling through life without a scratch. Don't get me wrong, I didn't want to die; I just couldn't understand why Alfie had.

Time for a new plan. I was cramping the old man's style, being an Olympic-sized stone in the tread of his tyre. I couldn't bring any more trouble to my parents' front door, and I was hurting like mad from the loss of my best mate. You would hope that now I would make the right decision, but no. I needed a hit and I needed one tonight. The heroin was calling and calling me strong. I was craving the brown stuff like a new-born baby craves milk from its mother. I went upstairs and ran myself a bath, then I left a note on the bathroom floor saying, 'Sorry, thanks for your help, but I wasn't and won't be ready to stop using yet'. I squeezed my way through the bathroom window and slid down the garage roof on to the grass in the back garden, leaving a hole that looked as though a comet had landed in it. I jumped the fence (which snapped) and legged it up the road. I needed to cook up.

The first hit after you've been clean for a while is just awesome. You get a very warm fuzzy feeling, like your first dram of whisky multiplied by three billion. I no longer felt any pain; it doesn't matter what your pains are in life, they all fade away, and then you just melt and sink into the abyss. The pain only comes back when the smack wears off. But I wasn't going to let the smack wear off for a very long time. I was now a fully-functioning addict again.

The next few years went by in a blur as I spent them in a drug-induced near-coma. Most of my time was spent in different grotty bedsits chasing my next hit, and then waking up from my opium bubble with all sorts of filth stuck to me. If I had the energy I would brush away the filth and go out to raise the cash for the next dose in the next grotty bedsit; twenty-four hours a day, seven days a week. That is the life of a person hopelessly addicted to heroin.

It took me until the year 2000, two trips to rehab and three stays in a psychiatric ward before I finally stopped using. In the case of heroin addiction you have to reach an all-time low, not known by normal mortals, before you realise that enough is enough and say goodbye to it once and for all, draw a line in the sand and move on. I had reached it twice already.

It was now my third time; the two previous rehab centres I went to didn't work for me. I lasted two days in the first before jumping out of yet another window and legging it once again up the road to get one last hit. In the second I managed one night. I took a final hit with me and crept into the toilet to settle my nerves, forgetting to lock the door. As I was about to self-administer, one of the other inmates decided he also needed to go to the toilet, and caught me in the act. He turned and headed back down the stairs, screaming blue murder, with me in hot pursuit. I tripped on the second-to-last stair and ended up on my face, the syringe still in my arm. Quite rightly I was sent packing the next day.

But here I was again, looking forward to another stay at a mental home, trying for a third time. If you want to get into rehab for any reason, be it alcohol, drugs or gambling, the big three, you have to go through the mental home first, to purify the soul and get yourself clean. Thus, when you arrive at the rehab of your choice, you won't unsettle any of the other inmates with your withdrawals. They have a whole programme to change you from raging addict to clean but very shell-shocked human in about two weeks.

I had been here twice before so I knew the script, and I was really, really dreading it.

CHAPTER EIGHTEEN

THREE DAYS TO LIVE

There was a nervous tension among us as we stood watching the sun rise on yet another day in captivity. The reason we were a little edgy this morning was that the tribal drums were being beaten rather more fiercely than usual. The mob seemed depressingly happy, and Commander Jackson was setting up his big gun. He was taking great care to position it in line with where we normally sat. We watched the proceedings huddled anxiously together, trying desperately to put a positive spin on them. The drums quietened as the Preacher led the mob into their morning prayers. Prada, Denzel and the Secretary were discussing something in raised voices and looking at some newspaper article, while Commander Jackson pointed his favourite weapon in our direction and looked down the sights. The raised voices weren't necessarily a worry, as they would normally debate even the most mundane things as if they were about to commit murder.

The Secretary summoned us over with that cold, smug expression of his. I had a sinking feeling in the pit of my stomach and I could sense the others shared my apprehension. Our fears were confirmed when we were told to stand in front of Commander Jackson and his menacing gun. The atmosphere amongst the rest of the mob was electric as they all gathered round and jostled for the best vantage point. We stood there like four statues rooted to the spot, just a slight twitchiness to the features betraying our outwardly calm front. The mob was beginning to bay for blood. Men with whom I shared a cigarette just the other night while listening to the Preacher's plan to kidnap George Bush were now calling for me to die; everything here was so fragile. The newspaper was handed over to us and Plooy was told to read it aloud. He cleared his throat and began.

'MEND has issued a three-day ultimatum to the federal government to release Alhaji Dokubo-Asari by 29th May. Failure to do so will result in the deaths of all foreign hostages.'

It had turned political and we were in the shit. All the while it was just about money we had every chance of getting out, but now a happy ending was slipping out of reach. It's hard to explain the despair I felt, but it was absolute and all-consuming. These people had complete power over whether we lived or died. The death threat we had just received was now backed up and delivered by the Secretary in a serious business-like tone: 'You see, you will all die in three days.'

This last statement seemed to please the mob and they all cheered, giving us the finger across the throat. Commander Jackson was standing behind his gun with those cold, intelligent eyes, looking a little pissed that he was not going to get to use it today.

After receiving verbal death threats every day, actually reading about your own forthcoming execution in a newspaper was freaking scary. Plooy nudged me in the ribs and whispered, 'Check the date, check the date.'

I did as he asked, and it said 29th May. 'What about the fucking date, what about the part where it says we're all gonna die?' I asked.

'Well, it's now 2nd June; that deadline has been and gone and, correct me if I'm wrong, but we're still very much alive.' Plooy was right and the mob was four days late. I'm sure there was a comedy moment there somewhere, but all I could think was, 'Bloody hell, this man Plooy knows his onions. I don't even know what day of the week it is, let alone what day of what month.'

'How do you know what the date is?' Noor whispered.

'Look, it says so on my watch,' and it did, quite clearly, say 02-06-2007.

I wouldn't have said we were totally relieved at this point, or put at ease with Plooy's new findings – the mob still wanted us all dead and Commander Jackson was still standing on the wrong side of his shooter. But it did give us a sparkle of hope and, if nothing else, it showed us that these guys were a little, if not totally, behind the times.

With their point firmly put across the mob dispersed, congratulating each other and pretending to read and understand the newspaper article, but they were just kidding themselves; one of them was scrutinising the newspaper at arm's length, holding it upside down while nodding at it approvingly. We were pretty sure the Secretary was the only member of this gang who could read and write, and he was no Charles Dickens. We were left alone on the edge of the yard next to our rubbish dump feeling somewhat deflated, wondering how to react to this latest turn of events. The camp went about its business of getting stoned. Prada looked particularly happy with himself, sitting with his groupies over where the boats were moored. This was the mood that Prada and his little splinter group liked us to be in: downbeat, pliable and yielding to their campaign of bullying. It was not long before small stones and sticks came sailing over from their direction, followed by a few overhead shots from their AKs. When you can feel the breeze of a 7.62 bullet whistling past, you know it's getting a little close.

The four of us stayed there for the rest of the day waiting for the sun to sink below the jungle canopy, not daring to venture any further than the river bank for a quick piss and then straight back again. No one said much; we just sat with our own private thoughts, clinging on to the hope that Plooy was right, that the date of our executions had indeed come and gone, and that MEND had had a change of heart. We had shared some pretty lousy experiences together since we were taken from our vessel some eight days ago, but sitting there in the dirt was the lowest we had felt so far. We were in desperate need of a morale boost.

'Fuck me, now it's starting to rain,' said Noor, offering the palm of his hand to the sky. All the militants ran to their huts as the heavens opened and the Delta began to receive one of its tremendous downpours. It rained hard in the Delta, with big fat drops that soak you through in seconds. The locals hated it and you would never catch them outside when it rained; at the first drop they high-tailed it to the nearest shelter.

We also picked ourselves up and headed for the shelter of our cell. Once inside we huddled by the open window and watched the downpour. The weather outside matched our mood perfectly. 'Let's have a shower,' I said.

'A what?' came the reply.

'A shower, come on, it will pick us up, be better than washing in pit water. We can just stand under the roof.'

The rain was running off the corrugated roof in torrents, more than enough to wash in. 'You gotta be kidding me, I'm staying in the dry, thanks,' said Bob.

'OK, Lekka!' said Plooy. So we stripped off and went outside naked as the day we were born, to wash in the cold, fresh rainwater.

The water felt great, better than any power shower, and our spirits were immediately lifted. We washed our bodies, mine still covered in nasty bites, and filled our bellies with some rain water too. The lack of clean drinking water was turning my piss all sorts of colours not found on any Dulux paint chart, so the chance of a bellyful of fresh was most welcome.

As we were drying off in our cell Plooy announced that tomorrow we would build the camp some rain traps to collect gallons of fresh water.

'You wanna do what? Just this morning they wanted to shoot us all to death, and now you want us to do some home improvements for them? Well, fuck that; let Christian Aid come in here and build wells for the fuckers if they want fresh water.'

I'm ashamed to admit that little outburst came from me, but Plooy was quick to point out the benefits of building rain traps. One, we needed fresh water to drink, and two, it would be a good 'hearts and minds' exercise, maybe even endear us to them and make it harder for them to kill us. I didn't think it would work with Prada but never mind. Also, no-one would think we were about to do one over the wire if we were busy building rain traps, so the guards should relax a little. Plooy had a way of making things make sense, and it did now sound a worthwhile project.

'Count me in then,' I said at last.

'Yeah, me too,' said Noor.

The rain had stopped and it was getting dark; it would stay damp and muddy tonight, as the sun hadn't had a chance to dry everything out. The NAFy would also come in their droves tonight; they seemed to love it after a good rainfall, especially if it was still damp in the evening. The militants started to appear again on the yard to stretch their legs and continue drinking; one or two lost their footing and slipped in the mud, laughing at each other. We also made our way outside to find a very forlorn-looking Gastro Pod sitting in our space by the ever-growing mound of rubbish. 'What's up, who's died?' we asked.

'Huh?' came Gastro Pod's response. He didn't quite get the joke so we tried a different tack.

'Why are you so sad?' we asked again.

Gastro Pod's answer was very disheartening for us. 'I'm no guard no more, they've taken my gun.' This was bad news for us as we had just lost the most useless guard in the whole of the Delta region; the Terracotta Army could give him the slip. We were sympathetic and asked him why. 'Kept falling asleep,' came his sorry reply.

'Nothing to do with all the kai-kai and marijuana you take, then?' came ours.

Today was just full of bad news and I didn't know if I could take much more. Not only had we been promised a quick death this morning, but the 'best' guard in the whole world had lost his job and would no doubt be replaced by an Eagle Eye II. I needed a walk to sort my head out and started to lap the yard, head down, shoulders slumped, hands in pockets and kicking stones: a proper dejected stroll with feet that still hurt like hell from having the life sucked out of them by the NAFy. After my third lap I was joined by Noor and Plooy, who quickly fell in step and encouraged me to get a grip. We walked like this for maybe an hour, trying to find some positives from today but achieving nothing. We were just about to turn in for the night after completing lap five hundred and sixty-eight, when I caught a glimpse of polished black out of the corner of one eye. It was way over in the distance outside Hut Three. I stopped dead in my tracks and reined in Noor and Plooy. 'Look, can you see? Over there outside the hut,' I gestured.

They both looked but couldn't make out what I was getting so excited about. 'Over there, look, Jackson's boots,' I said. Commander Jackson must have been having himself a little lie-down because there were his boots, neatly parked side by side outside Hut Three.

'See, I told you no one sleeps in his boots,' I said. All we had to do now was hope they were there on the night we escaped and then nick them before we legged it.

'That's it. We've all got a pair of boots. If things still look grim tomorrow, and there's no reason why they won't, I think we should make our last arrangements and be prepared to go over the wire tomorrow night,' said Noor.

'You think we're ready?' I asked, feeling a little apprehensive.

'Not much to be ready about, we know what direction we're going in, all we need to do tomorrow is each save a bit of rice from our meal and organise our escape kit,' said Plooy.

'What about better clothes for Noor?' I asked, trying to stall.

'Just have to make do, won't I? The insects don't seem to be as fond of me as they are of you, and I'll just have to be careful about getting scratched by the jungle foliage.'

'Bob's watch?'

'Sort that tomorrow night,' replied Noor.

'That's it then, bon voyage!' I said, sounding more confident than I felt.

We did, though, have nearly every piece of the jigsaw titled 'Dick' in place; only the odd detailed centre-pieces were missing, but those we would just have to do without. We did one final lap, a lap of honour. This time in two days we might well be stumbling around in the bush heading to God knows where, but it would be better than sitting in here; that much I did know. After the lap of honour we returned to our cell and settled down for the night.

I lay down squashed up against Plooy under the NAFy net, trying hard not to let any part of me touch it. If I could help it, I wanted to try to limit my contact with the mosquitoes to a bare minimum tonight.

CHAPTER NINETEEN

REHAB

It was the end of one millennium and the start of another. The predicted cyber-crash never occurred; New Year came and went and not a single circuit board sizzled, and as the end of the world never happened I had to follow through with my plan. The day had arrived for me to take a new path and set a course far from my past, but before I made my way to the funny farm, there was something I needed to do. I had to have one last hit, a hit to end all hits, one to remember. It is after all a junkie tradition.

I locked up my bolt-hole, a one-man cesspit in the sky, and posted the keys through the letter box; I wouldn't be needing them any more. I left the block of flats without a hint of nostalgia, I didn't even bother looking back, and started heading in the direction of the funny farm. Not too far away, just a small detour from where I was heading, was a nice little crack den I knew, run by a right pair of eccentrics. I hadn't seen this pair for a while and I thought my credit with them was pretty good. My inbuilt satnav was re-programmed and my feet put me on a new heading.

My whole body was trembling with anticipation, every hair and nerve-ending standing to attention. It had been nearly twelve hours since my last hit and I was already coming down. The four flights of stairs I was climbing to flat 507 were devoid of life. Graffiti tags led the way up the cracked and crumbling steps with paint peeling off the walls. The stairwell was strewn with litter: dirty discarded needles, soiled condoms and fast-food wrappers, and the place stank of stale piss. I reached level five and knocked quickly on the door, not wanting to hang around in the well for longer than was necessary; not everyone welcomed my sort round here.

The door swung open and the emaciated youth on the other side let me in with a courteous nod. As I walked down the hall to the main room I took in the scene. One of the eccentrics, Edgar, greeted me at a hundred miles an hour, babbling about this, that and the other. There were three more lads on chairs, and a comatose girl on the sofa. It was definitely not a scene from a country living magazine. The vacuum had not been run round in a while, and the place smelt of corruption. The faces that could focus on me were gaunt, pale and vacant.

After greeting all the nearly-deads I followed Edgar through to one of the bedrooms where they kept and sold the drugs. They called this guy Edgar after J Edgar Hoover, the FBI man, not because he was good at solving crimes but because he could hoover an unhealthy amount of powder up his nose. As we exchanged money for gear, I noticed dried powder and crystals of sorts stuck around the rim of his nostrils, gripping his nasal hairs like stalactites. My credit here was good and I knew by this afternoon I would be gone forever, so after handing over my last ten-pound note in the whole world I put the rest on loan, telling Edgar that I would be back in the afternoon to pay him back and buy some more – lying still came very naturally. In return I got two rocks of crack and two bags of brown. I nearly wet myself, it was so exciting.

Back in the main room I found myself a space on the floor and got my kit out. One of the rocks went straight in the pipe, crackling ferociously as I inhaled, hence its name. Now crack is another of those nuisance drugs; it is highly addictive and very powerful. In my view it can be more destructive than heroin, but this morning I was just using it as a confidence-booster. The hit was immediate and extremely intense but, unlike heroin, it only lasts a little while, one

156

or two minutes, leaving the user wired and beside himself for another rock, stopping at nothing until he gets one.

Out of my two rocks I made six good pipes. With them finished I moved swiftly on and started cooking up. My first hit was everything it should have been and I was in heroin heaven, all the stress of the crack comedown long forgotten. A half-hour later I managed to summon the energy to fix my last-ever hit; this one was going to be good. I went through the ritual of putting my hit together, taking my time, getting it right.

I found the perfect vein running up the inside of my left forearm and pierced the skin. I depressed the plunger, and my bloodstream was flooded.

'Fuck, it's the Old Bill. Raid!'

The shout of warning had come from the voice at the door and had pierced everybody's brains like a full metal jacket. A blanket was hurled into the air from the corner of the room. It was Pete, the other eccentric; he was called Pete because, well, that was his name. Pete was alive again and so was everyone else in flat 507. I didn't care, though; I was not enjoying my last hit in the relaxed fashion that I would have liked, but it could have been worse. The raid could have started before I'd had time to administer it.

Pete and Edgar were flapping big time, with their emaciated morning watchman shouting through updates from the front door, his eye stuck to the spyhole. The police were running up and down the stairs, then lining up outside the door, then going upstairs again. All the details seemed a little confusing and no-one had time to listen. Everyone inside the flat had one thing on their mind and that was to get rid of the merchandise. The only place for that was the bathroom, to flush it down the bog. If it was an organised raid, which this one seemed to be, the police would have cut the soil pipe and would

157

simply catch the class As as we flushed them away. But when you're high and desperate you still go through the motions.

They needed help, and I wasn't going to let them down. I grabbed a rock from the sideboard and lit up my pipe, then took a handful of powder from one of the mirrors and started snorting. I switched from Edgar to Pete and back again, helping in the destruction of their contraband. We must have been nearly three-quarters of the way through their stash when the shout went up.

'False alarm?' This time the voice sounded more as if it was asking a question than shouting out an update, and rightly so; I wouldn't want to be in his shoes if he got the 'Old Bill, it's a raid' warning wrong. Not after what I had just seen flushed away into the sewerage system. Everyone was stock-still, no one making a sound. The place was silent apart from the cistern refilling. The voice called back, 'They're bringing three men down the stairs, Pakis; they've arrested three Pakis.'

Pete called back to him in a hushed tone, 'Can't be, there aren't any Pakis living upstairs.'

'I'm telling you, three Pakis have been led down and the police are all following them down, we're in the clear, they're not after us,' the voice pressed home. Everyone relaxed apart from me; I was too wired now from all the unforeseen extras I'd had. Time for me to go. It was heart-breaking to leave and witness the looks on the two eccentrics' faces turn from relief to despair when it dawned on them just how much this fuck-up had cost.

'Still, it's better than having the filth come crashing through the strong door,' I said, falling out into the stairway. The lookout was right, though; three Asian men had been arrested. As I made it outside I overheard two old biddies and a single mother deep in gossip about the three 'Pakis'. They could have been from anywhere in Asia. People round there were pretty racially ignorant: as far as they were concerned people were either white, black, yellow or Paki. There was no grey area.

According to what I overheard in the car park, an old lady on the top floor had phoned Rentokil thinking she had monster rats in the attic. When Rentokil arrived, they popped up into the loft space with their extermination gear and were greeted by the sight of three illegal immigrants, cold, hungry and just as scared as the rat-catchers. They all stayed there until the police turned up, and thanks to them I got the best last hit ever.

That wasn't it for me, though; I couldn't turn up at the lunatic asylum looking like a lunatic. I had to sort myself out. I needed to make one more detour to a friend round the corner and get some downers. I was thinking blue ones, or possibly yellow, a couple of Valiums just to smooth the path on my first night.

I arrived at the institution feeling nervous and vulnerable, as I should have been when I turned up for the ill-fated operation on my ears. My overnight bag was also smaller than it was then, because by now I had sold the last of my possessions to raise the money for my final hit.

When you first arrived on a ward like this, the rules were explained. No drugs, no alcohol, no leaving the grounds, no fighting or getting too friendly with any other patients, no this, no that; every rule had a 'no' in front of it. Next came the search of your bag, followed by your person, for contraband and weapons. When that was complete and you had been given the good-to-go, you were shown to your bed to fill out the forms. My bed was in a dorm shared with about ten others. These were troubled people; some were considered by the authorities to be a danger to themselves or the public, but they were normally just very confused, scared, and in most cases very sad and unhappy people, with all sorts of different problems and mental health issues.

When you got your head around that you could slowly start to integrate with the others on the ward. With all the administration out of the way I lay back on my bed contemplating the next two weeks, and swore to myself that this was the last time and that I would never use again, ever. But I had promised myself that before, so only time would tell. I heard a noise coming from the next bed. There was a curtain pulled around for a bit of extra privacy, but there was no mistaking that sound; the guy next to me was jerking himself off. Just my bloody luck, my next-door neighbour was a masturbator. I closed my eyes and sank deeper into my bed and despair; this was going to be a long two weeks.

After a restless sleep filled with strange dreams I woke to a daytime nightmare which was all of my own making. Opposite me was an old man who looked like Captain Birdseye, with a big off-white bushy beard and a blue skipper's cap with a gold embroidered anchor on the front. He was pulling his bed sheets up under his chin with all his strength, as two nurses tried to wrestle them away from him and convince him it was time for his weekly bath. Two beds up to my right and the old man there was pulling out his hair and laughing hysterically at Captain Birdseye, stopping only to recite bits from the Bible; and next door to my left Master Bates was choking the chicken for the fourth time in a little under twelve hours. Sometimes if you've made your bed you just have to lie in it, but I decided to get up and have a cup of tea.

Leaving the dorm after a wash, I made my way to the TV room with a mug of steaming tea. I passed a few stragglers bouncing gently off the walls, also heading in that direction. As I opened the door to the TV room a huge cloud of cigarette smoke escaped, followed by a tall man with nine-o'clock shadow and eyes pointing in different directions. Inside, women sat in small groups crying and consoling each other and men just sat, staring vacantly at the small TV with long-burnt-out cigarettes between their fingers. The mornings seemed to be the hardest time of the day for the inmates of the Farm; I guess it was the morning blues, or just waking up and knowing they would have to live through another day of torment. Whatever the reason, there was no getting away from the scenes of early morning grief and despair. I never was one for TV anyway.

Two things happened here that you could set your watch to. One was meal time, the other was drug time. Both took place three times a day, and neither needed an alarm or a nurse to announce it. It was just built in to anyone who stayed here for more than a few days. At the designated time for drugs everyone stood up from their chairs and headed down the corridor, forming an orderly queue outside the best room on the ward: the drugs room. One by one they took turns to take their cocktails of pills and potions, the best part of everyone's day; even the women stopped crying for a bit. I took my place in the queue and waited patiently for my daily ration, a meagre 30ml of methadone. No way near enough to get me through a normal day, but nothing about this place was normal and it was the best I could hope for. I gratefully took my hit in one, savouring the thick, sickly, cough-mixture taste, and headed for the canteen. At the canteen I grabbed some toast and another mug of tea and headed back to my bed to read a book.

Time passed slowly in a place like this, but when you're withdrawing from heroin time slows down even more. Even though you got a dose of methadone it was only enough to keep the worst of the cold turkey at bay, to take the edge off. The reason you get addicted to heroin in the first place is that it is an endorphin, and the human body naturally produces its own endorphins. They're what make you feel good after exercise for example, but after months of giving your body the artificial endorphins it will give up producing its own. When you take away the heroin the body can wait about

161

three weeks before it starts producing its own endorphins again – the longest three weeks of your life. Cold turkey is very hard on the human mind and body, the most uncomfortable and painfully drawn-out process. Night-time is the worst; you don't sleep, have constant cramps and sweats and your feet get all fidgety and tickly, causing you to kick out. That's why they call it kicking the habit, because people going through cold turkey, or doing the cluck, are constantly kicking out with their feet. It was so bad, I was always up and walking about at night. This was also the time when the police rounded up the day's stragglers, people who had absconded and thought they were well enough to be set free. It was a sorry sight to see them being led back in with their sad, defeated faces, but you couldn't help admiring their spirit, for they would be at it again tomorrow. It was a very lonely time.

On my third morning, I woke up to complete pandemonium. One of the old girls had finally managed to kill herself. She had tried twice already before I had arrived, first by hanging and then by electrocution in the bath; both were unsuccessful. But that night she had cut her wrists with a concealed razor blade. Third time lucky, and I sincerely hoped she was now in a better place. I don't know whether you've ever seen anyone try to mop up a lot of blood but it's not easy, and much of the morning was taken up with nurses spreading the thick redness around the white tiled floor of the ladies' toilet.

Whilst that clean-up was going on, there was an even bigger incident in the TV room. Pulling his hair out and laughing hysterically, the man from two beds up and to the right from mine was trying to watch his re-runs of Minder on the top-loading video player; but during the night someone had spoon-fed it raspberry jam and the VCR was now far too sticky to work. Jam was not a good lubricant for electrical entertainment equipment, so he was seriously

162

pissed off and kicking up a jolly good force-nine storm, unsettling all the rest of the TV fans. In the middle of all this a new patient walked in. She was absolutely stunning. Young, long blonde hair, blue eyes, a button nose and a body that could surely bring an end to all the conflict around me; but no one else even noticed.

I hadn't had a decent hit in forty-eight hours, and the small world that was now my home seemed to be going mad with blood and jam everywhere. People were screaming and running about as if the world was about to come to an end, but there she was, a pretty young thing standing in the middle of it all. It took me a millisecond to size her up as I checked her from head to toe, as she tossed her long blonde hair and turned her head towards me.

She was mental, completely nuts. On the cuckoo scale of one to ten, she would be an eleven, but a very hot eleven indeed. I don't mean this in a nasty way, but she was as crazy as they come. It might sound as if I'm making this up but I'm not; you'll just have to trust me. Within the next few hours she had stripped butt naked and streaked across the rooftops of the neighbouring buildings, crying out to nobody in particular that she was the Queen of Sheba. Don't ask me how she managed to give the nurses the slip and get out to the flat roof opposite but she did, and it was a very beautiful sight against the grey, depressing backdrop we observed from the window on every other day. It took the nurses a good two hours, and another four cups of tea for me, before they managed to talk her down, but it wouldn't be the last time that she would treat us to such sights. Perhaps the next couple of weeks wouldn't last so long after all.

Over the next few days, and with the right medication, the Queen of Sheba came back down to Planet Us and settled into a normal routine – well, normal for this place. She was still a little away with the fairies but I was in no position to judge her, so I started talking to her. There were a few young girls there: anorexics, self-harmers and

163

some that were just plain mental. Give me the just plain mental any day, much less maintenance. I could sit and chat with Sheba for hours and marvel at her beauty; all the other patients and the depressing surroundings would just disappear. I'd find myself wondering how someone so lovely could end up in here. She was similar to a crushed petal, a little damaged for sure but still very pretty, and she smelled divine.

Sheba told me that she'd been studying very hard at university and was spending long periods of time alone at the computer; but after a while she thought the computer and TV were taking over her body, all the wiring boring itself deep into her body and soul, turning her into the Queen of Sheba. Even as she was talking to me the TV was communicating with her, not as loudly as it had in the past, but it was still asking her to do things. I asked her the one question that was playing on my mind. 'What drugs did you take?' The answer blew me away; she hadn't taken any, it was just a case of the human mind malfunctioning – mental illness. I felt really sorry for her, but was glad she was here to brighten up the days. We would go for short walks around the grounds, or sit in the coffee shop and chat over a slice of cake and a cup of tea. It was the first time in many years that I was doing normal things and feeling normal with it; it was just a little ironic that the first time I did some normal stuff it just happened to be in a mental home with someone completely round the twist, but life's never perfect.

When your mind and body begin to be weaned off heroin, you start to regain normal human emotions and feelings. These emotions feel alien at first as you've been years without them. One of these emotions is your sex drive – heroin kills it dead. For years I hadn't cared whether I got any sex or not; I was actually happier without it. Now, though, as my body purged itself of the poisons my sex drive returned with a vengeance. I was getting strange warm feelings in

164

my tummy and trouser area every time I saw Sheba. I was back and horny as the devil, and there was only one woman on my mind.

I don't think Sheba noticed the change in me or the efforts I would make to be in her company, but then she was ill and probably had more important things on her mind. As each day passed I grew in confidence and desperation, and threw all my best moves at her in order to seal the courtship. I opened doors for her, pulled out chairs; I even made her a friendship bracelet, for fuck's sake. I had it bad, I couldn't get her out of my head. It was hard work, this trying to woo a girl, and very tiring. After one particularly hard day at it I went to bed feeling a little frustrated. I lay in my bed with the curtains drawn round fully, trying to block out the rest of my roommates and reading a book in the hope of dozing off. Tomorrow I was definitely going to make my move on Sheba; I couldn't keep dilly-dallying around the issue. I liked her and she was too ill to know any better; it was a match made in heaven.

My eyes started to grow heavy so I closed my book, slipped it under my pillow and looked forward to tomorrow's love-match as I started to drift off. I lay in my bed for a long while, tossing and turning, dozing in and out of consciousness, grabbing five minutes here and five there. Just when I managed to pass out for another spell, my curtains were pulled aside and in swept Sheba, letting the curtains fall back in place behind her. I went to sit up and speak, but she put one finger to her lips to quieten me and pushed me back down with her other hand. She left her hand on my chest as she straddled me; her touch was electric and I had no control over the sudden surge it gave me. She had noticed my best moves after all.

Sheba had made an effort for she was dressed in character, fashioning a crisp white hospital bed sheet as a toga, tied at the midriff by some gold lace, which accentuated her firm high breasts and slight waist. She was tight, tight like a tigress, gggrrr! She was wearing golden sandals which showed off her delicate feet with their gold-painted toenails, and her long hair was held back from her heart-shaped face by a gold-leaf tiara. If my senses were correct she'd left her panties back in the female dorm. She was beautiful. Arching her back, she tossed her head and lost the tiara, her golden hair tumbling down her shoulders. Letting go of my chest she reached behind her and released her toga. I was rock solid and completely at her mercy.

With her bed sheet fallen around her waist, I reached up and took hold of her naked breasts, a fully erect nipple between each thumb and forefinger. I rolled the nipple quite roughly now, as she let out a low moan which made us both hold our breath. Trying to keep the noise down to a minimum made us both let out a giggle. Every move made a noise, the rustle of bed sheets, the squeaking of springs and bedstead. We couldn't hold back now, though, and the animal instinct took over. I gripped her tightly and thrust my hips upwards, entering her, and again she let out a small moan, biting her lip for quiet. I was back in the game.

I was thrusting in deeper now and quickening my pace; I didn't care about the noise any more, I was close to an exploding climax and God it had been a long time. Sheba sensed the moment and leant forward to lock her mouth on mine as I came inside her. I grunted as I came again and again, my whole body pulsing in time with my orgasm. I opened my eyes and 'Fuck, who's that?' A face was looking at me over Sheba's shoulder with the same expression as mine; he was also coming. It was my neighbour, Master Bates, and he was watching us while jerking himself off. I sat bolt upright to protest and lost my grip on Sheba; she was gone and I was awake. Sweeping away the confusion, it finally dawned on me with the sound of a scratching vinyl what had just happened. What's the story, morning glory?

166

Next door I could hear my neighbour easing back after going at it hammer and tongs, and I had just had a wet dream – shot my load in my PJs. I actually think we came at the same time. I felt confused, dirty and disgusted with myself. I lifted up my covers and sure enough, a little sticky map of Calcutta was pooling on my navel. Oh no, please not this; I felt like I had been violated. I felt sick, ashamed, and I desperately wanted to go back to sleep and finish this properly, lie in her arms and share a post-shag cigarette; but it was not going to happen. Master Bates next door finished up and rolled over to get some more sleep. I couldn't, not now. I cleaned myself up, crawled out of bed and went to find myself a key worker. I needed some counselling.

It took a couple of days before I could look my sweetheart in the eye again, but Sheba really helped make my stay a lot easier and she was and still is the best shag I never had. For that I thank her and wish her well, wherever she is.

It was coming to the end of my stay and I had big plans to make. I was on 0ml of methadone a day, drug-free and clean. I had two days left of my self-imposed sentence, and my next decision about where I went from here had to be a good one. I hoped the age of making crap decisions was over. I had tried rehab twice before and didn't relish it for a third time. I was thinking more along the lines of phoning my folks, just to see if I could stay for a couple of days until I sorted myself out. I hadn't seen them since I squeezed out of the bathroom window and legged it up the road some three years ago, and in that time they had moved to Devon, probably to get away from me and all the horrible baggage that came with me. It was a very hard call to make but I knew it was my best option, moving as far away from all my old haunts as possible and getting some country air, to take time out for my mind and body to heal. I had been completely

167

off my head on drugs for ten years; that was a whole decade I had lost, a ten-year blank in my head.

The phone call went well. I spoke to my mum (dad was still pissed off with me) and she laid down the law. As long as I kept my head down, stayed clean and didn't cause any scandal, I could stay as long as it took for me to sort myself out. The old man would pick me up from the funny farm and take me back to Devon with no stops for cigarettes. My last day at the institution arrived and I said goodbye to all my loopy friends. Saying goodbye to the Queen of Sheba was emotional.

The whole of the naughty nineties were a mystery to me. When they started West Germany had beaten the Argies 1–0 in the World Cup final. East and West Germany were reunited after the Berlin wall was pulled down. And London was in the grip of the Poll Tax riots. When I walked down the steps of the institution into my old man's car, the world had moved on. It was the year 2000 and Al-Qaeda held a three day summit in Kuala Lumpur to discuss and plan future ops, including the attack on the twin towers. Harold Shipman was found guilty and sentenced to life for the murder of fifteen of his patients. And a tree fell on and killed the last wild Pyrenean Ibex (a sort of mountain goat), rendering the sub-species extinct.

CHAPTER TWENTY

NEGOTIATION

It was day ten in the Big Brother Camp and also the tenth time I'd woken up feeling like crap after a very shitty night's sleep. A half-dozen of the NAFy's elite had slipped through our mosquito net and dive-bombed my head all night, leaving me sleepless and my body with a multitude of fresh, angry red bumps, so as a result I was itching all over. When I did finally manage to snatch the odd slice of slumber my dreams were filled with the living dead in the form of decomposing French tramps.

On the flip side, though, I was feeling very excited about getting out of this horrible place within the next twenty-four hours. I'd just had a shit, shower and shave, without the shower and the shave, and finished wiping my arse with my hand. I now considered myself an expert at this and could complete my business with minimal fuss. I made my way over to the others who were waiting together on the edge of the parade ground for this morning's theatrics to begin; if I thought yesterday was a little strange, well, it was fuck all compared with the weirdness that was going to visit us this morning.

We were all relieved to see that the ritual before morning prayer-time was back to its normal dull procession of a half-hearted conga to the patter of drums. We hoped that this was a good sign, and that maybe we might be able to get through the day with no more death threats. After the conga and the drums were through, the procession picked up a gear when the Preacher took to the stage to preach this morning's sermon, dressed only in a small thong, a leather string around his waist with an inadequate flap of material covering his

169

modesty. He wasted no time in whipping the mob into a frenzy, screaming and shouting to the heavens praising the Lord Almighty Jesus Christ; he was a pro, this guy, and he knew exactly what buttons to press to get the flock jumping to his tune. At times he danced so close while delivering his sermon that I got a whiff of his naked cock which was bouncing out from under his thong to say hello. It smelt like a block of old blue cheese smeared in layers of budget fish paste. It was about a foot long and he had the balls of a circus lion. I tried to ignore it, but it's hard when it's waving around a few inches from your face. If you can smell another man's penis it generally means it's way too close. After about ten minutes of over-the-top preaching which sounded more as if he was dishing out a bollocking, he finally brought the prayers to a close, to many cheers and hoots from his audience; they had all been sufficiently blessed for another day of criminal activity and they got the ball rolling right away by diving into the drugs.

We were also getting the ball rolling, and hurried over to the rubbish dump to put the finishing touches to our master plan, Dick. During the day, whenever we got the chance and when Eagle Eye and his new partner (who at this time seemed to be any random guard) were not watching, we were going to unearth all the pieces of our escape kit that were scattered about the yard and then hide them together in one easy-to-grab place, deep in a cavity of the roots of the tree where we aired the mattresses. We still had the empty bottle for carrying water; we had to lay our hands on another which we were going to fill with rice and beans from that evening's meal. After we had completed these rather menial chores we had some slightly more complex tasks to take on. We had somehow to come up with a way to steal Commander Jackson's boots, and also to try and find some better clothing for Noor. Noor had the most daunting job of all:

he had to swap Plooy's watch with Bob's and tell him that we would hope to see him on the other side.

We carried on as usual so as not to raise any suspicions, cleaned out the cell, carried out our mattresses to air in the open and settled down to play some draughts and go over Plooy's plan in more detail. And that was when our plan got well and truly blown out of the swamp. Coming up the river at high speed was the unmistakable sound of the General's gunboat – the only other traffic up and down these waterways were the canoes paddled by the river people, mostly honest, hard-working fishermen and their families.

The General's boat was tied up as soon as it docked, and everyone jumped on to the river bank and started for the camp. There was all his usual entourage in tow, and a couple of new faces I didn't recognise. We stopped our game of draughts, but stayed seated by the rubbish mound and waited to see what the General had planned. He went through his customary entrance to Camp Horrid by shouting a few 'Isowannas' and getting a few enthusiastic 'Wannas' in return from the mob. He lit up a big fat spliff and drank some Monkey Tail whilst offering a small capful to the ground to keep one of the many gods happy, and made the two new faces do the same. He then headed in our direction.

The General walked or rather minced over to us with the Somali and the rest of his bodyguards, who were chaperoning two very nervous and uncomfortable-looking individuals. These two were dressed smartly in traditional African costumes and were obviously not at home in such company or surroundings, so we eyed them hopefully. Commander Jackson led Sachin and Aditya out of their hut and they also joined us over by the rubbish heap. The two new men shook all our hands with warmth and reassurance and offered us some food parcels that they had brought with them. While the General and his crew looked on, we eagerly accepted the parcels but

171

put them to one side for a minute, not wanting to appear too keen until we knew what this was all about.

They introduced themselves as doctors who were acting as middle-men for both MEND and the Nigerian authorities, and they asked us how we were being treated. We told them we were fine but missed our families terribly, and that we just wanted to go home. They were particularly keen to speak to Aditya, the diabetic, whose health had been deteriorating a little more every day. Even if you're relatively fit the sort of environment we were all being forced to live in isn't very good for your health, but if you are unfortunate enough to get sick, injure yourself or have an ailment that requires medication, then your health can go south very quickly indeed.

It's only when you're stripped of all your home comforts and luxuries that you suddenly appreciate the very basics that support life, like clean drinking water, medication and good, fresh, healthy food. I'd made a promise to myself, since I'd been on the rice and bean diet, that when I made it out of here I would never again be choosy with my food; if it was put in front of me I'd eat it, simple. While the two quacks checked over the Indians, Noor, Plooy and I opened our food bags. I looked in mine and then quickly shut it again, looking up at the doctor who gave it to me and then at Noor and Plooy to read any reaction on their faces.

They did the same and looked first at each other and then at me with puzzled expressions. They were difficult looks to decode. Did they have the same as I had in my bag? Was it a look of joy or horror? I opened my bag and cautiously peered in for another look, but the contents were still the same.

'You've got to be fucking kidding me,' I said aloud.

These two doctors must have been the most stupid people on the planet, or they might just have thought they were the funniest, you decide. Knowing full well they were on a mercy mission to seek out hostages in a militant stronghold, one of whom they knew to be in very poor health and the rest probably underfed and close to being malnourished, they chose of their own free will to bring with them tubs of Neapolitan ice cream, bearing in mind they had a four-hour boat journey under the oppressive African sun to contend with, and packets of Jacobs Cream Crackers. The ice cream had probably turned to soup by the time they pushed their boat away from the jetty, and crackers? Even when you add a bit of cheese and a glass of port, they still aren't the most nutritious of snacks.

I felt like grabbing the doctor and rubbing his nose in it, telling him the next time he went on a humanitarian mission to leave his good intentions at home, idiot! I was just about to throw my food parcel on the rubbish heap when I remembered the promise I had made to myself – just eat whatever is put in front of you. So I started to break off small pieces of cracker and dip it in the ice-cream that had turned to soup. Even after I'd soaked the cracker it still stuck in my throat as I burned valuable calories trying to swallow it down. It would probably have taken us the whole day to finish them if it wasn't for the General, who was lacking in patience and saved us from the whole sorry affair.

'Who is going to speak to company? We must negotiate,' he said. This was the last thing we were expecting, and for a moment we were all stunned into silence. When no-one spoke the General tried again.

'I have satphone; one of you speak and then me.'

We pulled ourselves together and quickly nominated Plooy, who had worked for the company the longest. This wasn't hard, as it was Noor's and my first tour of duty with them, but Plooy knew the people in the office who would hopefully be on the other end of the phone, so that was that. We followed the General out to the middle of the yard with his bodyguards in tow, while the Indians were still being given the once-over by the quacks. Bob was also getting his

173

nose looked at; I couldn't help thinking that even if my arm was hanging off I wouldn't let either of those two clowns anywhere near me.

The General gave Plooy a strict script to follow for this most important of phone calls, and he wasn't to stray from it at all. He had to tell the man on the other end of the phone that we were being held in squalid conditions by MEND, that we were being denied food and clean water, and that we were in fear of our lives. Plooy didn't need to lie much. Noor and I stood back, very excited at this unexpected twist in the game, and waited for Plooy to connect to the outside world. The psychotic General stood next to Plooy and once again placed his pistol against his own head.

When we first arrived the General had said that he would keep us here for at least three months before he would let us speak to anyone, but here we were after just ten days, about to make contact with our company and maybe proceed with a ransom demand.

After what seemed like just a couple of rings, Plooy started to speak and stuck to the script word for word. Whoever was on the other end must already have been briefed and been waiting for the call, as after what seemed like only a few moments the phone was handed back to the General. As he took the handset he flashed Plooy a smile that looked as if he wanted to eat him for dinner – which of course he did. He slowly placed the phone to one ear while keeping his pistol trained on the other one. Plooy joined Noor and me and slapped us both on the shoulders, beaming from ear to ear; the call must have gone well. We all hugged each other while Plooy shared the good news with us. The General was just starting up his conversation on the satphone.

'All our families have been informed, they're all worried but okay... he told us all not to worry, to sit tight and not to do anything stupid... they will meet any demands made and get us out as soon as possible.' We all continued hugging each other and slapping each other on the back. This was great news and we would be on our way home soon, we were sure of it.

'Five hundred million dollars and some boats,' the General demanded confidently down the satphone, as though he were ordering this winter's quota of coal. We all broke from our group hug and made a step towards him.

'What!' we all said in unison. 'No, General, no, that's too...' The General swung the pistol from his ear and levelled it at our heads, meaning 'Back the fuck up, stay out of this and let the General work his magic.' Just to reinforce this message, his bodyguards all took a step nearer and blocked our way with Mr Kalashnikov.

It was one of those 'light at the end of the tunnel' moments and then utter darkness again, a total cave-in. Noor put his head in his hands and walked off, totally frustrated with it all. Plooy and I stood stock still in the middle of the yard, not quite able to come to terms with what we had just heard. We watched the General hang up the phone, after shouting something about used bills, fast, or die, and then mince over to Sachin and Aditya and march them in the direction of the dreaded A-frame. There were many times when you just wanted to throw back your head and scream like a banshee at the top of your lungs, pull out clumps of hair and beat fiercely on your chest like a gorilla who's lost his bananas. At that moment I think we were all feeling it.

Plooy turned to face me with a look of worry and total bewilderment on his face and asked, 'What do you reckon, Phil?' I took a moment to think.

'Well, to be brutally honest mate... we're fucked.'

'Hmmm,' was all Plooy could come back with.

'Listen mate, we all know it's a bit of a game; they start high, we start low and then at some point we find middle ground. But there's

175

starting high and starting high… with five hundred million dollars and some boats as the starting figure it could take a couple of years to find that middle ground.'

'Hmmm,' was again all Plooy could reply. But for once I was right; it was a game and, like a quality wine or a fine woman, it wasn't to be rushed. Governments and private companies are always whining on about how they never 'negotiate with terrorists', but with a starting bid like that I can't say I blame them. To put this obscene amount the General was demanding into some sort of perspective, an oil tanker named MV Sirius Star, worth $150,000,000 and carrying a multinational crew of twenty-five plus some $100,000,000 in crude oil, was captured by Somali pirates in 2008. The pirates demanded twenty-five million dollars and gave the Saudi owners just ten days to cough up the money, but after nearly two months of haggling the vessel and crew were released unharmed after a three-million ransom was parachuted from a light aircraft to the Sirius Star's deck.

The General was in the jungle by the A-frame for a good five minutes before we heard the two persuasive shots from his pistol. The shots made me and Plooy duck our heads a little and vacate the yard to seek refuge with Noor. This time, though, we were pretty sure that the two shots were just for show, and we did not fear for Sachin and Aditya's safety. Nevertheless the sound of gunshots still had us cowering under whatever cover we could find.

The General had finished with the Indians and now came over to fetch Bob, so he too could contact his paymasters; although we all worked on the same barge we were employed by different companies. The Indians came and sat by us, looking quite pleased with the way things had just gone for them, and updated us on their situation while Bob took his turn on the satphone. The General and the Indians' petro-chemical company had reached a price that they both agreed on; Sachin and Aditya didn't know the figure, but we were guessing it was a lot less than five hundred million dollars and some boats. Sachin seemed to think that one of the two doctors was also going to be the middle-man for the money side of things. I tried to hide my misgivings over this bit of news, but Sachin thought it could be just a matter of days, and not weeks, before they were set free. I hoped so for both their sakes.

The General had also let Sachin speak briefly to his wife on his satphone. She was sick with worry and not eating properly, and as soon as Sachin was returned safely to her she wanted to Foxtrot Oscar back to India. We couldn't blame her for that – what she had been through was enough to make anybody high-tail it back to wherever they came from – but this extra piece of information did give Plooy another of his ground-breaking ideas, which he shared with us as soon as the Indians had gone back to their cell.

Poor old Bob got two shots from the General's Glock right by his shell-like that near enough burst his eardrum. Apparently Bob strayed from the well-written script and was halfway through telling his paymaster that he was being treated just fine and that they had nothing to worry about, when the General thought he'd step in to put Bob back on the right path. I think Bob got the message after that.

When the phone call was finished the General came over to the three of us and asked what we thought of his first demand. We said that we were very sorry, but it was far too much money and that not even the President of the United States of America would fetch such a princely sum. This seemed to hit a nerve with the General, who looked to be chewing this over in his psychotic mind like someone might chew on a rubbery tube in a piece of lamb's liver.

'Next time, we make it four hundred,' he snapped, and then spun on his heels and was gone, his entourage in hot pursuit, doctors and all.

Left alone, Plooy set about telling us his hot new idea, but before he did I told him it had to be better than his last one about building rain traps for these morons. He replied that we were still going to do that later, but to listen up. I was going to like this one, this was a crackerjack.

Our escape plan Dick was to be postponed, for the moment anyhow; we had a lot of new information to take on board and we would have to let the negotiations play out for a bit and see where they took us. Negotiation was still by far the safest route out of here. Plooy's idea was this: the next time the General let him talk to our paymaster, he would ask if he could speak with his wife, just as Sachin had, and as he and his wife both spoke Afrikaans he could talk without anyone else understanding. Once the pleasantries were out of the way, he would instruct his wife to contact a certain man in the company whom Plooy knew well, and tell him that if we had no joy by 20th June we would make our escape. He could then alert the security services to keep their eyes peeled for us on the beach directly opposite the production platform, where we would wait to be picked up. The plan was good and it gave us an even higher chance of success, but it meant we had to stay put in Camp Horrid and play the game a little bit longer – over two weeks longer – and to me that felt like a lifetime.

Now that we'd got a price tag on our heads we felt a bit safer. We were not quite sure how one day it was political and we were threatened with death, and the next day it was all just a sordid business deal; but we did feel a lot better being viewed through dollar signs rather than being used as counters in a game of political tiddlywinks. Hopefully it meant we'd be treated with a little more respect, as they wouldn't want to damage the merchandise. Five hundred million dollars and some boats is a lot of money in anyone's language, and for now I would just enjoy having a third share on my head; that worked out to be one hundred and sixty six million, six hundred thousand dollars and, say, one boat. That's three-and-a-half times more than the great David Beckham was worth when he was sold to LA Galaxy in the same year, 2007. I would like to say that we now strolled around the camp as if we owned the place, but we didn't want to push our luck; we were a highly-valued asset but we were still surrounded by unpredictable morons, rapists, cannibals and tattoo-haters, who were armed to the teeth and for the most part completely off their heads on drink and drugs.

We located the Secretary, who was about the only man in the camp who wasn't permanently off his face, and asked his permission to build some rain traps which should put an end to the problem of having no fresh water in camp. After explaining in as much detail as we could, we got a 'Do what you want, I couldn't give a rat's arse' sort of response from him. We certainly weren't expecting him to jump for joy at our idea, but we were expecting him to be a little more enthusiastic about it. Maybe he would be more excited after they were built.

Plooy set us to work with his usual infectious enthusiasm. Behind our hut we found some corrugated sheets of tin which were left over after they had made the roofs to the huts. We made four two-metre lengths of guttering by cutting strips about twenty centimetres wide with machetes that we borrowed from the guards; of course, they guarded us even more closely all the time we held their machetes. We then shaped each one to catch water by bending it in to a U-shape and tying it in place with twine from the rubbish pile. The guttering was then hung at an angle, as it is at home, so the water caught running off the roof of the hut would drain down into an old oil drum placed at the lower end. We took four empty fifty-five-gallon plastic fuel drums and cut the lids off. This was the hardest work of all and took most of the afternoon, as we only had machetes to saw through the thick plastic. Once we had cut the tops off and cleaned out the barrels we stood them on end under the gutter. And right on cue, as soon as the last barrel was put in position, there was a big bolt of lightning that lit the sky followed by an almighty clap of thunder, and then the heavens opened. The militants all ran to take shelter and we stood back and admired our handiwork, letting the rain fall on us while watching the barrels fill faster than we could have hoped, with more fresh drinking water than they could ever dream of. After thirty minutes or so of continual rainfall, the four barrels combined held exactly two hundred and twenty gallons of water. That should be more than enough to save the residents of Camp Horrid from venturing into the pit for drinking or cooking water. We put one trap outside each hut and the cook had his own set up at the lean-to.

The Secretary finally got the idea, and stood with us and marvelled at the magical engineering ability of the white man. He even got out his cigarettes and offered them to each of us; we all took one, and of course Plooy and Noor gave theirs to me. I lit one, taking a light from a guard, and smoked while Plooy explained to the Secretary, and to the others who were showing an interest, that as long as they didn't go silly with the water they should hardly ever run out. As Plooy and Noor began demonstrating some of the simple construction methods used in building the traps, the rain stopped and the sun came out, bringing the Teacher along with it.

On seeing the new traps the Teacher started a little rain dance around the barrels (shutting the stable door after the horse has bolted sprang to mind), slapped us all on the back and vigorously shook us by the hand – this was a bit more like the gratitude I was hoping for. He slipped away for a while, all excited, and we watched him disappear into the jungle before we also headed off to our tree for a rest. The Teacher rejoined us there just in time to watch the sun set on this quite remarkable day, and offered us each a Star beer. We must all have looked very suspicious, for he had to offer the beer a second time before we most gratefully accepted. Leaning against the tree, we popped the lids and wasted no time in pouring the first warm mouthfuls down our throats, but then we took our time; this was one of those moments we wanted to eke out for as long as possible.

BA, Denzel and a few of the guards also came to sit with us, and the conversation soon turned to the astronomical ransom they had demanded. We were curious as to how they would spend the money after the ransom was paid, and BA was first to answer. 'Hummer,' he said, 'I want a Hummer so I can get all my soldiers in the back and go to war and rob bank.' We pointed out that there were no roads in the swamp and that it would be impossible to drive it here. Denzel joined in, shrugged his shoulders and simply said, 'You don't need roads to drive a Hummer.' He was of course correct, you didn't need roads to drive a Hummer, but you would need at least some sort of a track; even some boats got stuck out here. Hummers are some of the world's most durable vehicles, but in the Delta swamp I would think that the life expectancy of one would be about half a day.

We also wanted to know how they proposed to pick up and transport such a large sum of money – you can't just stuff that amount in a couple of briefcases – but yes, that was exactly how they planned to carry out the drop. We tried to explain that they would need a whole fleet of Hummers to carry all that dough, which pleased BA and Denzel no end – as far as they were concerned, the more Hummers the better. They just couldn't get the concept that five hundred million dollars and some boats was a little over-priced for three smelly divers.

Plooy's idea had worked a treat, though; putting up rain traps had served us very well as a 'hearts and minds' campaign, and seemed to have won us some new friends. As we sat there laughing and joking with the mob, leaning with my back against the tree trunk, it suddenly hit me what a most bizarre moment this was. Here we were, being held against our will, drinking lager and having a grin under the jungle roof with some of the most dangerous men the world has got to offer, and also without doubt some of the world's most stupid!

CHAPTER TWENTY-ONE

A DOG'S LIFE

Three big ugly belt-fed machine guns, thirteen AK 47s, eight other kinds of rifles, two full boxes of dynamite, half a dozen home-made hand grenades and boxes and boxes of spare ammo and magazines. That was the number of guns and gun accessories I had just counted while sitting over on the opposite side of the yard outside Hut Two, as the militants were using our normal spot by the rubbish dump for weapons drills. Hut Two was where most of the goon squad lived, and it smelt like a typical teenage boy's bedroom. It was squalid to say the least; there weren't any of the proud housekeeping skills that we displayed over in our cell.

Every morning after prayers we would take it in turns to sweep out the dirt, dust and dead mosquitoes from the day before. Then we would take out our mattresses, bang them out and air them, fold up our mosquito nets and mend any holes, and dust away the cobwebs to keep the big, hairy man-eating spiders at bay. Anything that we felt would go towards keeping ourselves in good nick.

Just sitting outside Hut Two was making me itch, or was it the thousand or so love-bites the NAFy had given me? I could no longer tell. We were going to stay put, though, all the time those idiots were mucking about with guns and high explosives in our normal spot. Commander Jackson was in his element, fussing over all his weapons and conscripts like a mother hen. However, their weapons drill was making it abundantly clear that none of the conscripts who served under Commander Jackson had any formal training. All the ideas they had of military combat, tactics and strategies were taken from a pirate DVD which they played in the rec room over and over again until it wore out. I had a feeling that the only shooting these guys would be any good at would be into a Kleenex.

I'd also watched a fair few war films myself, and didn't ever recall ones that showed soldiers plugging their fingers into, or looking down the end of, the barrel of a gun, which was what I was witnessing in front of me. Back home six-year-old boys were taught by their dads, older brothers or even mums never to point their toy gun at anything they didn't intend to say bang at, and for whatever reason you definitely don't go sticking your face in front of it or looking down the barrel. It was just common sense, which seemed to be lacking in all but a few of this ragtag army.

After getting very damp when the roof of the armoury leaked, the dynamite and home-made grenades were left out in the sun to dry. I'm not sure whether explosives are meant to be submerged in water and then left in direct sunlight time and time again, or whether this makes them volatile and unpredictable. There was no health and safety officer to advise them any differently. While the bangers were drying out, all the rifles and machine guns were cleaned and oiled, and I mean oiled. Cans of the stuff were being poured directly down the barrels, hopefully to reach the working parts of the guns; if bullets come out then surely oil must go in. Everything I watched was an education in how not to do things, and reinforced my belief that you should never mix together dysfunctional, untrained men and weapons of mass destruction.

Commander Jackson appeared to be satisfied with the crew's maintenance on the hardware, and it was now time to test-fire the weapons. We were already sitting on our arses but we managed to get even lower when they began to fire. Covering our heads with our arms, we pushed our noses into the dirt as they unleashed Armageddon in all directions. Tree trunks, branches and leaves were shredded, disintegrating under a massive barrage of fire power. All the animals for miles around that hadn't already been eaten must have been on their toes and scattering further into the jungle.

This barrage into the bush lasted three or four minutes before Commander Jackson called a ceasefire, trying his best to pitch his voice above the blitz. All the militants stopped firing and stood a pace back, panting like overweight Labradors. Chests were swollen with pride, and in their trousers the old flagpoles were flying at full mast. The barrels of their guns were smoking red-hot and the smell of burnt oil and cordite was filling the air. Bits of tree were still falling to the ground as we started to pick our faces out of the dirt. That was another of those Delta experiences I never wanted to go through again.

Commander Jackson called for all the arms to be put back in the armoury – apart from the guards' personal weapons, of course, those they kept with them at all times – and we sat up and thanked our lucky stars that we hadn't been hit by a stray, or a well-placed round from Prada, who was one of only a few who could shoot straight.

As soon as our area by the rubbish pile had been vacated by the now fully-trained firearms unit, we crossed the yard to fill it. We wasted no time in getting it into a habitable condition by cleaning it up again. We kicked the damp patches with dust to soak up the spilt gun oil, threw the thousand or so bullet casings onto the rubbish heap, then sat down and made ourselves comfy. Still a little shaky, we hoped that firearms training didn't happen too frequently. Today was going to be one of those days where we just sat down and tried to blend in with our surroundings. The mob was still full of testosterone and strutting confidently about the yard like peacocks, ruffling their feathers with their hard-ons on display, play-fighting with each other and firing make-believe rifles at the sky, and us.

The Teacher ambled through the yard, which at that moment resembled a school playground, clutching a few sticks of dynamite and a fishing net; he was going fishing militant-style. We were running worryingly low on food supplies, and the Teacher had taken it on himself to top them up. We were guessing that the reason the General had brought forward our negotiation was because they needed the money. We could cope with the dwindling stocks of rice and beans if it got us out of here faster. The only one of us that was a little concerned was Plooy, who had good reason to be worried as he was at the top of their menu.

Every now and again we would hear a loud boom that suggested to us that the Teacher was still fishing. The real fishermen, the honest, hard-working ones who lived in the villages and plied their trade up and down these waterways, must have hated the way this ragtag army went about catching fish. There they were, fishing with conventional well-worn nets, catching a few meagre fish to take back to their families, perhaps having a few left over to sell; and then you had the Teacher and his cronies blasting huge numbers out of the water. I thought the Teacher took the net with him to try with that first, and if that didn't work then he could fall back on the TNT. But no, the net was simply to help scoop out all the dead fish that were floating belly-up on the surface.

While we were trying hard to blend into our surroundings a long, thin canoe turned up with a long, thin sorry-looking man in it, who had with him an even sorrier-looking dog on a bit of rope. The thin sorry-looking man was met by Denzel, who was the latest militant to be wearing my booties, and BA, who never strayed too far from Denzel's side. After much haggling and raised voices they exchanged the dog for some money, and the dishevelled man turned around his canoe and paddled back the way he had come. He never looked back. The dog was led into the camp. I immediately had a bad feeling for this dog, who seemed to share my misgivings. Her ears were back, her tail was down between her legs and she had the sort of walk where she had to be more pulled than led.

As we sat through the afternoon it was becoming clear that we were rapidly losing the war for the hearts and minds of our captors. Our rain traps, such a big hit the day before, were already running dry and causing small outbursts and arguments. If they had just used the fresh water for cooking and drinking they would never have run out, as it was pretty much topped up daily with fresh rain, but they were going through the stuff like shit through a goose. Where they used to wash their clothes and themselves in the pit-water or river, they now helped themselves to buckets of fresh from the barrels. As soon as they discovered it was there, they used it and then it was a free-for-all, a race to use it up. Only the cook was trying to manage the water properly, but he soon got pushed aside and his barrel too was now nearly empty.

The last bucket to come out of his barrel caused a full-on fight. Two guards were swinging badly-aimed punches and kicks at each other, fighting over this bucket of water as though it were the last precious energy source left on earth, going at each other like a pair of evenly-matched cockerels. While they were scrapping on the floor, Frog Face picked up the now half-empty bucket and walked back to where he'd been sitting listening to hip-hop music and smoking joints. He didn't appear to want to do anything with it; it was just there, so he took it.

This was most definitely not good for us. As soon as the camp grew excited, or law and order started breaking down, we began to get scared, very scared. We really feared for our lives at times like this. Apart from Frog Face everyone else was at fever pitch and we couldn't understand why; it was only a fight. But the two guards involved were now being charged by the rest of the mob on the orders

187

of a very disappointed-looking Jackson. We moved back further out of the way into the shadows, as this thing was threatening to spiral out of control. The two guards were dragged and dumped unceremoniously in the middle of the yard, and everyone rained kicks and blows down upon them. Gastro Pod, also not liking this explosive atmosphere, came and found refuge with us.

'What the fuck is going on?' we asked. Gastro Pod was rocking back and forth, trembling and blowing bubbles with his bottom lip. 'Arrrh, very bad this, big crime, fighting amongst ourselves, very bad,' he stammered.

As it had turned out, the last bucket of water we supplied caused the most heinous crime that could be committed in Camp Horrid – guards fighting between themselves. I suppose they had to have at least one rule in the camp, or the whole place would just descend into complete anarchy. Rules are rules, and if they were broken they shouldn't go unpunished, even if the punishment was going to be dished out by your mates, African style, which is both swift and brutal. Now I should have rubbed my hands together, sat back and enjoyed watching a couple of these fuckers get some of their own medicine; but as I said, too much in-camp excitement just gave us the heebie-jeebies. But this was what they did.

The Teacher had returned from his fishing expedition in time to oversee the delivery of the punishment and to make sure justice was delivered in the Delta way. Although he had shown us nothing but kindness since we had got here, he was not inclined to offer any to his own. He didn't even have time to show off his catch and sacrifice the biggest and best fish to the river gods.

The two guards were stripped naked and softened up with a beating, some of the mob taking their time to aim a blow accurately or to take a run-up. Jackson disappeared and came back with some whips and handcuffs. The whips were just lengths of electrical flex and the handcuffs were the sort you could buy in any Soho sex shop. We sat huddled with Gastro Pod, more than a little concerned as to just how this would play out.

The two accused guards cowered on the edge of the yard. They looked really scared, with big wide eyes, clasping their hands together in prayer begging for clemency; I for one couldn't blame them. The Teacher was no longer content with just observing. He and Prada were wrapping the electrical cord around their wrists to get a better purchase on their tools of correction, and then they took a couple of practice swings in the air. Satisfied with the 'swoosh' that the cord made they turned to their prisoners, who were still getting slapped about and beginning to leak a little blood.

The aim of the game was this: both the naked guards would start on the side of the yard where we sat by the rubbish dump. They were to hold on to their ear lobes with both hands and they weren't allowed to let go; if they did the consequences would be severe. Once they had hold of their ears they were to do frog-jumps all the way to the other side of the yard and then back again; it sounds easy, but there was more to it than that. Lining the whole distance on both sides was the mob, baying for blood and eager to get stuck in. To their rear, encouraging them to keep going and not give up, were the Teacher and Prada with whips at the ready.

Bang! And they were off; both the prisoners were quick off the blocks and started frogging frantically across the yard, trying desperately to get as far as they could before the first crack of the whip. They didn't get far. *Thwack, thwack;* the noise of electrical flex on flesh was nauseating. Some of the mob, stimulated by the whipping, started digging with their bare hands, pulling green roots from the ground and lashing the two frogs from the front. I looked at Gastro Pod, who didn't appear to be enjoying the show, and nudged him. 'Why aren't you joining in?' I asked.

He shook his head and lowered his eyes. To us and the world in general Gastro Pod had the wit and guile of a whelk, but he was a very sensitive soul and more human than this lot put together. God, I wished he was still our guard.

One of the frogs had reached the halfway mark and was already on his way back, but the other one was struggling. With his strength and energy fading fast, he kept letting go of his ears to block the lashes from the flex and green roots that whipped and slashed at him, earning himself an extra barrage of blows that just slowed him down further. There was no let-up for either frog as lash after lash came raining down on them. The Teacher had to hand over his flex, as he was spent and wanted to catch his breath. He handed it to BA, who picked up an awesome strike rate to encourage the failing guard to get a shift on and catch up with the other. The way BA was motivating the guard with his whip, you would be forgiven for thinking he had a wager on him, such was his enthusiasm.

The first guard to cross the finish line was rewarded with a beating, and the loser got dragged by his ankles over the line while being beaten; the end result was the same. The race was over, and thank the Lord for that. I wasn't overly keen on any of the guards, and I certainly wouldn't be suffering from Stockholm Syndrome any time soon, but that was a little strong for my particular taste in entertainment.

The torment may have been over for me and my comrades, but it was far from over for our two frogs; their suffering was to continue right through the evening and into the next morning. The two of them were dragged, bloodied and broken, over to *our* tree, where they were manacled together using the handcuffs, belly down in the dirt facing each other, so that the tree stood tall between their arms and both their heads. Sprawled in the dirt they looked like two heavyweight boxers who had just knocked each other out. A single light bulb was hung a few feet above them to attract as many of the jungle creepy-crawlies as possible, and there were many. I had brushed and slapped all sorts of weird and wonderful creatures from my body, some just having a walk over me but most wanting a feed. Soldier ants with pincers like digger buckets, millipedes the size of a man's finger and man-eating spiders. These two men would stay tied immobile all night at the mercy of these creatures, the light from the bulb and the metallic smell of their bloodied bodies attracting the fiercest and most bloodthirsty of them all.

Frog Face waited until the mob had dispersed, finished his joint and then made his move. He carried the last of the water that he had rescued earlier over to the two guards at the tree, and ceremonially poured its contents over their faces, dropping the bucket when it was empty. That was the very last of the fresh water. Then he walked off to join the others, who by now had found a new target to plague: the dog on a rope.

The bullying mentality seemed infectious that night and was spreading like an epidemic through the camp. The sun had sunk below the horizon a long time ago, and it was just a few campfires and one bare bulb that penetrated the dark. Fresh supplies of drugs and drink were being dished out with no thought for our dwindling stocks of food. The cook and two of his kitchen assistants brought us over four pathetic plates of rice, as the beans, our only source of protein, were gone. I got stuck into my rice and tried hard not to watch the poor dog being kicked and beaten with sticks. She looked wretched and resigned to her fate; when they came up with the phrase 'At the end of your tether' it was meant for this poor bitch right here. To this day I can still picture her sorry-looking frame: big drooping teats that proved she had borne more than one litter of pups, and big pitiful Disney-like brown eyes that seemed to hunt me out, pleading with me to save her. But there was nothing I could do to help.

Although I was feeling very bad for the bitch I was extremely hungry, and although I wasn't quite ready to eat dog I couldn't help wondering whether she had any liquor left in her teats. A nice glass of fresh milk full of protein would definitely hit the spot. What would dog milk taste like anyway?

I liked my dogs and had two waiting for me at home; walking them in the fields was one of those many simple pleasures that I now missed terribly. On the other hand, I have nothing against people eating them, which was what this bitch had in store for her; better her than Plooy. But you could still treat the animal with a bit of humanity and respect and kill it quickly. I just wanted to walk over, pick up one of their AKs and put a bullet in her skull or better still, theirs. Apart from the very first night in Camp Horrid this was the lowest I had felt. I was completely filled with despair and a new loathing for our hosts. I could really relate to this animal, because we too were totally at their mercy and had suffered the same treatment. If the General suddenly desired it we could also end up on the menu.

After an hour or so of being heckled, the bitch was finally dragged across the yard and over to the A-frame by some of the more cowardly members of the goon squad, who doused her in petrol and set her on fire, turning her into a huge ball of flames. The last sound to come out of her throat was one of sheer terror and pain that cut through to my very core.

The mood amongst us that night was sombre and woeful, each of us picking at our plate of rice that long ago went cold, with lost appetites and a vacant stare, as the mob tore excitedly into roast dog. We thanked the camp boss as he finally collected our plates, as we were too scared tonight to take our own back to the galley where the remains of the bitch's carcass were being picked to the bone.

We chose our moment carefully and then dashed back to our cell, picking our way through the party; none of us relished the thought of being accosted by the mob tonight. Back at the cell we grabbed the two bottles of water we had saved earlier in the day and hidden in the roof space, one for Bob and Noor and one that Plooy and I would share once we had climbed under the mosquito net. I lay next to Plooy on our mattress listening to the noise all around, drinking from the bottle and then passing it back to him. When the mob was fired up like this the party could last all night and well into the next day, so I shut my eyes, thought of my family and a better place, England. God, how I missed it.

CHAPTER TWENTY-TWO

BIG DICK

It didn't take the jungle drums long to get the news back to my parents' place where the phone was manned at all times, either by my mother, father or Sophie. The call was made by the man Plooy spoke to on the General's satphone, and he passed on the news that although he didn't get to speak to me, Plooy had assured him that I was alive and well, that we were all being kept together and a ransom had been demanded. This was very important news for them, as they hadn't heard a squeak from anyone since the statement saying we were to be executed on 29th June, and that date had by now been and gone. So to hear I was okay and a money demand had been made was about as good as it could get for them at that moment.

The news filtered its way down further, making it to the Torcross Tavern, Kidnap HQ. My brother John made the journey to the bar where some of my friends were drinking and eagerly waiting for some proof of life. John now knew he had a slight chance of getting back the money I owed him, but was apprehensive about telling the patrons of the Tavern that I was alive and kicking. He had cashed in the other night, accepting sympathy pints from everyone after he'd told them my execution was imminent. After this latest turn of events he feared he would have to buy them all one in return.

The lord and landlady of the manor were called Julian and Sally, and they were both holding their breath for my safe return as they were very fond of me. As well as running a pub they had links to the Metropolitan Police. Sally was an ex-plod but Julian was still out there solving crimes, and only helped Sally run the pub during his time off. As it was a school night tonight for Julian, Sally was on her own pulling pints when John walked in to pass on his good news. Sally responded, 'Well, they will either kill him out of frustration or pay a ransom themselves just to get rid of him. Your brother is the most annoying man I've ever had in here; he gets under people's skin like a slow-moving fungal infection.'

This sent a chuckle round the bar. 'That's a bit strong, Sally,' said my brother. 'Get us a pint of bitter please, and you'd better get this lot one as well.' Sally was busy pulling ales and bitters for various patrons when a voice came booming down from the other end of the bar.

'Yeah, your brother left a shit in my cup.'

'What do you mean, he left a shit in your cup?' John asked with a morbid interest.

The booming voice began to explain and everyone in the bar was now listening. 'Well, we had a fall-out when he was skippering my crab boat, and on his last day he took a poo in my Incredible Hulk mug and then smashed the rest of the cups. So when I went to sea the next day I either had to wash out my Hulk mug and drink from that, or I had to go without a cup of tea for the day.'

My brother was next to speak. 'Sally, you'd better get Big Dick one as well... so Dickey, did you drink from the cup then or...?'

'None of your business,' Dickey cut in, 'but I did have the last laugh; silly sod still had two weeks' wages owing to him.'

CHAPTER TWENTY-THREE

BACK ON THE STRAIGHT AND NARROW

The year was 2001 and Devon was now my home, my place to relax, get my health back and rethink my life. It's a beautiful part of the country, with rolling green hills lying next to freshly-ploughed, chocolate-brown fields. High hedges hide narrow country roads, and the smell of the ocean rises up from a wild, rugged coastline. Perfect conditions for me to start a new life, put the past behind me or just chill out.

For the last ten years I had tried nearly every drug known to man, and enjoyed 99.9% of them. But for all the good they did me I may as well have smeared myself in dog crap on some street corner and sacrificed myself to the flies. No, if I had the remotest chance of a half-ounce of happiness or normality I couldn't fall off the junky spoon again. If I did, it would no doubt mean another wasted decade.

For the first couple of months after leaving the Farm I didn't venture out much from my parents' house; I spent most of the time on the sofa shaking like a little puppy dog gagging for a biscuit. I was still withdrawing from the heroin. Sleep was restless and uncomfortable, and I still had the sickness and flu-like conditions, cramps and vomiting that came with withdrawal. However, I could tell that I was winning the war; as the days passed the symptoms eased, and I sneezed less and less. During the most severe parts of the detox you have sneezing fits, and you might sneeze thirteen or fourteen times in a row while stamping your foot and gasping for breath; but with time, that number comes down to just seven or eight, and then just three or four, until you are out on the other side.

After all the physical symptoms have passed you are left with just the mental battle, which some say is the hardest; but for me the very thought of heroin now filled me with dread. It had messed my life up enough and caused me endless amounts of trouble and besides, the world is a great big place with many adventures to be had. You can't spend it all wasting away in some dingy bedsit off your head. No, it was right to move on now and try to make up for so much lost time.

After all the years of drug abuse I was extremely unfit and as weak as a kitten. It would still be a few weeks before I was back to my fighting weight. Mum was feeding me well, but my body was just not used to it. I had spent years skipping meals, and the ones I had managed to fit in were lacking somewhat in nutritional value. At times I must have gone for days without eating a single morsel. I was now being fed three to four home-cooked meals a day and my body was saying no, so I was also having three to four poos a day or throwing the food back up. It took a while, but in the end my body grew accustomed to the healthy diet, and eventually I started to gain some weight and recover my strength.

The next stage was exercise and getting out of the house, as I was still in danger of becoming institutionalised. Baby steps at first though. Mum and I would take a stroll round the block a couple of times a day, chatting about the last decade and trying to piece it all together, obviously holding back on most of the gory bits; there are certain things your mother just doesn't need to know. It felt weird talking to my mum about drugs and depravity but it helped a lot; it all went towards that healing process.

The days went on and I grew fitter and stronger. I was now having just the one poo a day at around zero-nine hundred-hours, regular as clockwork. You ask any doctor and he'll tell you that this is a sign of good health. I was managing to go on longer walks now,

197

on my own, walking the cliff tops without cramping up or hyperventilating. My old man was still carving furniture in an old pig shed which was now his workshop, so I helped out for a few hours a week which went some way to pay for my keep, but it was not enough. I needed to get some work of my own, to get out in the real world again. My skills were non-existent; all I could offer was that I would get stuck in and work hard, but I didn't think that area of Devon had very many work opportunities. There were just fields and coastline, and I didn't think anyone was going to pay me to bum about around those. I needed to take myself down to the local pub, have a couple of pints, show my face and see what came up. Some say you will never find the solution to a problem at the bottom of a bottle; I disagree. There were two pubs within walking distance, The Church House Inn and the Torcross Tavern.

It was in The Church House and an hour into my drink when I met a bloke at the bar. He was six foot four and weighed in at about seventeen stone. He was a larger-than-life character with a round, stubbly Desperate Dan face, a ready laugh and fists like frozen armadillos. For a big guy he was extremely agile and light on his feet, and he had a quick wit and a sense of humour to match. I took an instant liking to him. His name was Richard, but I came to calling him Dickey or Big Dick. As I shared a few pints with Dick I learned that he was the owner/skipper of a crab-fishing vessel called The Newbrook, which fished out of nearby Dartmouth. A few pints and a game of cards later, I had been press-ganged as a new member of his crew.

Big Dick was no fool. He had seen me about and knew there was an underlying reason why I was living here with my parents, but he was still willing to give me a try. I was to start at the beginning of next week, on a two-week trial basis with no wages. After those two weeks he would then decide whether or not I had the minerals to make a crab fisherman. You don't find men in every pub who are willing to give an ex-leper a second chance, so I figured it must be fate and told myself to make the most of the lifeline he had thrown me.

It had only been three months since I'd left the Farm, and although I had put on weight and grown in confidence I still didn't know whether I was ready to embark on a new career just yet, especially one as demanding as crab fishing. But what was the worst that could happen? After the success of my pub visit I felt a lot more positive about my future. All you needed sometimes to turn things around was some hard work and a bit of luck, and I seemed to be on a roll at the moment, so I decided to push it some more. The Torcross Tavern was over on the other side of the village, so I went to chance my luck there as well.

I was nursing my second pint at a table in the corner of the bar, battling a sudden and unexpected craving, when a young lady caught my eye. My drug craving quickly passed and was replaced by a very nice warm glow. I hadn't managed to do anything about that feeling since my fumble with Sheba at the Farm, but it was back.

She was beautiful: bright, funny and holding the attention of all the young farm hands standing about her. She did glance in my direction now and again, but I was still a stranger in those parts so the glances could have been ones of suspicion. She was not like any girl I had ever been drawn to in the past. Most of the girls that I'd had sexy feelings for had either been off their heads on drugs or just plain mental. This young lady was at the bar gently sipping a glass of mineral water, with bubbles!

Over the next few days I found out a little about the girl who had so captivated me. She was called Sophie and came from the next village. And the reason she was drinking mineral water and not downing shots of tequila was that she was too young to drink alcohol;

in actual fact she was way too young to do anything, she was fifteen. What was I thinking? I was twenty-six, an immature twenty-six year old, but still twenty-six. Nothing ever seemed to be straightforward. I would, however, keep an eye on her from a distance and see how she developed. Anyway, I had promised my Mum not to cause any scandal, so I would concentrate on the fishing for now.

My last week of recovery was over; I finally felt that I had beaten the hold that drugs once had over me, and could now look forward to discovering all the other things the world had to offer. I still didn't know if I was ready for my next challenge, but there was only one way to find out. The morning of my new job had arrived and I knew absolutely nothing about boats. The only boat I had ever been near was the little inflatable rowing dinghy on that murky little pond all those years ago, and I remembered all too well what happened there.

I had set my alarm clock for the first time in over ten years, at the uncivilised hour of three in the morning. The thing about setting your alarm clock so early in the morning is that it comes round very fast. I hadn't even had enough time for a saucy dream about the foxy young filly who drank fizzy water down at the Tavern. But you can't ignore the *beep beep beep* of the clock, so I rolled out of bed and pulled on the work clothes that had been regimentally set out the night before on the obligatory chair that stands in the corner of most bedrooms. I then collected my pre-made sandwiches from the fridge and headed outside, trying not to wake my parents on the way. About fifty yards up from their house was a bus stop with enough room to shelter two, but at that time of the morning I had it all to myself.

There were no streetlights so I stood waiting for Big Dick in the pitch black, worrying about what the hell I had got myself into. Since the mining industry had been sent up the Swanee, fishing had become the most dangerous industry we had. The ocean after all is a big scary beast, impossible to tame. Going from an unemployable skag-head to a crab fisherman was going to make me or break me; but, as they say, 'Time and tide wait for no man', and it was not long before Dickey rounded the corner in his pick-up to collect me. We made our way to Dartmouth harbour to meet the other two deck hands and to start the day's fishing. The deck hands were just as I would expect fishermen to be, a bit rough (you have to be) and of a strong and confident character. These two were called Matt and Stu.

The work started straight away. In the back of the pick-up were seventy to eighty stone of fish to bait the pots with, which had to be hand-balled down the steps of the quayside while Dickey and Stu got the tender (small boat) to go and fetch The Newbrook from its moorings. I had my first glimpse of The Newbrook as it came alongside, and we quickly passed all the bait across and jumped aboard ourselves. The Newbrook then pulled its forty-eight ton bulk away from the quayside and headed along the River Dart and out into open sea; there was no turning back now. From sharp end to blunt she measured twelve metres. Her wooden hull was painted light blue with white gunwales, most of the paint now peeling and streaked with rust from the fittings and the hand-rails that run around the gunwales. The wheelhouse sat slightly back from amidships on the deck and was painted a darker blue; the inside was dark and damp.

Depending upon the tides and wind it could take between one-and-a-half and two hours to reach our fishing ground, where pre-baited pots from two days before were waiting, hopefully filled with crab. But the journey was not a time to catch up on a bit more sleep; there were many chores that had to be completed before we reached our destination. Seventy-odd stone of fish needed defrosting and cutting up into single bait sizes, crab pots needed to be repaired, and cups of tea needed to be made in the wheelhouse – the shed – that was the skipper's job.

As we reached the open sea, walking around the deck became increasingly difficult. I hadn't got my sea legs yet and was forever falling against the gunwale and bouncing off the shed, with Matt and Stu racing around me like gazelles on roller skates, preparing the deck for the first string of pots. The smell of the boat was just as overwhelming as the work, and sat in the back of my throat threatening to gag me. I felt a little out of my depth to say the least, and to be honest I just wanted to go home; but no-one was going to take me to shore so I just had to get on with it.

After about an hour's steaming the tea was ready and we all went inside the shed for a quick sarnie and a brew. Inside the shed was as disgusting as the bow and the stern of the boat. It was damp, smelly, dark and extremely cramped for four men. These people had to be joking; this was absolutely horrible and I wasn't even being paid. I sat in silence eating my sandwich and drinking my tea, listening to all the piss-taking and banter around me. As soon as the sun was up I would be swimming to shore, fuck this.

Not long after our brew Big Dick told us we were nearly there and gave the order to go, and we made our way on deck. I had been given a pair of sea boots, which were the same as normal wellington boots but yellow or blue in colour and with a softer grip on the sole. I was also handed some dirty yellow oilskins, which smelt horrible and were covered in fish scales. They were made up of two parts: bib and brace leggings which were in the style of dungarees and a smock, a zipless garment that you had to pull over your head, and a pair of thick rubber gloves to protect your hands. Together they went some way towards keeping you dry. The deck lights were on and the boat was bobbing about like a cork. I was stumbling about on deck holding on to the rails and anything else I could grab.

'Let's go fishing!' shouted Big Dick; this was the part Dickey enjoyed the most, the part where we started working and he started earning.

Stu, Matt and I were standing on the rails looking for a luminous orange pellet buoy; we called this a 'dan' and it marked the start of the string of pots we were about to haul in. There were sixty pots on a string and we had nine strings to haul today, five hundred and forty pots in all. A powerful spotlight on top of the shed soon picked out the first dan with the guidance of one of the crew, and the boat swung round to come alongside. We used a long gaff (boathook) to bring the dan on board. It was connected to about forty fathoms (one fathom = six foot) of rope called a baush, which we put through a winch to haul the end weight on board.

All the rope that came on board had to be coiled down perfectly, for it was to go back over the side in the same manner. When you look at the decks of a fishing vessel they generally look like a right medieval mess of scrap, but everything has its place and must be stowed accordingly. Once the end weight was on board and stowed in its position, we waited for the first pot. It took two to work the deck on The Newbrook: one to lift in the pots and clear them of crab and old bait, and one to re-bait them and stack the pots in their allocated spot on the deck. There would be sixty pots and one and a half miles of back line (rope) on board by the time the string was finished, so it was essential to get it right – and of course Big Dick oversaw this in the shed on the levers (the controls), running the winch and keeping the boat on course.

The first pot was lifted aboard by Matt, and he gave a shout of delight for it was jammed full of crab and a couple of blues (lobsters). Not all pots come up like this, but it was a good start and a good introduction for me; my spirits were lifted. Matt cleared the crab with lightning hands, throwing many back to the sea, selecting only the crab of a good quality and of legal size to drop into the bin by his feet. The pot was then tossed to Stu who re-baited, and I then stacked it under Stu's supervision. Everything on a crab boat is extremely heavy, and it was not long before my body was screaming for me to stop. But that wouldn't impress the skipper much, or my new crew-mates, so I grinned and ignored it.

The pots kept coming one after the other. The winch was going flat out and I was racing back and forth, placing my pots in the designated places that Stu had indicated, trying to join in the banter to hide my increasing pain. It was such brutal work; each pot seemed to get heavier and heavier as one pot followed the next. The deck was both slippery and unsteady under my non-sea legs; it was going to take everything I had just to make it through the first string. At the end, when the whole string of pots was on board, there wasn't any room left to swing a starfish, but we did have two bins of hens (female crab), six or seven individual cock crabs and three or four blues. I dragged the catch to the stern and went inside the shed, totally exhausted, to grab myself and my new mates a cigarette.

Big Dick gave me a thumbs-up and a 'Well done', and I returned on deck with an enormous sense of wellbeing to dish out the smokes to Matt and Stu. Smoking helped the bonding process and I was starting to feel like part of the crew.

Big Dick swung the boat around and Stu got ready to shoot the pots away. This was the most dangerous part of the job, as every pot had to go back to the sea bed in exactly the opposite way it came to the surface; if Stu selected the wrong pot, or if I stacked one incorrectly, we could have a bit of a mess, and although the boat would only be doing about seven knots, Big Dick still wouldn't be able to stop it in time. If the back line took a turn round Stu he was going down with the pots, and it was cold, wet and very dark down there. Big Dick was back on the fishing ground we had originally hauled the pots from and gave the command to release the second end weight, the last thing that came aboard. Matt was back aft watering the crab and cutting more bait, and I was helping Stu shoot the pots.

The end weight went over and the back line instantly snatched up and started snaking up the ramp, overboard and into the deep. Anything attached to the rope was going to follow. Stu rolled the pots on to the ramp and the back line took them overboard with deadly force, giving Stu just enough time to select the next pot and roll it to where the one before had stood, taking care to keep his feet out of the way of the unforgiving rope. Pot after pot was sent to the sea bed with fresh bait to entice more crab; the last thing to go over was the other end weight, the baush and then the dan. Big Dick turned The Newbrook and headed to the next string. The whole process had taken about one hour and we had another eight to do.

As we started hauling the next string of pots the deck lights were switched off as the sun was coming up. What greeted me was a beautiful sunrise, like nothing I had ever noticed before on land. The whole sky was lit by a fiery, swirling mass of red and orange as the sun crept over the blue horizon. I was hooked. All thoughts of swimming back to shore had long gone, even though the work just got harder and harder as we ploughed through the next few strings. I had cuts and bruises all over my body, but I didn't care.

I was starting to get my sea legs, and there were too many things to do and look at to worry about my depleted energy levels. Weird sea creatures which looked as if they'd come straight out of the Star Wars bar were falling off the pots and crawling around the deck wherever I looked. Everything in the sea wants to eat everything else and a little bit of fresh bait in a pot attracts any creature that happens by. Conger eels and fish of all colours and shapes came up in the pots amongst the crab, and had to be killed and cut up for extra bait. Full bins of crab were stacked back aft and replaced on deck by empties; so in short everyone was happy. They were all earning money, and I got to look at weird shit.

When the last pots of the day had been emptied of crab, re-baited and sent back overboard to the sea bed, The Newbrook turned and steamed for home. Big Dick made another round of teas and we had a quick sit-down and got some food down our necks. Getting back up to go out on deck proved a little tricky, for I ached all over. I felt as if I'd been stuffed in a sack and beaten with baseball bats. I was walking around the deck like the Tin Man in need of a little oil on his joints. But the deck had to be prepared for landing our catch to the fish merchant, who would meet us on the quayside. All the crab had to be pulled back up to the bow, covered and watered, the lobsters had to have their claws banded and the cock crabs had to have their claws nicked to stop them scrapping to the death with each other. This meant cutting the tendon in the join where the top claw meets the bottom claw. If they were dead they were not worth any money.

The conger eels had to be gutted and hung up on the 'A' frame for drying, and any other bait had to be cut and covered for the next day's fishing. Pots needed mending and the decks and gunwales had to be washed down. The work was endless, but just as we reached the mouth of the Dart, The Newbrook was restored to some form of order.

After the day's catch had been weighed by the fish merchant and loaded into his wagon, we could finally tie up at our moorings and head home. Matt and Stu lived in Dartmouth so we left them on the quayside and Dickey and I headed back in his truck. We stopped off at a pub called the Start Bay Inn for a well-earned pint, and as we stood at the bar the whole place started to sway from side to side. It felt as if I was still on the boat. Dickey looked at me and knew straight away what was happening, and gave a chuckle. He told me I had done well for my first day and that if I wanted to carry on my two-week trial I would be more than welcome. What the hell, I thought, I had nothing better planned and it was just what I needed, so we clinked our pint glasses together and made a toast to many more days at sea.

The two weeks flew by and I was then made a full member of the crew, on a share of the catch. Big Dick had got me a new set of oilskins, boots and gloves, and took it out of the wages that I would now be paid weekly. So, not only did I get to look at weird shit all day, now I got paid for it, too.

CHAPTER TWENTY-FOUR

BREAKFAST WITH A WARLORD

The next morning it was either my imagination or the camp smelt of dead dog, and it was an altogether worse smell than wet dog. Last night's fire-bombed hot dog and TNT-caught fish had brought a whole new meaning to everyone's favourite combo, 'Surf & Turf'. The whole camp was suffering from a Vegas of a hangover, with only half-dozen militants bothering to turn up and jig, down-trodden, to the drums. They needn't have bothered, such was their lacklustre performance. Including the drummers, I counted nine men on the parade ground, the ones who'd stayed on guard last night I presumed, and who therefore weren't allowed to go to bed. The tree was also looking bare; gone were the two guards who'd been caught fighting. Perhaps the night crawlers ate them whole; we could only hope.

This morning's half-hearted ritual was by far the worst yet, but the best for us. Fewer people meant less noise, excitement and intimidation. We were looking forward to a quiet day with no distractions, a day of reflection, to regroup and perhaps come up with a new game plan. This 'Stay put and see how the negotiations pan out' plan was not really floating my boat. I realised it was still the sensible option, but to be fair I would rather have a threesome with Fred and Rose than hang around here.

As with previous visits, the approaching gunboat was only seconds away when we first heard it, because of the dense jungle foliage absorbing the sound. The camp was either not expecting guests that morning or, as I suspected, had been caught with its pants down. The sound of the General's advancing boat penetrated the sleeping minds of his foot-soldiers and brought them bleary-eyed and scurrying from their huts, hastily hopping into pairs of pants and slipping into flip-flops. Many of them were desperately trying to smooth out their bed hair. The General entered the camp in the same cocksure way he always did and headed straight in our direction. His beret was at the same jaunty angle as his devious smile. He thrust forward his elegant, girl-like hand for us to take, which of course we did. The rest of his entourage was not far behind.

'We have breakfast together,' he announced, just as the first spots of rain started to fall. The General wouldn't normally have been my first choice of company over breakfast, but this wasn't an invitation. If the General wanted you to do something, you did it with a big smile stretched right across your chops. The skies blackened over and the rain began to fall, which started to replenish our empty rain traps. The militants who had just raced out to welcome their General hastily made their way back under cover.

Our cell was the chosen venue for the breakfast engagement and the General chose my and Plooy's mattress to sit on, which meant we were relegated to the hard and cracked concrete slab. Our mosquito nets had already been shaken out, mended and folded away ready for tonight; maintenance was next to godliness.

Noor and Bob sat on their mattress opposite the General, waiting for him to speak. In the cell next door to us were Sachin and Aditya, who had been enjoying a morning in bed but were now gate-crashed by about four of the General's bodyguards. They didn't want to talk or enjoy the company of our two Indian friends, they just wanted to keep out of the rain; they saw themselves as above sitting in the rec room with the rest of the mob and watching Delta Force, which seemed to be the latest training film for the younger recruits.

We spent an agonisingly uncomfortable ten minutes while the General stared us all out in silence, placing the dangerous end of his pistol at his temple, in his mouth and in his eye-socket. I was trying to think who out of various war movies he was trying to impersonate; there was always someone they were trying to mimic. Either that or he was a fan of Russian Roulette. His little slimy lizard tongue snaked about his lower lip while he eyed each of us in turn. The silence was threatening to tip me over the edge. I didn't feel I had the resolve left for playing stupid games, but these games were important to the General. They let him dominate us and made him who he was, an unhinged psychopathic warlord, so we had to play along.

I tried never to raise my eyes and connect with his and I was submissive in all my actions, as were my cell-mates; everyone knew the rules to this game. He stared at one of us and we all looked away: at the wall, at the ceiling but mostly at the floor. To hold his stare would have been very disrespectful and I would imagine would have upset him greatly. I made a secret wish, trying to rustle up a little juju and make the gun discharge on its own, sending a bullet right through his eye-socket and blowing his brains clean out of the back of his head, painting the wall behind him pink and grey.

The General suddenly shouted out to someone outside and we all flinched, our nerves at breaking point. A large fresh pineapple was passed in. Breakfast, I presumed. The General was also passed a big shiny knife, and once he had finished digging something out of his teeth he set about peeling the pineapple. He was sitting with crossed legs, elbows on knees, pineapple in the palm of one hand and blade in the other, slicing away at the hard skin and making a right ruddy mess on our mattress. The man didn't give a damn and continued meticulously cutting into the yellow flesh of the pineapple, occasionally popping a piece into his mouth, chewing slowly and then swallowing, all the while dripping a sticky mess onto our bed. The pineapple is among the juiciest and stickiest of all the fruits, and now a big pile of peel, flesh and juice was pooling on our bed, and on my side of it. I sat watching him, seething, and a great rage burning inside me. I just wanted to reach across, grab his gun from between his crossed legs, put it under his chin and let off a volley of shots up through his skull, screaming, 'Haaaaaaaa!'

I found myself fantasising about the sort of things you would normally only expect madmen to think of – maiming and killing on a large scale. I was starting to realise I harboured all these qualities – a primeval instinct lurking deep within us all – and these fuckers were slowly bringing mine to the surface.

We watched with our mouths watering as the last of the juicy pineapple disappeared into the General's mouth, and the chance of a few nutrients for us was lost with it. I'll never know why the General chose to eat that pineapple in front of us, or why he chose not to share it; it was after all his idea for us to have breakfast together. All I do know is that he made one hell of a mess doing it and made me feel hungrier than I'd ever felt before; I hoped he'd get the runs. All you could hear in the cell was the sound of four rumbling tummies as he swallowed the last mouthful and wiped his sticky hands on our mattress. He made to stand up and beckoned us to do the same, which we did obediently, keeping our eyes on the scraps of pineapple left on the bed. He pointed at Plooy. 'You phone boss man now, you tell him four hundred million dollars or we kill you all.'

Plooy either saw this as his chance or felt he had nothing left to lose. 'I'll ask for your four hundred million but I want to phone my wife afterwards, to tell her I'm okay.'

The General acted as if he was debating Plooy's request for a moment, sucking on the end of his Glock and looking up at the roof space, before he looked back down and said, 'Yes, you talk to wife.'

Getting the answer we were all hoping for, we made our way outside with the General and his satphone. First Plooy would make the call to our company, and then a call home. I couldn't even begin to imagine how that call would go.

Rain was still falling when Plooy dialled the number and waited to be put through. We stood around barefoot in the mud. I was enjoying the sensation of it squelching up through my toes, and as I looked round I could see that the water butts were overflowing at the brim with the most precious of life's resources once again. The rest of the mob was still trying to stay under shelter, even though the rain was now easing to just a few drops.

The first call didn't really go the way the General wanted, so therefore it didn't really go the way we wanted. The General thought he was being more than generous in dropping his ransom offer by a hundred million dollars, and so did I; that's a hell of a discount, a right bargain in anyone's language. So he was really quite insulted when our company came back with a piddling five million, and that wasn't even in dollars but in Nigerian naira, and at the time that worked out to be about $33,333. That's a piddling $11,111 each and no mention of any boats. My self-worth had dropped from three David Beckhams to one Paul Gascoigne in a single phone call.

The General was wounded and let off a volley of shots from his Glock to let his mood be known to the negotiator on the other end of the phone. To be honest we were also a little pissed off at this pitiful sum, but life here was cheap and negotiations had to be played out, as a game all of its own.

The gang that kidnaps a hostage opens the negotiations by putting in a ridiculously large ransom demand, only to be rejected by the company or family that wants his safe return. The company/family will use excuses: we haven't got that sort of money, we are not a rich company/family, and we need more time to raise that sort of capital. The kidnap gang doesn't give a damn whether or not the company can afford the ransom, that simply is not their problem, but they are all the while being worn down. The company/family then comes back with an equally ridiculously low offer, one that can only be dismissed but buys more time. This can go on for weeks, months or even years, until one day both parties reach an agreed amount somewhere in the middle. It's just another game, but one that has to be played out in its entirety if you want to make it home in one piece. It is just a little frustrating when you are stuck in the middle. All you want is for everyone to get along, a price to be agreed, money to change hands and to be allowed home, all inside the first week; but it ain't going to happen. Not when you're inside one of the most corrupt nations on the planet, a country where every man and his dead dog wants a slice of the half-billion dollar pie.

As angry as the General was, he was true to his word and let Plooy make the call to his wife, while he stomped up and down looking totally miffed as to why his well-thought-out and calculated ransom had been dismissed out of hand. I was beginning to wonder just what was on the General's CV and whether he had done this kind of work before, because to conduct this sort of murky business takes a lot of patience; even I knew that. I was starting to get a little nervous about the General's attitude and obvious lack of experience in these matters. The last thing we wanted was a pissed-off warlord looking to make an example to the world about who was calling the shots.

Plooy looked a little distressed when he finally cut the line with home, and we gave him a few minutes to gather himself. The rain had passed on to another part of the Delta, leaving the camp bathed in warm sunshine again, but even this failed to brighten the General's mood. He was now busy with the other business of Bob and the Indians, so we took ourselves off to the rubbish dump to interrogate Plooy on how his phone call had gone.

Plooy said the missus took some calming down and reassuring at first that he was well and that everything was going to turn out all right. Then in Afrikaans he outlined the information she was to pass on to Plooy's mate in the company. She was very brave throughout the call, and kept a cool head as the information was relayed to her. Now we had to hope that she passed it on word for word, or we would be stuffed and have a good 200-kilometre walk to Cameroon to look forward to. It was out of our hands now, though; we had done all we could and it was up to Plooy's wife and the man to whom she was to pass the information.

The camp, as always, let out a huge sigh of relief when the General completed his day's business and disappeared down the river. The mob got straight back on the booze; this lot were certainly not going to make old bones, they could burn the candle at both ends and the middle. We tried to unwind with a game of Hangman and then a chuck-about with the Frisbee. Bob's chat on the phone had gone about as well as ours; we agreed that the outfit he worked for was running to the same script as our company, and both were going to do their damnedest to get value for money out of us. We had until 20th June, the date Plooy passed on to his missus, to make our rendezvous on the beach, and we figured it might take us as long as a week to get there if our navigation techniques weren't up to par. So at the very latest, and if we had no good news and feared for our lives, we would have to make good our escape by 13th June. Today was the 5th and that meant we had another shitty week to look forward to; I couldn't for the life of me see that a ransom amount would be agreed in that time.

Again the mood in the camp had brightened, just like the last time negotiations had been made and large sums of money had been discussed. Talking of ransoms seemed to make it all worthwhile for this sorry bunch of militants, and they could once again dream of Humvees, fast boats and travelling to the UK to steal themselves a bride. Some of the mob even joined Plooy, Noor and me in a game of Frisbee, leaving Bob to relax in the sun and Sachin and Aditya in their room; they didn't come out much with Aditya as ill as he was. Sachin was pleased with his phone call, though, and was hoping that he and Aditya would be on their way home in a week's time at the very latest. We hoped so for Aditya's sake; we felt that he wouldn't last a lot longer in here without his medicines.

As the evening wore on, more and more of the guards had put down their AKs to join in with the Frisbee. It was like trying to teach a four-year-old how to fly a helicopter, but it was fun watching their delighted, smiling faces when they did get it right. After the game we all went and sat by the fire that the Teacher had lit, drinking a beer with them; and after Plooy started humming Bob Marley's 'Three Little Birds', everyone broke into song. I wasn't sure whether the song was very apt for our present situation, but we all knew the words so we sang along anyway.

'Don't worry... about a thing,

'Cause every little thing... gonna be all right,

'Singin' don't worry... about a thing...'cause every little thing gonna be all right!'

And I think old Bob Marley would have approved of us that night, if he was looking down on us drinking beer, with some of his black brothers smoking big fat riffas, singing along to the feel-good lyrics he had written many, many moons ago. I may well look down on them as a bunch of dangerous terrorists who had all cut their teeth on crimes including armed robbery, kidnapping, extortion, gunrunning, gangbanging and black-market oil-bunkering, to name a few. But to others they would be admired as freedom fighters; such is our world.

I tried to pass on some of my own drug-taking knowledge by making them a bucket bong, so they could really get off their chops; but when I had finished making it none of them would try it, as they were all too suspicious of the white man's magic. It was just as well really, they were making a pretty fine job of getting stoned on their own. This was probably our most relaxed night since we'd arrived in camp; not even the NAFy could chase us back to our cell that night.

As the mob around us got tipsy and stoned on weed we started to press them for information: innocent-sounding questions about what lay beyond the jungle walls of the camp, and in what direction and how close were the nearest villages: anything that might help us once we were on the outside. We learned that there were two villages, one either side of us, and that most of the men here came from these villages; so we had to assume the villages were hostile and sympathetic to MEND. We also found out the average wage of a militant in these parts – not particularly useful intel, but it made us realise just why most of these guys ended up becoming gun-toting pirates and not hard-working fishermen. Not only did they get to drink and smoke drugs all day, use guns and hang out with their mates watching war DVDs, but they were paid a monthly wage of 30,000 Naira, about £130, a staggering amount of money when you lived in a swamp. I dare say most of that money found its way back into the organisation once the drink and drugs expenses had been deducted, but many of them did say they were saving for their bus fare to England – not such a comforting thought before bed.

Negotiations day was always going to be a very tense and stressful affair, especially for Plooy, who would be speaking to his wife. With the General at the helm you never knew what direction they would take, or whether he would just lose patience altogether and end it all with a bullet to the head. But it did always leave us with fresh hope that we hadn't been forgotten out here, and that the wheels were in motion and working hard for our release. Tonight, as we readied ourselves for bed, I didn't know whether I was feeling the effects of one Monkey Tail too many, or whether I was genuinely feeling a lot more positive; but I really thought that just like Bob Marley's lyrics everything was going to be all right. How stupid was I?

CHAPTER TWENTY-FIVE

DEADLIEST CATCH

All of a sudden life seemed rosy again; my sense of right and wrong had been magnetised and my moral compass was pointing true north. I was being trained to ignore pain and adverse weather conditions, to live off a boat and to eat things that would make a billy-goat puke. I was living in the country by the sea, still with my parents; it was not ideal, but I needed a little more time before I could afford a place of my own, and all the while I was keeping my nose clean. I was not really noticed. If I was not up at three a.m. and out on the boat all day, I was down the pub, walking over the fields or helping the old man carve furniture in the pig shed, so I was really no trouble at all.

There were two things that took up most of my time. One was watching and waiting for my sexy young filly down at the Tavern to reach some sort of age of civil decency – she was just sixteen but soon to be seventeen which sounds a whole lot better, almost an adult. The other thing was of course my job. The more I put into it the more I was getting out of it. I was very much enjoying being a crab fisherman.

Big Dick alternated skippering The Newbrook with a man called Mark, on a day-on, day-off basis. Matt, Stu and I worked two days on, one day off. The Newbrook herself was at sea every day, stopping only for breakdowns and extreme weather.

On this particular morning it was Mark's turn to skipper and Stu's and mine to work the deck. The day started like all days at sea: first I heard the *beep, beep, beep* of the alarm clock, then I washed, dressed and grabbed my lunch before sleep-walking up to the bus stop and waiting for Mark to pick me up. It was November and I was dressed for the season – I had my sea boots, thick scruffy trousers and a warm waterproof coat with a woolly hat pulled tight over my ears. It was drizzling slightly and the wind was fresh, so I huddled deep inside the bus shelter.

After a few minutes I heard a vehicle approaching, stuck my head out to see if it was Mark and came face to face with a police car. My natural reaction was to jerk my head straight back into the shelter and pretend I hadn't seen them, looking directly at the floor and feeling very guilty even though I hadn't done anything. With that, there was a screech of tyres and two doors going *thump, thump*, followed by a rush of heavy boots on tarmac. How does anyone get himself into trouble at three o'clock in the morning, in the middle of winter in the middle of nowhere, waiting for a lift to go to work?

As soon as two of Devon and Cornwall's finest reached me they grabbed for their radios and started babbling all sorts of cryptic coded messages to their colleagues. I understood enough of what was being said, though, to give me something to ponder over. Reading between the lines the message was, 'We've got him.' Got who, though? Within half a minute another two panda cars arrived carrying some angry-looking coppers.

There were far too many coppers here for this to be just a random stop and search. And who the hell does random stop and searches on a country road in the middle of nowhere? Nothing about this felt right. I was normally pretty good at weighing up situations, and there was definitely something askew about this one.

Police now completely surrounded me. It was blatantly obvious they thought they had their man. Where the hell was Mark? I needed an alibi; he could explain things. Once the officers had secured their prisoner in the bus shelter, the questions started.

'What are you doing out at this time, on a night like this?' asked the nearest.

There were five of us squashed up inside the shelter built for two, with another three officers loitering around just outside, talking on their radios and shuffling their feet from the cold. I looked down at my yellow sea boots and gave one a wiggle whilst lifting it slightly off the ground, held up my lunch bag and replied, 'Going fishing.'

'What's in the bag?' the policeman fired back.

'What's all this about? I'm just waiting for a lift to go to work.'

The policeman ignored me and started searching my bag. 'Take off your boots,' another demanded.

'What the hell for?' I asked, but they were not listening to me now, they just wanted to search me. It was very cold and I hoped they were not going to go all the way with a full strip-search. My boots came off and my lunch was emptied onto the bench. I had two hands groping inside my coat and searching my pockets. 'Have you been in trouble with the police before, sir?'

I lied, 'No.' I didn't like the way he had called me 'sir'; in my experience that meant I was in trouble. They took down my details to run through the computer, which wasn't the best thing that could have happened, but it was pretty much running its own course now, completely out of my hands. I thought for a moment about the tiny lie I had just told and started to back-track a little.

'Well, I may have got into a spot of trouble a year or so back, once or twice.' They couldn't shut me up now and I continued down my own line of inquiry. 'I moved down here to get away from all the trouble, and I was doing bloody well until you lot showed up.' I started waving an accusing finger at them whilst blubbering what a good boy I had been.

'Have you got anything sharp on you, sir?' Bloody hell, they had read my file. 'No I haven't, Constable … I've…' They cut me off.

219

'What's this blade for then?' he asked, holding it high between his thumb and forefinger for everyone to see. When they said 'something sharp' I thought they meant needles and syringes.

'It's a knife. I'm a fisherman, and like I've already said I'm on my way to work.' This wasn't getting us anywhere and I was starting to run out of patience.

I told them that I had been standing in this bus shelter for no more than five minutes before they showed up, and before that I was tucked up safely in bed at my parents' house. After they had forced the location of my parents out of me, one of them set off to check on my alibi. Six months I'd been here, and the police were once again knocking on the door. Mother was going to be pissed off at this; surely this morning couldn't get any worse.

While we waited I picked up bits and pieces of information from the radio chatter, and started trying to prise a bit more out of another policeman, the good cop. He told me that I was their number one suspect for the attempted rape and battery of a seventy-four-year-old lady. Fuck me, just a small charge then. I took umbrage at this. I had been accused of all sorts over the years, but messing about with an old lady, well I was bloody speechless. If only I could have stayed that way I would have come out of the situation with some dignity left intact, but I didn't.

'Attempted rape?' I started. Shut up, Phil, I thought. 'Attempted rape, give me some credit. If I wanted to get it on with an old lady I'd like to think I'd be nothing but successful,' I said proudly. I didn't exactly mean it like that; I just wanted to put across to them that I wasn't some pathetic sex pest, but the look of disgust on all the officers' faces told me all I needed to know. By the looks on them you would have thought they'd just caught me finger-banging the neighbour's cat.

The officer came back from my mum's house and gave me the all-clear. All the police started back to their cars shaking their heads at me, just as Mark pulled up, leaning out the window and singing, 'You've got your man, bang him up!' All I needed.

He pulled up and I jumped in. Just as Mark was about to drive away one of the police came up to his window and leaned in to say, 'Your mate needs his head looked at, he's a sick man,' and turned back to his patrol car.

'What was that all about?' Mark asked me.

'Nothing mate, just drive, you're late.'

About two hours later The Newbrook was punching through the waves, bow into the wind. The wind was fairly strong, and the waves were breaking over the sharp end and crashing over the wheelhouse. Inside, Mark, Stuey and I were enjoying a cup of tea and having a laugh at my rather embarrassing run-in this morning.

Mark gave the signal to get on deck, and we ditched our tea and got ready for the day's fishing. Stu and I were there, struggling against the pitch and roll of the boat as Mark brought The Newbrook alongside the first string of pots. As soon as the end weight was aboard I started hauling in the pots and clearing the crab, tossing the pots to Stu to bait and stack when I had finished. On the third pot, a large wave crashed beam-on into The Newbrook, causing her to roll violently, just as I was about to lean over the gunwale to snatch in the next pot. I slipped on a piece of old scad bait and everything went black, cold and very wet.

I was no longer on the wooden deck of The Newbrook but splashing about in the middle of the English Channel. My head broke the surface and I took in a lungful – mostly of sea water, but enough air to keep me going. I turned my head as I drifted past the boat and just made out a blue-gloved hand belonging to Stu, my quick-acting deck mate. I had one chance at this and grabbed on to it, holding it tight as he pulled me back to safety. Another hand grabbed the scruff of my oilskin smock and both Stu and Mark, who had run out of the shed, hauled me back on board. I rolled on my back to the middle of the deck and stood up somewhat shakily, cold and very wet, but thankfully unhurt.

Mark looked at me and asked, 'What the fuck was that?'

'Dunno, boat rolled, I slipped.'

'Stu, get him in the shed and get those wet things off him, I'm going to send the pots back over and we'll head for home.' I wasn't in the water long, but once wet and in the middle of winter it wouldn't have taken me long to succumb to the effects of hypothermia. Mark started chucking pots back over and Stuey led me back inside the shed, shouting, 'Aye aye, skipper,' and laughing all the while.

As soon as we were inside, Stuey turned on the cooking hobs for some heat and to put on a brew. I stripped off my wet clothes and started drying myself. When it's cold and you've got a man overboard, it's essential to take off all wet clothes, get some dry ones on and keep him warm. You lose body heat twenty-five times faster through water than you do through air, and in the middle of winter it wouldn't take that long before my core body temperature started to go south.

Stripping off and getting dry wasn't a problem, but finding spare dry clothes on board our boat was. My teeth were chattering and I was shivering as well, so Mark and Stu dressed me in some of their clothes and sat me down with a cuppa. All three of us were sitting round in various stages of undress, drinking tea and having a bit of a giggle about what could have been. One thing was for sure, it had definitely been a strange morning. Word soon spread over the radio waves thanks to Mark, and the whole crab fleet was now having a laugh at my expense.

By the time we reached the River Dart and tied up, I had warmed up enough to put on my clothes that had been drying down in the engine room, and give Mark and Stu back theirs. Mark dropped me at home exactly five hours after he'd picked me up, and we hadn't earned a penny. No-one was angry though, not even Big Dick himself, just glad all was well that ended well. I did buy him a few pints down the pub, however, and told him and anyone else who'd listen a largely exaggerated version of the story.

Two weeks later and the wannabe rapist struck again. This time, however, he got a good kick in the balls and was apprehended by the police – who did turn out to be Devon and Cornwall's finest – and was put away where he belonged.

As Christmas approached in 2003, The Newbrook was in dire need of a refit. Every time we went to sea a different part of the boat would fall off and float away or sink to the bottom. The deck was rotten and the hull was like a piece of Swiss cheese; she was taking on water all the time, the bilge pumps could barely keep up. During the year we had had one fire, one near-sinking and I had cracked my head open on the winch, needing stitches.

The fire had started in the accommodation under the back deck and filled the wheelhouse with smoke, disabling Mark and leaving the two of us on deck to put out the flames. We then limped back into harbour for repairs. The near-sinking happened sometime after. There were fairly rough seas so the leaky deck was constantly being swamped, and one of the bilge pumps packed in, leaving the other one unable to cope. Again, it was back to harbour for repairs. The cracking of my head, well, that was my own fault.

Big Dick had booked The Newbrook to be lifted out just after Christmas, so we worked like slaves up until then, had a jolly good knees-up over the festive season and then cracked on with the refit. I had to say goodbye to my deck-mates at this point, as they were

223

getting the sack. Dickey was keeping me on, not because I was better than them, but because he knew I could survive on the pittance he planned to pay me. Matt, Stu and Mark were released to go and earn on the other boats which worked out of Dartmouth.

The refit (or to start with, the demolition) was not only interesting but very rewarding. The Newbrook was on stilts in a dry dock and we effectively got to rip it to pieces. Everything was coming off: 'A' frames, wheelhouse, decks, even the engine and all the hydraulics. All that was left after the demolition job was an empty hull. Tons and tons of wood had to be burnt and that was also my job. I loved a good fire, but it couldn't be burnt on site so I had to transport it back to the beach in another of Dickey's work vehicles, a VW LT35 which had a flat-bed back with an old transit-type cap. The wagon had no second gear and drove like a piano; it leaked like a sieve and the brakes were shite.

I had just finished burning the first load of the day and was returning for my second; it was still quite early, and the roads were frosty. The road I took was a back lane – no chance to overtake or pass oncoming traffic – with high hedges on either side. But they were relatively quiet, especially when it was early, so you could make good progress.

My mind wandered a little and I switched to autopilot. Whilst thinking of nothing in particular I came round a sharp right-hand bend and face to face with a massive, bright green John Deere tractor, with one of those large, black, shiny counterweights sticking out in front. I slammed the practically non-existent anchors on at the same time as Old McDonald, and what can only be described as an involuntary game of chicken ensued. The pair of us were gripping our steering wheels like demons while staring at each other with mirrored faces, shocked open mouths and eyes like dinner-plates with high arched eyebrows.

The LT 35 was managing to slow a little, but the mean green tractor machine just kept on coming. With a ten-ton trailer full of cow shit pushing up its rear, it had no chance of stopping. I thought there could be only one outcome, the total destruction of Big Dick's wagon, and probably me with it. The tractor's counterweight ploughed straight into Dick's truck and ripped right through the centre of the grille and bumper as if they were made of cardboard, then started folding everything inwards. The wagon came to a shuddering halt and then got shunted about ten metres backwards. As I was not wearing a seat belt, I just kept on going forward.

There's only one thing that goes through your mind when you're staring at a lump of metal such as this, and that is, 'This is going to hurt'. I left the seat, flew straight at the windscreen, put my head through it and bounced and landed on the passenger seat. Old McDonald still hadn't taken his eyes off mine, and was trembling like a leaf. He had a dead man's grip on his steering wheel, knuckles bony and white. He spoke to me; no sound came out, but I could make out the words, 'Fuck me, mate'.

He clambered out of the cab and helped me out of mine. I brushed myself down and gave myself a bit of a shake to clear my head, and then we both turned to survey the damage. The LT35 lost in spectacular fashion; there was not a mark on John Deere, not even a noticeable scratch. Big Dick's wagon, though, was smashed, a crumpled wreck, a total write-off. We didn't even exchange numbers as it was generally considered that down the back lanes it was knock for knock, so I had just lost Dickey a wagon and he was not going to be pleased. All that was left for me to do was climb inside, put it in reverse and peel it away. The farmer did the same. It made a terrible noise, metal scraping against metal, but we managed to separate the two vehicles and I gave the farmer a cheery wave as I backed the wagon up, turned it round in a gateway and limped my way home.

On the way back I placed a call to Dickey who was already on site working on The Newbrook. I told him that I had totalled the wagon during a jousting match with a tractor, but there was no need to worry as I was A-okay. Dickey didn't seem angry – he simply replied, 'Nothing surprises me about you, when are you going to show for work?' I said, 'I'll make a plan.' I arrived home and Mum made me one of her world-famous fry-ups, and then I waited for the pub to open.

That was my only day off in the three months it took to complete the refit. We worked tirelessly, seven days a week, wind, rain or shine. Everything at sea has to be built to a higher standard because of the inhospitable environment, and I like to think that that includes the men who work there. This was certainly true back in Nelson's day, but I'm not sure whether the phrase 'steel men on wooden boats' stands its ground today, especially after what I've brought to the table.

Come the end of March, The Newbrook was ready for sea. It was on time but well over budget, three times the original estimate. It was time for us to catch some crab, and we needed lots of it to pay off the shipwrights and engineers who helped rebuild the boat. Dickey designed, and we built, a gunwale rolling system that would let the pots come aboard on their own, so now we only needed two of us to man the boat: me and Dickey. It meant a little extra work but my share of the catch went up, and Dickey needed his extra to pay the mounting bills.

A spanking-new boat re-christened The Newbrook was launched back into the Dart, and we were ready for sea. The first couple of weeks back had the normal sort of teething problems you got with a new vessel: a burst hydraulic hose, malfunctioning electrics, that sort of thing; but we managed to nip them in the bud and iron them out quickly. In addition, after leaving the pots for so long on the sea bed through the worst part of winter, we were left with lots of tangled back line and crushed pots, all of which had to be sorted out before any money could be earned. But once we were back working to full capacity we started to coin it in. Not only were we putting in maximum days, we were also getting bumper catches. We were catching more crab and lobsters than you could shake a pointed stick at, more than I had ever seen anyway.

Week after week the pay cheques came in and I religiously placed them in the bank. After a few months I was rich and Dickey was making major dents in his bills. All through the summer and autumn it was the same, maximum days and bumper cheques.

With three strings to go on a bright, calm day at the beginning of November, things turned a little hairy. The back deck was full of crab and Dickey and I were in a good mood, enjoying the rare good weather for this time of year. The day was passing fast, going like clockwork; Dickey and I were like a well-oiled machine. Bait was running a little low, so all the fish that had been caught in the pots needed to be cut up into single baiters. Now that there were only two of us on the boat, Dickey had to cut the bait back aft while I shot the pots away on the main deck.

The Newbrook was steaming at about seven knots on autopilot, and I was rolling the pots on their sides on to the shooting ramp, when one of the pots bounced off the gunwale and rolled back towards me. My foot shot out instinctively to nudge the pot back on to the ramp. Now, nine hundred and ninety-nine times out of a thousand I would have got away with such a heinous crime, but not today. Today I would face the full force of the law.

As my foot moved to kick the pot, the back line jumped off the deck and took a turn around my ankle like an angry boa. It bit down hard, turned me ninety degrees to starboard and whipped me up the shooting ramp in the same way a water-skier is pulled off the jetty. There was always a knife jammed in the bait tray, for cutting bait and

227

for emergencies just like this one. I was on my back, getting dragged feet first up the ramp, fast. I made a hasty grab for the knife, a one-chance shot, and missed. I shot off the ramp in mid-air, clutching a fish. I had a second for one last action for my survival, and shouted, 'Dickey!' at the top of my lungs. That was also my last breath before – *splash.*

Dickey heard my cry and was a little taken aback when he looked up and saw no-one on deck. He was even more miffed when he raced forward to see a bright yellow blob being dragged out to sea and then disappearing under the surface. Dickey later said he stood motionless on deck scratching his head and thinking, 'What the devil am I gonna tell his parents?'

I slipped beneath the calm surface and started making my way to Davy Jones' locker. To work in the fishing industry you have to go on a sea survival course, and on that course they will tell you that if you find yourself being dragged to the bottom of the ocean by rope or net, stay still, don't panic and conserve your oxygen. In other words, keep calm. No chance! I was thrashing around, panicking as I had never panicked before. It was dark and wet but I didn't feel the cold; my body was completely numb to the elements. My mind was more alive than it had ever been, racing around and trying to come up with a survival plan.

After two seconds of thinking I realised that there was no plan, I was doomed and all that was left for me to do was carry on panicking. The pots were spaced every sixteen fathoms along the back line, and another pot had just dropped overboard into the sea. This tightened the back line and spun me several times, taking more and more turns up my leg. I was now wrapped up from my ankle to my thigh. It dawned on me that I was going to die. I didn't think of my family or the foxy little filly who drank water with bubbles that I had just started courting, now that she was of an acceptable age. I just felt scared and even more panicky. I was straining every part of my body to try and get my head above water, but it was no good; the pots were going to the sea bed and so was I. My ears were starting to hurt from the pressure as I got dragged even deeper, I'm guessing around two to three metres.

Sixteen fathoms – another pot entered the ocean and tightened the back line once again. This time, though, it snapped me back the other way and the back line let me go. I shot to the surface, broke through the gentle swell and pulled in a great lungful of air as I looked into the bright blue sky; what a beautiful sky it was.

As soon as I broke the surface Dickey snapped into action. He cut the back line, sending the pots to the sea bed. Using the controls on deck he turned The Newbrook in a one-hundred-and-eighty-degree arc, and came back round to pick me up. He made one pass, threw me a Perry Buoy (orange life ring) and screamed, 'Get yourself inside!' followed by 'You twat,' in a lower tone that I only just caught as he passed by.

Bloody hell, he looks angry, I thought, but I was looking forward too much to getting safely back on board to worry about him. Dickey had turned back round, and The Newbrook was bearing right down on me; she looked massive from down here with my head just bobbing about on the surface. Dickey held out his arm and I held up mine; we locked hands and he pulled me back on deck with little effort, as Dickey was as strong as an ox. We both fell on our backs; Dickey was laughing with relief and I was coughing and being sick. I rolled on to my hands and knees and continued coughing up sea water. Dickey got to his feet and then started taking the piss: 'You're crying, you big bloody girl!'

'No I'm not, I've got salt water in my eyes and it stings, you big fat fuck. What took you so long? I thought I was gonna die.'

'Dry your eyes, princess, and stop being such a drama queen; we've got pots to haul.'

He was right, we did have pots to haul, another three strings. Dickey let me take five minutes out to recover before I grabbed the gaff and got in position to haul on another string. We laughed our way through that whole string, more out of shock than anything, but it was bloody funny. After I had shot it away Dickey said we'd leave the other two and get ourselves off home for a nice pint. Good call.

Those couple of pints tasted good, as we told the story over and over to anyone who would listen. It was a damn good pub yarn, and by the third pint Dickey was already the hero of the day, and rightly so. After five pints we went home for a feed and an early night, for tomorrow we had the extra two strings to haul on top of our normal day's work.

The next morning I woke up feeling as if I'd been in a car crash, I was so stiff. Every muscle and every joint was screaming at me, from thrashing around and straining to get my head above the surface the day before. I was seriously thinking of jacking it all in and finding myself a normal job.

When Dickey turned up at the bus stop and I had climbed aboard, I relayed my concerns to him. I explained that in the short time that I had worked for him I had pushed my luck enough: a split head, twice overboard, one fire, one near-sinking and also a near arrest for the attempted rape, robbing and battery of a seventy-four-year-old lady. I continued that perhaps crabbing wasn't the right job for me. Dickey turned to look at me with a look of total understanding, and there was almost a hint of sympathy on his normally harsh, weather-beaten face, a look I hadn't seen on him before. Then he said quietly,

'Don't be such a fucking poof. Grow yourself a pair will you, for fuck's sake.'

I turned back to stare out of the passenger window, thought for a little while about the wise words my skipper had just given me, and decided he was right.

CHAPTER TWENTY-SIX

WHITE MEN CAN'T JUMP

The good times didn't roll for very long in Camp Horrid. During this morning's roll-call it emerged that Prada and a few of his gang hadn't taken too well to the previous night's bonding session between us and the guards, and had lodged a formal complaint with the Secretary. As a result the Secretary warned all the guards to keep a 'professional distance' from us.

That, however, wasn't the only reason why Plooy, Bob and I sat on our own by the rubbish dump feeling a little downcast. Just after the morning's prayers had finished two of the General's bodyguards showed up, the Somali and the Actor, and with the help of Commander Jackson, the Secretary, BA and Denzel, they dragged Noor from our clutches, put a sack on his head and took him on a mystery boat trip to we didn't know where.

We tried to protest against this and demanded to be kept together, but all it took was for one of their AKs to be thrust in our faces and we let them take him. It was so hopelessly depressing, knowing that a wave of the magic AK made us do whatever they wanted. We tried to find out where they were taking him and why, but they wouldn't tell us a thing.

Frog Face hadn't been around since the fight over the last bucket of water so BA was manning the outboards, and he steered the boat away from the camp and up the creek. The last we saw of Noor was a hooded figure with slumped shoulders sitting in the boat, surrounded by heavily-armed militants. He had guns pointed at the back of his head and was forced to keep low. Then they went round the corner and out of sight. We were not sure whether they were splitting us up into different camps, selling Noor to another gang or, God forbid, taking him off somewhere to execute him. We were very concerned for his and our welfare, as we were not sure what they had in store for any of us. We kept telling ourselves that negotiations were open and sums of money were being thrown on the table for our safe return, and if they harmed us or killed us then they would tarnish their good reputation for all future business dealings involving kidnappings. It was now starting to sound a bit hollow, as though we were just trying to convince ourselves.

With the backbone of the camp's hierarchy out of the way, overall command of the camp fell to Prada, which was about as irresponsible as the BBC letting Jimmy Savile front Top of the Pops. We hadn't yet seen the full potential of Prada's mean streak, but I had an inkling we were about to.

The Somali and the Actor had brought with them a new hot training DVD. It was called Black Hawk Down, and was the true story of a botched American special forces mission in Mogadishu, the capital of Somalia. In the film the Somalis, or Skinnies as the Yanks called them, shot down a couple of American choppers, 'Black Hawks'. Then a ferocious firefight raged through the night as the Americans attempted a rescue operation, leaving a couple of thousand dead. Most of the camp was now glued to this being played in the rec room.

Plooy and I finished banging out the mattresses and putting them out to air, and sat down for a game of draughts to try to keep our minds off what was happening to Noor. It was not working, though, and I lost three games in a row. We pushed the beer bottle tops to one side and tried our hands at Hangman. I was in control of the noose and chose the word 'abscond', which was what we should have done days ago. Plooy had guessed three of the letters correctly, A, B and

232

N, but if he made one more incorrect guess then I would complete the drawing of the hangman in the dirt to win the game. For a minute all thoughts of Noor and our predicament vanished, and I focused on the victory that would surely be mine.

'Oh fuck, Prada,' said Plooy.

I spun round to where Plooy was looking and saw Bob encircled by Prada and his cronies, all of them poking him with their guns and slapping him about the head. Oh, fuck indeed. Under Prada's orders they were starting to behave just like a pack of wild dingoes snapping away at an abandoned baby, getting bolder and bolder, egging each other on.

'Stop that immediately!' I stood and shouted, putting on my best British officer's accent, full of authority and conviction, backed up by Plooy who was quick to stand up next to me.

'Hey, knock that off, leave Bob alone, he's a senior man,' said Plooy. This was quite a clever tactic as in most villages a lot of respect is paid to the older generation.

'Fuck off, white man,' shouted back Prada, his gun cocked and levelled directly at our faces. Prada was the worst type of bully and his face was full of pleasure, his shark eyes narrowing; he was going to enjoy this. 'What you going to do, white man, I'll fucking kill you.'

For a moment we just stood and stared, trying hard not to look intimidated, but Prada knew there was nothing we could do and that he was the one in charge. Bob was the next to talk. 'Let them have their way, goddam.' The voice was one past caring and reeked of acceptance of his fate. Bob knew Prada was going to have his fun; it was just a case of whether we let him have it the easy way or the hard. Plooy and I sat down in the dirt again, feeling pathetic and helpless. Prada turned back to Bob. 'You watched frog jumps the other night, you do them.'

Bob looked Prada in the eye and firmly said, 'No way'.

Prada jabbed the barrel of his AK into the upper part of Bob's leg and pulled the trigger, *click*. Prada pulled his gun away, put a round in the chamber and thrust it back into Bob's leg. 'I blow fucking leg off, fucking white man, do it!'

'Come on Prada, mate, don't do this,' Plooy and I both moaned, but it sounded just like what it was, a half-hearted plea that would do nothing to discourage a man like Prada from his natural instincts.

'Do it.' A nasty smile crept across Prada's face, and he pushed the gun barrel harder into Bob's leg and repeated the words more slowly and clearly. 'Do. It.' All Prada's mates were watching intently, surprised at just how far he was willing to take the game. We tried our hand again with the senior man card.

'Come on Prada, knock it off. Bob is a senior man, you shouldn't be doing this.' This seemed to please Prada and his smile widened, spreading across his whole face.

'Bob no senior man here, he's a fucking white man. Now jump.'

Prada and his cronies pushed Bob to the edge of the yard and forced him into the squatting position. They slapped him about until he held his ears in the correct position, and then kicked him between the shoulder-blades to get him off the mark. Some of the mob followed Bob, kicking him every time he stopped, and some stayed and covered us with their AKs, laughing and taking the piss. I wanted to do something to stop them hurting Bob, but I knew that I wouldn't. Instead, Plooy and I just sat and let the treatment of Bob continue. Bob couldn't go any further and collapsed in the dirt. He was exhausted and demoralised. Prada and his gang knew they were not going to get any more out of him and left him there on the ground. They walked off laughing with each other, mimicking Bob's efforts at frog-jumping and his subsequent humiliation. Plooy and I went to help him up, dusting him off and offering words of comfort while taking him back to the rubbish tip.

Prada swaggered over all cocksure, flanked by a few of his followers, to deliver a cold and chilling message to us. He towered over us as we sat on the ground and shouted rather than spoke: 'You never leave Delta, I will kill all you. Noor is already dead, you follow... Fucking white man.' He spat at our feet and the others drew their fingers across their throats and walked away. Prada and his band of merry men didn't want any money in exchange for us, they simply wanted us dead, and for the white man to get the message that he was not wanted here, now or in the future.

The rest of the day dragged on with us isolated on the edge of the yard, letting our minds run off with what could have happened to Noor and trying to avoid eye contact with any of the guards. We felt sick with worry and fear and struggled to eat our ration of rice, our appetites all but gone. As hard as we tried to stay positive, we could only come up with bad reasons for them splitting us up and taking Noor away; everything in the camp was starting to go sideways.

The mob were pretty drunk by now; they had watched Black Hawk Down for the third time straight and were now starting to act out some of the more violent scenes. *Whoop, whoop,* came the thumping of a chopper passing overhead, which got the mob very excited; they came rushing out in a group, pointing their weapons to the sky and play-shooting at the helicopter. Our moods matched the darkening skies as a thick oppressive covering of cloud threatened rain. Thoughts of the whereabouts of Noor and our own predicament filled the rest of our day, leaving us in a very dark place. We had all grown very close since working together, and even more so since we had been thrown together in Camp Horrid. I missed Noor terribly and hoped he was not suffering, wherever he was. To say it was like a physical pain wouldn't be too far from the truth, and I did feel I was hurting. I am not and never have been a religious man, but lying on my mattress that night, listening to the first spots of rain falling

235

on the tin roof, I had to think long and hard as to whether I should say a prayer for Noor. As the only time I went to church was to have a pint at The Church House Inn, I decided not to pray, but kept him in my thoughts and hoped I would see him again soon.

CHAPTER TWENTY-SEVEN

JUNGLE CREEPY-CRAWLIES

By the morning the camp was back under Commander Jackson's and the Secretary's control. The mood during roll-call and the morning's prayers was strained, and we were very scared because at first we didn't know why; we didn't want to be split up any further. However, one or two of the militants must have disagreed with Prada's treatment of Bob and complained to the Commander when he got back.

Bob was then singled out by the Secretary and told to pick out the man who made him do the frog jumps. This put Bob in a very awkward position; he didn't want to cause a stir and give Prada any excuse to persecute him more than he already had, and so he decided to keep mum and let Prada off the hook. Prada and his mates were all wearing mischievous silly grins on their faces, as though they knew they were not going to get any comeback from this, and were probably feeling untouchable. The Secretary knew full well who had instigated the attack on Bob and probably approved. He finished by telling everyone that no-one was to touch us until the General gave the word. It was a depressing thought that all that stood in the way of our being killed was a beret-wearing maniac who wouldn't even share his breakfast.

No-one in the camp was allowed near us now apart from the two guards assigned to look after us, which as far as we were concerned was just fine. After trying unsuccessfully to get some information about Noor out of the Secretary, we settled ourselves down for another long day by the pile of rubbish. It was a very hot day and the ground was baked hard. I shifted constantly, trying to find a more comfortable position, as Plooy drew out the draughts board in the dirt with a stick. The first game was over quickly and we repositioned the bottle tops to start another, occasionally chatting about what we thought had happened to Noor; we still couldn't think of any good possibilities. Bob was lazing on the mattress.

'*Cheep, cheep*,' we heard before a short pause, then came the sound again. *'Cheep, cheep.'*

'SSSShhhhhh, listen,' whispered Plooy. Then it came again. *'Cheep, cheep.'*

Two little chicks came walking out of the jungle straight towards us. *'Cheep, cheep.'*

We might have lost any chance of winning hearts and minds or making any human friends in here, but there was no reason why we couldn't turn all Doctor Doolittle and make friends with the animals. Our game of draughts was put on hold as we tried to entice the two freshly-hatched chicks to where we sat; they couldn't have been any more than a week or so old. The bigger, stronger one was black in colour, so we named it Ebony. The other one was yellow, so it got the name Ivory.

We hadn't a clue where these chicks had come from, but we were glad they were around to brighten our day. They spent their time scratching about in the dirt looking for food, and with good reason they seemed to prefer foraging near us to approaching the militants. We decided to adopt the chicks and help them in their search for something yummy to eat.

Near to where we sat was a collection of old logs which supplied great cover for all your belly-crawlers and super-bugs, and that was where we started. As I picked up the first log and moved it to one side, several bugs darted in different directions. The chicks were quick to react to the movement, and homed in on a juicy-looking millipede before he made it to new cover. Both Ebony and Ivory went for the same bug, snapping away as it changed direction to avoid the incoming beaks. Finally Ebony headed him off, and even though the millipede was nearly the size of my little finger, Ebony gobbled him whole, leaving Ivory to seek out new prey. Plooy lifted the second log and again the ground erupted into movement, dark shadows scurrying this way and that. Ivory trapped a weird-looking creature underfoot, but Ebony snatched in and stole the morsel literally from right under Ivory's beak.

'Come on Ivory, you've got to do better than that, little girl, or you're not going to survive long in the Delta,' I said.

'How do you know she's a little girl?'

'Because she's small and pretty.'

'Okay, fair enough, that must mean Ebony's a boy then.'

'Yes, I suppose it does.'

We lifted another log and again Ebony got in first, barging the smaller chick away and devouring the prize before Ivory got a chance. A different tack was needed if we were going to share the food out fairly, and I decided to test my theory about all animals being scared of sticks.

I selected a small straight twig with a V in one end, and got ready to fend off Ebony while Plooy lifted another log. As he raised the log Ebony, being a quick learner, strained his neck to pluck an insect that was sheltering underneath, but I showed him the V in the end of my stick to stop him in his tracks. Ivory seized her chance and moved in for the kill. Panicked by her earlier failure, she missed the first time and changed direction as the bug turned at a right-angle and headed towards Ebony, who was still rooted to the spot, unsure of how to deal with the stick blocking his path. If Ivory didn't home in fast and get her act together she would lose another meal. I couldn't hold

Ebony back much longer as he began ducking and diving, trying hard to outwit my stick.

'Hehe, lekka, lekka,' chuckled Plooy, 'she got it,' and Ivory lifted her beak triumphantly to the sky, holding a fine-looking millipede fast before she let it scurry down her throat into her belly. I moved the stick away from Ebony and let him re-join the chase. Sachin had just arrived to see what all the fuss was about, and Aditya had come out for a change and had joined Bob over on the mattress.

The chicks scattered into the jungle as militants came rushing out to defend their camp from the helicopter that was now passing overhead with the *whoop, whoop* of its rotors. We put our hands up to protect ourselves as our guards started manhandling us up and across the yard to some cover. These choppers had been flying over daily, and it was only since the Black Hawk Down DVD that it had been a problem for them, but it was now threatening to get out of control. They bundled us into our cell and covered us with their guns, while more guards outside covered the skies. *Bang*, a shot goes off, and then another, *Bang*.

'Oh, shit!' I mouthed to Plooy as I lay flat on the floor with a guard's knee in my back. Plooy, also pinned by a guard to the ground, shook his head ruefully at me, his head centimetres from mine, concerned at this new deadly game the militants had started to play. The chopper was gone in seconds, and when the guards had given the area the all-clear after a last- minute sweep of the perimeter, we were let back up again to go outside.

Sachin and Aditya had decided it was way too hazardous to come outside and had opted to stay inside the cell, but Bob was out and lying on his mattress. The chicks found us again by the rubbish dump after the camp had simmered down, and we quickly got back to fussing over them. We watered them with our own precious supply and fed them as equally as we could, holding Ebony back every now and again to let Ivory have her fill. When they tired of foraging they huddled in close to us for safety and slept, while Plooy and I continued our game of draughts. Little pleasures were rare for us in the Delta and when one came our way we had to make the most of it, trying to hold on to it for as long as possible. The chicks were a distraction and gave us a much-needed lift that day, just when we needed it most.

'This Black Hawk Down thing is not going to end well for us,' said Plooy.

'I know, these guys can't shoot for shit, but if they get an unlucky shot and down one of those choppers, this place will get levelled and us with it.' Plooy gave a sigh.

'What fucking next, hey?' he asked. 'I'm off to drop the lighties off at school,' he announced, which meant he was going for a poo. He caught the attention of Eagle Eye, who was sitting with his back against a tree, looking alert as always with his knees up and his gun resting across his lap. Eagle Eye climbed to his feet and slowly walked Plooy to the toilet, the river's edge where we all did our business. If you timed your poo just after high tide the area was pretty clear, but if your guts dictated you needed to empty your bowels after low tide, you had to navigate your way through everyone else's mess.

It was low tide, so Plooy picked his way through poo of all shapes, colours and smells, as the crabs all retreated down their holes. At the water's edge he found himself a perch on which he could keep his feet out of the water and squatted with his back to the river, facing the guard. Halfway through Plooy's toilet duties Eagle Eye muttered the first words we had ever heard him speak. I can't tell you what these words were, and neither can Plooy. It was a strangled sort of mumbling sound that came rambling off Eagle Eye's tongue in words we couldn't decipher; but it wasn't what Eagle Eye said or the fact they were his first words, but where they were directed, that got my

241

and Plooy's attention. Plooy followed Eagle Eye's words and looked back over his shoulder out to the river behind him, and, intrigued, I looked in the same direction. A long, thin canoe was just a few feet off behind Plooy, slowly paddling up the river, and Eagle Eye was chatting to the weathered-looking fisherman, his wife and three kids who were inside the canoe with him.

As soon as Plooy saw the family his head shot back round, and I could see him tense up with a look of embarrassment. The fisherman carried on chatting away to Eagle Eye as if it was the most normal thing in the world, holding a conversation while a big hairy white bottom was spraying neon-yellow waste on the surface of the river. I was rolling up with laughter; it was the first time in many days that I had felt I could laugh, and I'd almost forgotten what it was like, but now I'd started I couldn't stop. It might not sound very humorous, but at that moment I found it the funniest thing ever. By the time Plooy had washed his arse with his left hand with some river water, I was struggling for breath with an enjoyable pain in my ribs, and of course tears beginning to well in my eyes.

Plooy came sauntering back to the draughts board with a sheepish grin on his face, mumbling, 'How bloody undignified is that? You can't even have a shit in this place with a bit of privacy, that's the pits that is; we have got to get out of here.'

After I had recovered sufficiently and Plooy had sat back down, we continued to help the chicks look for food. Ivory's hunting skills were improving all the time and I didn't need to hold Ebony back quite as much. At one point both chicks had either end of a big fat millipede and used it in a macabre tug-of-war, both beaks eating away until they met in the middle. The chicks were great company and we had already grown quite fond of them. We were sitting playing draughts again, with the two chicks catnapping next to us after feasting out on grubs. Bob was also napping nearby on his favourite chair, fashioned out of a log, when *wallop*, something long and green fell out of the trees and landed smack bang in between where we were all sitting.

Bob opened his eyes and turned towards the noise, and it took him a couple of seconds to focus. 'Fuck!' we all shouted as we sprang up and legged it across the yard. The chicks and guards were running too. The Preacher had dropped his gun in his haste to be on his toes. And I'd never seen the old fella Bob move so fast; he was like Linford bloody Christie. There, in the space we had all vacated, was one startled-looking snake, rearing up and hissing at us angrily as we fled. We all stood about twenty metres away from the snake and watched it slither back into the jungle, stopping to look back now and again to make sure none of us had any silly ideas of following it.

We gave the snake a few minutes' head start before we got on with our game, and it was a few minutes more before Bob managed to rest his eyes again. The chicks settled down next to us and everyone relaxed, well, as much as you could in here. About fifteen minutes later, *wallop*, the same thing happened again. Everyone was back up and running to get clear of the snake as it hissed and spat venom. It was a lovely-looking creature from a distance, and would have made a great psychedelic wallet, but I was damned if I was going anywhere near it. One bite from that thing and it would be curtains. I wasn't clued up on poisonous creatures but the rule I follow is, if it's bright in colour, run; I couldn't exactly see the Secretary having a stock of anti-venom in the armoury. Plooy and I looked at each other.

'The chicks,' we said. 'They've got to go.'

Encouraging the chicks to hang around us must have been attracting snakes. So there was only one thing for it. It was a hard decision. The two chicks had supplied us with some good entertainment, company and sport, but we couldn't risk a snake-bite.

243

It is never easy getting rid of your loved ones, especially when they don't understand a word you're saying, so we had to encourage them with sticks and stones. It was a sad end to a very meaningful two-way friendship.

A big hairy tarantula finally chased us indoors. It was dark and time for bed, with the night's party just getting under way. We were sitting on a log chatting about our concerns as to where this jungle trip was heading and what might be happening to Noor, when the big stripy freak came creeping out of the shadows and across Plooy's hand. He never saw it but he felt it, and instinctively flicked his arm out in a panic; when we stood up to see what it was I nearly jumped straight into his arms. It was the size of a dinner plate, with about eight shiny eyes and a hairdo like Rod Stewart. That was it for the day as far as we were concerned. We were sick to the back teeth of this place. Ever since Noor had vanished things had gone from bad to worse, so we turned in for the night.

We lay under our net discussing plan Dick, and whether we should continue with it without Noor. Bob was lying on the other side of the cell, making the most of having the mattress all to himself, spread out on the stinking foam and snoring softly. We decided that we would sit it out and wait as long as we could, to try to find out what had happened to Noor. We just didn't feel we could do a bunk without him. But if we felt there was an imminent threat to our lives then we would go regardless. It was as good a plan as we could come up with.

It was about then that the generator went down. That in itself wasn't strange, as it always went down when it ran out of fuel. These guys wouldn't manage the fuel by topping it up now and again; they would literally fill it up and run it to empty and then fill it up again, but this time the generator stayed quiet. To begin with the sound of silence in the jungle was lovely – it was the first time in a very long while we had heard silence – but then the stillness yielded to the gossiping of nocturnal creatures: small squawks and cheeps at first, and then idle grunts backed up by high-pitched whining, screeching and loud cackles, all coming together as one bush-tucker orchestra. I much preferred the gentle hum of the generator. After our day of chickens, snakes and spiders these noises were filling my head with visions of all sorts of monstrous creatures. I moved in a little closer to Plooy, and prepared myself for some cheesy dreams.

CHAPTER TWENTY-EIGHT

LAND AHOY

At work Big Dick made an announcement. 'Due to all the crusties, hippies and fags,' as he called them, 'I'm gonna take all year off.'

It was the spring of 2004, and Dickey's favourite sport of hunting was under threat from the anti-blood sports brigade. I had been hunting with him a few times and I didn't really see what all the fuss was about, but it did look as if the antis were going to get their way and an all-out ban on fox hunting would be pushed through. So Dickey wanted to take the year off to make the most of the time they had left.

Matt Griffiths, my old deck-mate, was back on the scene. He'd been away touring New Zealand, trying to carve a new living for himself and his family out of fishing crayfish, but was now back in his home town of Dartmouth, totally skint and keen as mustard to earn some coin. Matt was born with a bait knife in his hand. He had naked chicks and shipwrecks tattooed on his forearms, a goatee beard, a gold hoop in his ear and a bandanna tied around his head; a fag dangled constantly from a smile that never left his face. He was a proper pirate and as hard as a coffin nail, a very dependable deck-hand.

When Dickey announced he was going to be missing in action, we both knew that he was going to expect Matt to step forward and take the helm; but Matt didn't. Matt didn't want the responsibility or the hassle that he knew would go with it; he was too laid-back, and struggled somewhat just saying the word 'responsibility'. So all eyes were shifted to me, not much of a second choice, but I still took it as a compliment and in stepping up to the helm I shrugged my shoulders and said, 'How hard could it be?'

In order to captain The Newbrook I needed a truck to get myself to and from the harbour and to cart around all the bait that was needed. I had my eye on one of those big old funky 4X4 monster trucks, all covered in chrome and other shiny bits, but had to settle instead for a clapped-out little white rust-bucket, a 1.3L Skoda pick-up. As my mother always used to say, 'It will do a turn'.

On day one of my training Dickey gave me a chart depicting the location of all the strings of crab pots, the shoreline and all the other points of interest that would help me navigate, drawn on the back of a Rice Krispies packet. He stood in the wheelhouse telling me what did what, and when to use it, all the different procedures for the day-to-day running and maintenance of The Newbrook, and all sorts of other pitfalls and dangers that were waiting to trip me up. It was enough to make my head hurt. Then the most important thing of all, the location and operation of the kettle.

After only two days of intense training Dickey came aboard and announced, 'I'm off hunting tomorrow, you and Matt will have to cope the best you can.'

'You're an arsehole Dickey, I could do with another day or so; go on, give us one more day, and I don't feel quite ready yet.'

Dickey snorted and then replied, 'Nah, sod it, you'll be all right. You've got Matt, he knows all there is, and besides, how hard can it be?' So with my own quote thrown right back at me, my training was complete. I was now the skipper of The Newbrook and to be fair I felt like the dog's knob. People get promoted for all sorts of reasons: some because they shine above all others, some because they're natural leaders and some, like me, because they're in the wrong place at the wrong time.

My first day at sea skippering The Newbrook with Matt went like a dream. We got the boat out on the river, which wasn't easy first thing in the morning with lots of cloud cover and no moon to light your way. The sky and the sea were as black as a black man's cape and the shore was just as black, all amalgamating into one sheet of blackness. Peppered all up and down the river were little yachts and other craft; you have what they call a steaming light, but that's not to light your path, it's so that other boats can see you. You had to rely on your instruments alone to guide you through. These were the GPS numbers, the radar, the sounder and Matt, who was standing high up on the bow keeping his eyes skinned. It was a little like walking through a forest blindfolded with a friend telling you which way to go; you have to trust him one hundred per cent. We made it to our fishing ground and hauled the gear with no dramas. I brewed the tea and we made it back home safely to land our catch, which meant we had made our money for the day. Nothing to it. If every day was like this one, I would make skipper of the year.

The next day didn't run quite as smoothly as the day before; everything started going a bit off-beam. Seamen all through the ages have been very superstitious creatures, and I woke that morning with a strange feeling in my tummy. The first part of the day went okay; it was a beautiful spring morning, with good seas, and our haul of crab was plentiful for that time of year. After the third string the autopilot went down, and then the radar. Not a big deal; it was a lovely clear day, I could see for miles and I could steer with the ship's wheel. It just made staying on the right GPS numbers a little trickier when we shot the pots away.

We were hauling the fourth string when we noticed a Customs boat taking an interest in us, which was also no big deal as we had nothing to hide. There were no illegal immigrants crammed below decks on top of bales of cocaine, but they boarded us anyway. They launched one of their small RIBs (ridged inflatable boat) with two officers on board and a pilot. As they pulled alongside they followed maritime etiquette and asked permission to come aboard. I pondered this for a couple of seconds before I granted them permission. I could hardly refuse them; these guys wielded more power than Lily Law, they don't even need a warrant to enter your house. In actual fact, depending on how you've kept up on your mortgage payments, they may have more right to be there than you have.

The two Customs men climbed The Newbrook's rails and landed heavily on the deck. I greeted them and welcomed them aboard. Matt was at the bait table cutting bait, and he turned to face them. With an eighteen-inch, slime-covered-bloodied blade in his hand he growled at the two of them, 'If you're looking for drugs you're too late, we've done them already.' He then gave them a crooked smile with a fag dangling from his bottom lip, opened his eyes as wide as he could just to put his point across, turned back to his fish and carried on chopping.

Nice one, Matt, these guys were born with less of a sense of humour than a bean counter. Matt thought it was the funniest thing in the world when they led me into the wheelhouse to pull my pants down. They gave me a grilling for a good twenty minutes before checking The Newbrook above and below her decks, while I replied 'Yes sir, no sir,' to everything they asked. Satisfied we were clean, they said their goodbyes and climbed back into their craft, giving Matt a wary look as they pulled away.

After another half-hour our whole world disappeared. Fog had closed around us fast, and it was as thick as green pea soup. By the time we completed and shot away the string we were working on, you could have stood a spoon up in it, and we could only just see the bow of the boat. It had turned cold too; the temperature must have dropped three or four degrees in about ten minutes. Fog wouldn't normally cause a boat much concern as long as all the on-board navigational equipment was working, but all our equipment had gone down. All we had left to find our way home was a compass and the sounder, but as I looked up at the sounder that started blinking and fizzing as well, so make that just the compass – and as that is not an electrical item I was pretty sure we could rely on it.

After double-checking all the instruments in the shed and chucking a few Fs at them, I went to meet Matt on the forward deck for a confab. We fell into each other's arms for a few minutes for a man-hug. Matt started sobbing, 'We're lost,' and 'It's not going to let us out'. I reassured us both that we would make it home and that no one was going to get left behind. We dried our eyes and set about finding our way home. Matt took his position high up on the bow to keep his eyes out for any vessels coming out of the gloom; I stood in the shed at the helm and set The Newbrook on a course for home. I knew the mouth of the river to home was north-ish, depending on the strength of the tide, and set us on that bearing, going at only five or six knots because I couldn't see my hand behind my back.

Matt might have looked like a bit of a brute, but he was a sensitive chap and a worrier to boot. He frequently came into the shed to voice his concerns, and each time I offered him words of comfort and sent him back out to continue his vigil with a cup of tea. After a couple of hours I began to wonder if we might be heading in completely the wrong direction, and started doubting myself. It was very eerie in the fog; everything was so still and quiet. There wasn't even the shrill from the seagulls as they had all gone home ages ago, and the only sound I could hear was the chug, chug, chug of the diesel engine.

Matt cried out, 'Seagulls, dead ahead.'

'So what?'

'They're walking!' shouted Matt, running back up the deck towards the shed. 'Hard astern!' he screamed.

It took me a couple of precious seconds to compute the significance of the 'They're walking' bit of Matt's sentence, before I slammed The Newbrook hard astern and whacked the revs right up as far as they would go. A cliff face loomed out of the fog, standing high and foreboding, its grey, jagged ledges jutting out at savage angles, with seagulls strutting about on them laughing down at us the way seagulls do.

We didn't know where we were, what depth of water we were in, or what sort of jagged rocks were waiting below the surface to tear a gaping great hole in the boat's hull. We should never have been this close to shore; that much I did know. Everywhere I looked I could just make out rocks pointing up out of the sea. I was shitting a brick now and I knew Matt had probably got his eyes closed. I had to get us the hell out of there as fast as I could, but could only guess as to which route out would not sink the boat and us with it. I didn't so much choose a path as let The Newbrook back out and find her own. It was a nerve-wracking few minutes, expecting to feel the hard rock demolish our wooden hull, until finally I felt we were a safe enough distance away.

Once I'd gained control of my jelly-like sea legs, I set a new course of north-northeast and tried to keep parallel to the shore on my left. Matt stayed up on the bow keeping a lookout while I stayed at the wheel, keeping us on our new course and praying it was the right one. I couldn't keep a visual on the shoreline; visibility was down to a few metres and I couldn't risk running aground. So I had to stay well clear and trust my compass.

Then, as fast as the fog had descended, it disappeared, and left us in beautiful sunshine again, about half a mile away from the mouth

251

of the Dart. I called up to Matt that he could stand down. 'Aye aye, skipper, let's be 'avin' that brew then!'

It was rewarding to be chugging back into harbour, drinking tea and with no damage to our vessel. I phoned Dickey to explain the problems we had with all the equipment, and that it might be an idea to phone for an electrician. Dickey was busy chasing his dogs, which were chasing Mr Fox, and couldn't speak for long but would sort it. Before breaking the connection he said once again, 'How hard can it be, hey Phil?'

I really enjoyed skippering The Newbrook; each day was totally different from the one before, and you never knew what the next would bring. There were a lot of challenges on the way, learning about the sea, the tides, weather, sea conditions, and having to improvise and plan in an instant for when (and not if) things got out of control. It's only you and the guys on board with you that can be relied upon, so you do form a very close bond with your deck-mates; comradeship they call it, and I like to think I worked with some of the best.

I continued taking The Newbrook to sea all through the summer, the winter and into the next spring, and enjoyed every minute of it. Life was good. I had a happy home life; I had purchased a house with my older brother John who had returned from New Zealand with his son George, and Sophie had now turned a very respectable nineteen and had also moved in. I loved my job and was earning enough to pay the bills and have a beer when I wanted one. This for me was a first, and I'll always be grateful to Big Dick for plucking me off the scrap heap and introducing me to a life at sea.

CHAPTER TWENTY-NINE

CHANGING OF THE GUARD

For once I was glad to wake to another day. Four times during the night I woke up from terrible nightmares, frantically brushing from my sweat-soaked body imaginary headless tramps stinking of corruption and riding bareback on tarantulas, and tearing at my itchy bites with my fingernails. I hadn't experienced such wild dreams since my days of going cold turkey; they were illogical and totally mad. There was no refuge, not even during sleep. I checked on Plooy, who was also just beginning to stir, and offered him a good morning.

'What's good about it?' he replied rather groggily.

'You all right, mate? You sound tired,' I asked.

'Yes, well, that might have something to do with you thrashing around all night, shouting about headless Frenchmen.'

'Sorry mate, how about I make you a nice cup of water and bring it to you in bed?' I offered with a sarcastic undertone.

'Ram it up your arse, I'm getting up,' Plooy shot back, and with that we crawled out from under our net, folded it, picked up our mattress and took it outside to air. Once the Secretary had brought the drums and morning mass to a close, the river was disturbed by the arrival of a boat. We hoped it was Noor as we were now into the third day of his second kidnapping. BA was driving, with another man sitting down and Denzel standing up in the bow with his assault rifle slung across his back. He threw a line to a guard who pulled the boat to the bank. The seated figure was the Juju man, and he climbed ashore with stiff joints, bringing a mystical air with him; this man put the weird into fucking weird. He walked with long strides slowly

253

up and across the yard into Hut Two, everyone watching him closely, a couple of guards shadowing him. He cast us just a fleeting glance without any emotion, no love, and no hate.

The Preacher came over to show us the AK47 that he had found part buried in the jungle. He said it had been there for many years before he unearthed it. I could quite believe it too; all the woodwork had rotted away and the metal frame and the moving parts were pitted and rusty.

'Works,' he said with a knowing smile.

'No, it can't do,' Plooy and I said together. I regretted the challenge immediately. The Preacher inserted a curved magazine, spun on his heels while sliding the bolt back and unleashed on full automatic. Plooy and I instantly ducked, turning from the threat and covering our ears, along with everyone else on the yard.

'So it does,' I said, straightening up. 'Can you put it away now?'

'What's the Juju man here for?' Plooy asked. The Preacher said a name we didn't understand, followed by 'has sickness.' After a bit of digging we found out that it was Frog Face who wasn't well.

'Oh dear, I hope it's nothing trivial,' I said mockingly. Plooy gave me one of his conspiratorial smiles. The sickness, we learned, was malaria, Africa's single biggest killer. I looked down at my body that was completely covered in angry little red bumps and shuddered, thinking, have I, haven't I? The Preacher left us and took his old AK over to show some of the goons. We stayed by the rubbish heap playing draughts, our guards nearby. The Juju man stayed in Hut Two.

All day long the brown river water was churned to a white foam by BA, Denzel and Prada coming and going in the boat, bringing new militants and taking away the ones we had become familiar with; it looked as though Camp Horrid was having a crew change. We sat, growing increasingly uneasy and a little more nervous with each new arrival; better the devil you know, we thought, even though some of the devil that went was in the shape of the three sisters. I was relieved to see the backs of them. The atmosphere in the camp was in limbo as we watched all the old faces climb into the boats and disappear down-river. The new faces were all shaking their heads at us as they crossed the yard, chests puffed out with bravado and full of hate.

'I don't like this, Plooy,' I said as I took three of his bottle tops.

'Me neither, I wonder what's going on?'

'Shall we get out of the way and go back to the cell for a bit?' I asked. 'What do you think?'

'Lekka idea, let's go and join Bob.' We collected our bottle tops together, picked ourselves up and retreated to the cell. We watched as yet another new crew of four was dispatched from the boat driven by BA. One of them came charging ashore doing spinning high kicks, low sweeps and shadow boxing. By the time we reached the cell my mood was sinking, along with Plooy who had just sunk down with his back to the wall just below the window.

'We'll call him Bruce Lee then, shall we?' said Plooy in a dejected voice.

'Here, come and look,' I said. Plooy slowly spun back around and pulled himself up to the window.

'Bloody hell,' whispered Plooy.

'What's going on?' Bob was on his hands and knees, heading over to the window, and by the time he got there Frog Face was already halfway across the yard.

'Goddam,' whistled Bob, 'the sonova bitch don't look too good, does he?'

'He looks very good from here,' said Plooy. I gave a chuckle. Frog Face was limp and being carried by four goons, a man on each limb, leaving his head to dangle at a deathly angle with no strength left in his neck to support it. He looked as if death was whispering in his ear. We watched the goons dump him as gently as they could into the boat; the Juju man, Prada, BA and Denzel all climbed in after him. BA flicked his cigarette butt away before gunning the engine and disappearing down-river.

'Do you think he was dead?' I asked with morbid enthusiasm.

'If he wasn't, he's not long for it,' Bob replied, heading back to his mattress; he was making the most of Noor's absence. Plooy and I left it a while for the yard to clear, talking about the likelihood of catching the sickness ourselves, before heading out to walk some laps, Plooy whistling 'we gotta get out of this place'. I was feeling itchier than ever, every bite now stimulated to let me know its presence. The Preacher walked up and fell in beside us, holding up a cup for us to inspect.

'This potion Juju man make for sickness,' he said proudly. I peered in and wrinkled my nose. Inside the cup was a muddy concoction of bark, twigs, leaves and essence of forest frog. I would have to be very sick to drink that jungle soup; it gave off a strong, pungent and disagreeable smell. For a brief moment I did consider asking for some, but the moment soon passed.

'It didn't do him much good, did it?' Plooy said. I smiled widely at Plooy and challenged the Preacher.

'Why don't you drink it?' I asked. 'It may stop you getting the sickness.' The Preacher looked at me and then looked at the potion, thought about it for a second and then necked it in one, using his teeth as a filter and wiping his lips with his forearm when he had finished. He shuddered as the potion found its way down.

'Nice,' he said, before heading off.

'Preacher!' I called. He liked his name and turned back to me, smiling. 'You have cigarette for me, I beg you.' He nodded and reached into his pocket, fishing out a packet of Marlboros and handing me two. 'Thanks,' I said with a nod of my head. I popped one in my mouth, got a light and squirreled the other to my pocket.

256

We continued lapping; with not much else to do, I smoked and Plooy whistled. Plooy had reached the end of his song and I had finished my cigarette when we felt that faint vibration from the sky.

'Ssshh, listen,' whispered Plooy.

'Helicopter,' we both said. Knowing the script well by now, we instinctively ducked and started for our cell. Two guards who hadn't been swapped came running across the yard to cover us. *Bang, bang,* two shots were let off and we flinched while doubling our speed, heads down till we made it inside.

'Bloody morons,' I said; 'they're going to get us all killed if they keep this up.'

'I can't believe they actually think these choppers are going to rescue us,' said Plooy. We stayed in our cell, hiding under our mosquito net, listening to the growing noise as the new guards took up positions in camp and settled themselves in with a monstrous party. It had all the hallmarks of that horrible first night, and I lay there, sleep evading me, expecting the worst.

CHAPTER THIRTY

TEA ANYONE?

The bright sunshine hit me as I staggered outside, forcing me to pull a face as though I'd just taken a spoonful of vinegar. I closed my eyes tightly before slowly letting them adjust, then opened them again, waiting for them to focus. We had endured a long, horrible night. No visitors had come into the cell but we had stayed awake most of the night expecting them. A few projectiles found their way through the window, but it was the noise and the open threats that really kept us from sleep.

'There's Noor over there!' said Plooy.

'So it is,' I replied.

We dropped our mattress by the tree and made our way over to a beaming Noor. I felt like giving him a hug but settled for a conservative handshake instead; everyone was relieved and overjoyed to be back together. Noor had been gone for three nights, and we had almost given up hope of seeing him again. We were very keen to hear his story and find out where he had been all this time, but first he had a little surprise. Noor pulled out a small bag and opened it so we could all take a look inside.

'Wow,' we said in a low, long, drawn-out theatrical tone. Inside the bag was a small tin of coffee, a few tea bags, a small pot of honey, and a tin of corned beef.

'Where did you get those?' we asked.

'Get a pan off the cook and we'll make some tea and coffee and I'll tell you all about it.'

Plooy got a saucepan and some mugs from the cook, and I put a fire together and got Bob up; Bob being a Yank wouldn't want to miss out on a cup of coffee. We boiled the water over the fire, made three cups of black coffee and one of tea, and put a dollop of honey in each. Noor opened the tin of corned beef and broke it into four pieces, offering one to each of us. We did wonder whether we should have saved the corned beef for our escape, but we couldn't; we were too hungry to risk losing it and all voted for an 'Eat it now' strategy. We asked Sachin and Aditya if they wanted any, but they said they couldn't eat meat on religious grounds. I suggested you could hardly class bully beef as meat, but again they declined. It was a genuine case of 'more for us then'! We made them each a cup of tea though, re-using my bag.

There are not many occasions when you can sit back and say, 'That was better than sex', but sitting against the tree with a mouthful of corned beef and washing it down with sweet honey tea was just orgasmic. I no longer cared what Noor had to say, I just didn't want it to end. After a couple of weeks on a diet of rice and water, the taste of corned beef and tea, even without milk, was out of this world. I washed the last of the corned beef down and turned to Noor.

'Come on then, mate, what have you been up to? We've been worried sick.'

Noor swallowed hard on his last mouthful of corned beef, washed it down with his favourite tipple of black coffee and began to tell his story. I got a light for the other cigarette the Preacher had given me and kicked back to listen to Noor's story.

Although he was very disorientated from being hooded all the way, Noor estimated the boat journey from the camp took around an hour. Not much was said during the boat ride as they were travelling pretty much flat out. When they arrived at their destination, Noor was dragged out of the boat and his hood was removed; it took a

259

while for his eyes to adjust. The General's bodyguards were leading him through an overgrown and very unkempt plot of land, littered with all kinds of rubbish. They led him up to a big house that was heavily guarded and self-contained within the plot, and hurried him inside. He was taken down a series of dark corridors and then locked in a small cramped room. The part of the house Noor had seen was very run down, and conditions were squalid.

Noor was locked in the room for almost a full day before they brought him any food and drink, which was the source of our morning's supplies of corned beef, honey, tea and coffee. Noor spent the time huddled in the corner, trying not to let his level of fear overwhelm him but to formulate a plan of escape. He came to the conclusion that this was the General's HQ, as he recognised a few of his bodyguards on the way in. The house also had that ambience to it which indicated that a maniac lived there. Not so long ago it would probably have belonged to a wealthy family and would have made a nice home, but since the General had taken up residence the whole place had slipped into decline. None of us could imagine the General buying such a property through legitimate means; he would probably just have told the family they had a day to get out. If they chose to ignore the General, then – this again was just our assumption – the family would have all been shot and dumped in the river.

Noor was kept locked up for a further day before he was brought before the General in the main room upstairs. The General was slouched in a filthy armchair, nursing a bottle of Monkey Tail and a big hubble-bubble pipe, and watching 50 Cent rap videos on a big plasma screen. His bodyguards and many of his foot-soldiers were lounging around on dirty, broken floorboards, drinking and smoking through glass pipes. Noor could only guess what was in the pipes, but I assume it was either crystal meth, which is very popular in Africa, or crack. The main room was very large, with high ceilings,

260

decaying cornices and big windows with the light blocked by heavy, soiled drapes. Down the far end of the room was a long heavy table covered with computer components, laptops, bits of desktops and all sorts of other junk. The General slowly looked at, or rather through, Noor with vacant, glazed eyes, and coughed up some smoke that he was holding in his lungs.

'We need internet, you fix for us.' He pointed one of his elegant fingers over to the pile of computer hardware and then his attention went back to his bottle of Monkey Tail and 'Fiddy', who was halfway through 'Take me to the Candy Store'.

Noor picked his way slowly over the mess that littered the floor and walked towards the table, a walk he didn't really want to complete as he had a nasty feeling that an impossible task lay ahead. Sharp as Noor was, he was no Bill Gates. When he reached the table he rested both of his sweaty palms on it, surveyed the mess in front of him and slowly muttered, 'Oh my God!'

There was nothing he could do with any of it. The pile of components was just like a big jangled heap of odd socks, a big pick-and-mix of circuit boards and wires. Even if Noor did know how to rebuild computers and set up an internet connection that worked, he was pretty sure he couldn't have done it with any of this equipment. I was just glad they hadn't chosen me to help with the updating and modernizing of their hideout; at that time I didn't even know how to turn a computer on. Noor was faced with an impossible task, and I'm not talking about the setting up of the internet, I'm talking about how he was going to explain himself to the General. Noor spent the next few hours pretending he knew what he was doing by picking up bits of circuit board and shacking them by his ear, then trying to mate them with other likely-looking components; but what he was really doing was thinking of a decent enough excuse to take back to the General.

261

50 Cent was blaring out another track while the General's foot-soldiers were coming and going, paying Noor little or no attention. They were more interested in getting out the pipe and getting off their heads than seeing what a hash Noor was making of the World Wide Web. It got to the point where Noor couldn't put it off any longer. He had to go and face the General and tell him that he couldn't make it work, that they didn't have the right sort of equipment. He half expected to have his head chopped off and his neck used as an ashtray for having the nerve to fail him, so was very shocked when the General just shrugged and ordered Noor back to his lonely new cell, without even taking his eyes off the TV screen. Noor spent the rest of the time locked in that room, which suited him nicely. Finally he heard a key turn in the lock; some guards rushed him and again pulled a hood over his head, bundled him into the boat and brought him back here.

Noor had just about managed to get to the end of his story when a helicopter flew overhead and the guards started firing at it. We were grabbed and hauled inside the hut, out of view of the chopper, in the same way as the Secret Service cover their President when he's threatened; I only just had time to grab my used tea bag. Not only is tea a superior beverage to coffee, in desperate times you can get more than one brew out of a bag.

'I can't believe Bristol hasn't changed the flight path of their choppers yet,' spat Plooy. I was about to agree when Noor jumped in.

'Will someone tell me what the fuck is going on?' Noor was confused and physically shaken, so we sat him down and explained all that had been happening in his absence.

We told him about Bob's run-in with Prada and being made to do frog jumps, Camp Horrid's 'Trooping of the Colour,' the crew change, the chicks and the snakes, Black Hawk Down and Frog

Face's" medevac; so much had happened. Sachin and Aditya came through to our cell and had some more news to add to ours. The Secretary had just told them their ransom had been released by their paymasters and they could expect to go home any day now. We congratulated them and shook them warmly by the hand; the only sliver of a silver lining to a very bleak cloud. The mood in the camp was becoming very unpredictable, chaotic and strained at best, and at times downright dangerous; but we felt a lot better now for just having Noor back with us and hearing the good news about the Indians' ransom. It was a huge boost to our morale.

Under the watchful eyes of our new guards we had one more cup of tea with honey at dinner time, which helped when it came to swallowing the stodgy rice. Although it didn't taste quite as good as that first cup, it was still most welcome. We also snatched a game of Frisbee during the guards' meal-time, just before the sun went down, and that helped to keep us alert and gave us a little exercise. We had a good twenty minutes with the Frisbee before the guards had finished their meal and started to wander back into the yard.

There were a lot of new faces in the camp, replacing some of the old guards whom we had grown to know and hate over the last two weeks. These new guards seemed a lot more unstable, and all appeared to want to make a name for themselves by being crazier and crueller than the last. A new idea had congealed in our minds: that the new guards were here to make it easier to execute us when the time came, as the others had come to know us and built up a rapport. However slight that relationship was, it might still have been enough to make it hard for them to pull the trigger; but these new guys didn't feel a thing for us and would gladly put a bullet in the back of our heads, especially if a promotion was dangled in front of them like a carrot.

The guards that watched over us were changed regularly now, every six hours or so, it seemed; so it was difficult for us to get a handle on their strengths and weaknesses before they were swapped again with another pair – which is how it should have been done from the beginning. The one Plooy had named Bruce Lee was looking over at us now; his eyes seemed to focus on each of us in turn, challenging us to some hand-to-hand combat. Bruce Lee had replaced Eagle Eye, who was now a fully-fledged lieutenant in the snatch squad, after a spot became available through Frog Face's sickness. The other guard working alongside Bruce Lee, who was yet to receive a name, was squatting on the balls of his toes with a face that suggested he wanted to rip our heads off.

Plooy and I were discussing the quality of our new guards over a game of draughts, while Bob was snoozing close by and Noor was chatting to a very sozzled Teacher. We knew it was good that Eagle Eye was no longer guarding us, but we missed Gastro Pod and hadn't quite got a feel for this new pair. I was about to clean up all Plooy's counters when the Teacher started screaming and going ballistic at Noor. The whole camp stopped to watch the scene unfold. The Teacher's once-friendly eyes were filled with a crazy hatred. He had lost control and was ranting and raving at Noor, who had taken to cowering in the dirt. Plooy and I left our game and calmly made our way over to Noor. We held our hands up so the Teacher could see them and quietly asked him what was wrong.

He was going bat-shit crazy and screamed in our faces, spraying us with spit that tasted of pure alcohol. He then spun on his toes and seized an AK47 from one of the new guards, who gave it up without a struggle, and immediately turned it on us, forcing us down on our knees next to Noor. The Teacher pointed the gun at each of our heads in turn, pushed the end of the barrel to our foreheads and dry-fired the weapon. My heart was racing like a hare being chased down by

264

a lurcher. As I knelt waiting for my turn, I realised just how tired I was. I was tired of being shit-scared all the time, tired of Camp Horrid and the squalid conditions. I was tired of the men who ran the camp and worked in it, and I was most definitely sick to the back teeth of people threatening to kill me. I just wanted to go home. I realised then that I would never get used to having a gun stuck in my face – each time I was filled with a fresh, unrivalled fear that gripped like a vice.

As he pushed the barrel of his gun to my forehead, I shut my eyes tight and found my home-made shank in my pocket, wrapping my fingers round the handle for comfort. I made a conscious decision that if he shot me in the head and I survived I was going to stab him right through the fucking foot that was planted in front of me. *Click*, the gun dry-fired. I couldn't make out what the Teacher wanted or why he had turned on us. He was rambling on about something and acting it out, tears streaming down his dirty cheeks, but he was far too emotional to make himself clear. When the barrel of his gun moved from my head I took a deep breath and opened my eyes. I looked to my right to see Noor and Plooy, both still with their heads bowed, and I lowered mine as well.

After the Teacher had spent all his anger he threw the weapon back to the new guard and stormed off into the bush, still zigzagging bow-legged and shoulder-barging militants as he went, and that was the last that we ever saw of him. We were left kneeling in the dirt, utterly shocked and speechless. The rest of the camp was buzzing from this and we sensed that they all now wanted a piece of us. We pulled ourselves together and took this as reason enough to scurry back to our cell – out of sight, out of mind.

'What the fuck just happened out there with the Teacher?' Plooy asked.

265

Noor's reply was quiet and sort of embarrassed. 'I told him I used to be a policeman.'

With that we all broke down laughing. 'Fuck me, Noor, you would have done better telling him you were a high-ranking priest in the Ku Klux Klan,' said Plooy. This had us in fits.

'Oi Noor, what do you call a black man with a gun?' I asked.

'Dunno.'

'Sir,' I said. We collapsed on to the mattresses that Bob had brought back in from airing and laughed the tension away. As bad as things got in here, if we could just keep venting it in this way then maybe we could keep some perspective, I thought.

Noor went on to explain what he and the Teacher had been talking about. Three years ago the Teacher was captured pirating the Delta waterways by the Nigerian Joint Task Force, and then handed over to the regular police. The police tortured him in ways not considered humane by the Geneva Convention or the western world in general. The Teacher in his fury had been trying to act out one torture method for us: the police placed a wooden stake horizontally under his knees, with the insides of his elbows under the stake and his wrists shackled above the knees. Bound in this fashion, he was then hung for long periods either on a meat-hook or a reinforced rotating fan, while being beaten with rubber batons.

Noor tried to convince the Teacher that not all policemen behaved in this way, and when he announced that he used to be one, well, the rest was history. I think the Teacher should have counted himself lucky; it was not that long ago that even in Western countries piracy on the high seas meant capital punishment, and the noose was your reward.

Being held hostage was proving to be very hard work, but with the new militants all looking as if they wanted to kill us, and with the only man who offered us some form of protection (and the odd bottle of beer) gone, I was now thinking that perhaps it really was time to put our plan into action and escape. Plooy wanted to give it one last chance and see if a deal could be struck; it was our safest and best chance of getting out alive, but I honestly just wanted to get away from these people now. I lay under the mosquito net next to Plooy, listening to the new guys settling in and getting ludicrously drunk. The stress was starting to show in us all, and it was a job to hold it together. You do manage to find extra resources from within, but it's not a bottomless pit and I seriously thought mine was beginning to run dry. Any moment now I was expecting the floodgates to open and to have a bit of a wobble.

CHAPTER THIRTY-ONE

A QUICK PINT

When you get to a certain stage in your life and everything is moving along quite nicely, you've got to be very careful not to fall into your comfort zone. When you feel comfortable in your work, get used to managing your allocated budget and are happy in your home life, it is very easy to sit back and let life pass you by without ever taking that extra risk and seeking out the adventure you have always craved.

I was now in such a position. I was feeling very comfortable in my life, so was quite prepared just to let it drift by. If I was honest I would have been quite content with that, and why not? I had all I needed: a nice house, a beautiful girl to share it with and a job I enjoyed with an honest income earned from it. I also had a little dog, Alfie the Jack Russell, and all the outdoor space I needed in which to walk him. So there was no way I was going to get myself off my backside and go forth in search of that adventure.

What I needed was a gentle push, a bit of persuading, and an opportunity even, to start me on a new path. On the way back from another gruelling but successful day at sea, I popped into the Torcross Tavern to meet a mate and have a chat over a couple of pints of Guinness. It was the tail-end of summer and there were lots of people milling about on the beach, taking advantage of the last of the year's warm evenings. The pub looked out over the ocean, so my mate and I took our beers outside and sat on the sea wall to chat and enjoy some people-watching, which was another of my favourite pastimes.

It was a nice place to sit when the weather was good, passing the time with a couple of beers, a mate and a chat, and after beer number two I was starting to get the taste for a session; but my mate had to be somewhere else ten minutes ago, so he was off. I was also about to leave when another mate turned up, so I decided to stay for one more. Looking back, that was bad decision number one.

Before I knew it the tide had come in and it was getting dark; the chill in the air had driven us inside, where DJ Night Hawk was setting up a disco for somebody's birthday. It was well past seven and both of our dinners were being digested by the dog at home, so we got comfy at the bar and settled down for the night. I don't care what anybody says; you can't beat a good disco. Like any party, it didn't get going until about nine and was now peopled with happy, drunk funsters, singing and dancing their way through as many eighties tracks as DJ Night Hawk could throw at them.

If you've ever been to a disco in a Devon pub, you will know that at least once during the night you will be surrounded by ten to a dozen psychotic farm hands, screaming at the top of their voices along to the track 'Who the Fuck is Alice', much to the delight of DJ Night Hawk. After the young farmers have bastardised the Alice song there is normally only one way for the party to go, and that's downhill. Drinks get spilled, punches are thrown and then the landlord calls last orders.

It was past home time, the landlord was ushering everyone out and DJ Night Hawk was packing up all his gear after another near-fatal evening on the wheels of steel. A couple of mates and I lingered at the bar for a nightcap whilst the landlord locked up. By the time we staggered out of the side door it was well past two in the morning. I watched my mate stumble home, bouncing off the sea wall, as I pondered my next move. I headed off to find my Skoda pick-up, thinking, 'Shall I or shan't I?' Even in the cold light of day when I'm

269

sober, I find making the right decision a bit of a handful. I'd been awake for twenty-four hours, missed my evening meal and been on the piss for nearly eight hours, so I hadn't got a hope in hell of making the right decision at that point. I had to be back on the boat and at work in an hour or so, and decided to drive. That was bad decision number two.

I located my Skoda about fifty yards away from where I remembered parking it, and climbed in. I started the engine and pulled out into the road; I had convinced myself that it was only a mile and a half to my house – what was the worst that could happen? The windscreen was all fogged up and I couldn't see a thing. I'd covered about thirty yards when I thought to myself that perhaps it would be a good idea to pull over and clear the screen. I travelled another ten yards and *bang*, the Skoda lifted up and slammed back down on the road, refusing to go any further.

I had to get out of the truck to see what had happened, as I couldn't see anything from the inside. I opened the door and fell out into the road, trying to sober up and get a handle on the problem. I had just crashed my Skoda into the local butcher's shop on the corner, a couple of doors down from the pub. My truck was lying at a funny angle in the road, a big enough drama at this time of the morning, but I was sure I could sort it. I just had to get my vehicle out of the way and off the road fast. Although these roads were deathly quiet you could guarantee someone would come along when you didn't want them to.

I checked that the coast was clear and that I hadn't woken anybody up, and climbed back in my Skoda, but it wouldn't budge. It wouldn't go forwards or backwards. In my drink-addled state I came to the conclusion that I must have run out of fuel, even though I was revving the pistons off it, but the fuel light was glowing red and that was now the sole focus of my attention. All I had to do was siphon some fuel out of my mate's quad and Bob's your barnacle, I'd be back on my way. If I'd looked at the passenger front wheel I'd have seen that no amount of fuel would get this Skoda running again; it was lying at a ninety-degree angle from the rest of the truck.

Off I went, though, to find some fuel, just as another car came around the corner. It slowed to go around the dead Skoda and stopped to see if I needed any assistance. They were an old couple and I told them in my best sober English that I was 'Shfine' and that I'd run out of petrol; that was a close one. It took me about thirty minutes to find a container, fumble some fuel out of what I hoped was my mate's quad and return to the scene of the crime, just in time to meet two patrol cars full of Lily Law. I turned sharply on my heels, dumped the fuel over the butcher's shop wall and headed in the other direction, only to be met by another patrol car.

I was well and truly bang to rights. The law surrounded me with a sense of amusement at my predicament, and wasted no time in trying to piece this little mess together. 'Have you had anything to drink tonight, sir?' he asked.

I replied with my head bowed, looking down at my feet, 'Yes, Officer, shlots.'

An officer then handed me a small black box with a white tube attached. 'Can you blow into this then for us, please, sir?' I held the breathalyser in my hand, took a deep breath and held it for a second or two, knowing that as soon as I breathed into that box my life was going to change for the worse.

I blew hard for what seemed like an age until all the right lights glowed on the machine. 'Thank you, sir.' The Officer took the black box and held it up to read the results. When the results came through he looked skyward and let out a whistle; that was not a good sign. 'Yes, you have had a drink tonight, sir, haven't you? You'd better come with us.' I was manhandled into the back of one of their cars;

271

my mouth felt dry and my head was already starting to hurt with a premature hangover. It took an hour to drive to the main police station, which was Torquay nick; all the local ones were closed at that time of night due to cut-backs and the general lack of crime.

After we arrived the first thing they made me do was a second breath test, for which I was rewarded with a round of applause: another high reading. After that I gave them my personal details for the computer to check. Through all this I was on my best behaviour, very humble, with just the right amount of remorse. It wasn't an act; I was genuinely sorry, I had fucked up badly. I was then supposed to have my prints and DNA taken for records to be kept on file, but before that they wanted to search me for any sharps or contraband, which I submitted to. At this point we were still getting along famously with a bit of banter being thrown back and forth; they were starting to feel like my new friends.

I've got no hang-ups with the law and I've been on the wrong side of it a number of times, having my collar felt for numerous misdemeanours. In my eyes if you do wrong and get caught, well, it's your own fault and you have to put your hands up and take the consequences. 'Do the crime, do the time', blah, blah, blah and all that bollocks; but now they wanted to strip-search me and I told them in no uncertain terms to 'get fucked', and then went on to say, 'This is just a drink-drive charge, it's got nothing to do with drugs'.

The Officer in charge then tried to inform me that it was normal procedure to strip-search all young males who came through their doors. Stupidly I told them again to get fucked and then raised the bar by telling them, 'Well, it's going to take more than you three'.

'That's no problem, sir,' came the Officer's reply, and with that he pressed the big red button and a few more of Devon and Cornwall's finest came crashing into the ring, well up for a row – and that was just what they were going to get. That was my third and final bad decision. It ranked right up there with the best of all my other crap decisions.

I am neither built for fighting nor consider myself tough, so what happened next was completely out of character.

As the Officer led his crew in towards me, I put one on him. I head-butted him. A cracking little blow caught him just above the bridge of his nose, and as he went down I jabbed with my left, caught him a second blow in the solar plexus and then turned to face the next man, just before the rest of his crew overpowered me and kicked the living crap out of me, and rightly so. Striking an officer of the law is inexcusable; putting the head on one is just taking the mick. I was on the floor now, being sat on, knelt on, kicked and punched; the situation ran away from me completely and was way out of control. My clothes were being ripped off my body with no thought given to my dignity, I had about seventy stone of the law on top of me, and I thought one of them had just pushed a gloved finger up my bum; well, that's what it felt like anyway. They dragged me naked down the corridor by my ankles and through a cell door, threw a paper suit at me and slammed the door shut.

When I woke up a few hours later I felt as if I had been beaten around the head by a twelve-inch rubber cock. I also had that sinking feeling. I was quite used to this feeling, even though it hadn't visited me for a few years. There was light streaming in through the thick glass, made up of lots of small squares that passed as a window. You couldn't see out but it let light in. This particular cell had had a man called Bez and a cop-hater as previous tenants, as I could see 'Bez was here' written underneath the window and below that, 'All coppers are bastards', which was a must in any busy cell. Another guest wasn't very fond of a lass called Vicky, as 'Vicky is a slag' was scrawled in big letters on the door. I was left wondering how these people managed to smuggle a pen in here. The other furniture was a stainless steel toilet in the corner and a bunk, which I was lying on.

The walls were bare and cold, with clumps of plaster missing. My mouth was as dry as the floor in my cell and my head hurt like hell; my body was stiff and covered in bruises.

I forced myself to think, and as I raised my arm to scratch my head I noticed for the first time that I was wearing a paper suit – not good. I tried to play back the events that had brought me here. At the moment all I could recall was crashing the Skoda and getting a capture from the law. I got up off my bunk and paced the cell, before banging my fist on the door to try to get someone's attention. The custody sergeant came to my door after about ten minutes.

'What do you want?' His tone was only just tolerant.

'When are you gonna let me go?' I replied softly.

'You won't be going anywhere for a little while yet.'

'Why not, I only got done for drink-driving, the butcher can't be that pissed off with me?' I asked him, with a little desperation to my voice now.

Then came the bombshell of an answer. 'You can add assault of a police officer to last night's charges as well.' With that he walked away.

I leant with my back against the cell wall and sank to the floor. 'Fuck, fuck, fuck'. Everything came back to me then: the drinking, the crash and the slap and tickle with the law. My head really started to hurt now. All my hard work of the last few years was gone in a flash through one stupid mistake – but that is all it takes. I was no longer going to be known as the hard-working skipper of a crab vessel, but the hard-drinking idiot who crashed his Skoda pick-up into the butcher's shop and then assaulted a Police Officer.

They let me out a day later after handing me back my sea wellies and my smelly old fishing threads. Bollocks, I hadn't even made it home to change. I looked a right mess walking out of there and smelt like a mermaid's vagina. I went straight to a phone box to ring my brother; I needed a lift. I'd be in need of a lift for the foreseeable future.

CHAPTER THIRTY TWO

DOT TO DOT

A wave of fear had flooded the cell. We were awake but still lying on our mattresses, apart from Plooy, who was peeking out of the window. 'It's the General,' he said in a hushed voice, 'and he seems really pissed.'

I crept out of the netting and squeezed up next to Plooy to look out of the hole that was our window, closely followed by Noor; together we all snuck a peek outside, Bob remaining quite still on the mattress. Sachin and Aditya were kneeling down, facing away from us with their hands clasped behind their backs and their heads bowed, in a classic execution pose. The General was going nuclear, stamping up and down and shouting into his phone, his bodyguards keeping at a strategic distance. Outraged and clearly upset about something, he stopped behind Aditya and let a shot off by his head, close enough to make his hair move. We all turned and sank to the floor with our backs hard against the wall and our knees to our chests, breathing heavily.

'Holy shit, what the fuck is going on? I thought the Indians were sorted, their company had paid the money, right?' I said.

'I don't know, but it doesn't look very sorted to me,' Noor whispered.

'I can't handle this place anymore,' said Plooy, shaking his head. 'Fuck the ransom and fuck the General, we've got to get out of here.' Plooy had been a rock for both Noor and me throughout, and now I could see a chink in his armour. If Plooy lost it I feared we would all follow.

We waited inside our cell listening to the General outside, all of us far too scared to venture out. Whatever was happening on the yard, it was quite clear that Sachin and Aditya weren't out of this yet. I was very relieved when I heard the General's fast boat roar into life and pull away from the bank. Sachin and Aditya were led inside the hut and pushed by the guards with the stocks of their rifles into their cell. The old guards had treated both of them well enough, but these new ones were cruel and wholly disrespectful towards them.

Once the guards had gone we left it a few moments before we crept across the tight corridor to their cell. We wanted to find out what had gone so wrong. Sachin and Aditya were slumped on their mattresses and looked completely wrecked, all the hope drained out of them. It was an emotion they just couldn't hide and it was horrible to see. We gently asked them what had happened. A shell-shocked Sachin briefed us on what had just occurred.

The Indians' paymasters had released the agreed amount in used notes to the middle-man, the 'doctor' who had brought us crackers and ice cream. He had then vanished with all the cash to somewhere not on the General's radar, leaving Sachin and Aditya up the creek without a paddle or, indeed, a canoe. Some doctor – I wonder what oath he swore? The General was now demanding more money from their company or he would kill them. The company, which had already paid once for the safe return of Sachin and Aditya, had quite rightly told the General they had no more cash and that he should choose his doctors more carefully, perhaps even go private. Sachin and Aditya were stuck between a jagged boulder and a rock-solid place, and back to square one.

We boiled up some water and shared out the last of the coffee and my last, rather used and limp-looking tea bag, in an effort to calm down our Indian friends, who were understandably beside themselves. The disappointment felt by Sachin and Aditya and the damage done to their morale was impossible to quantify. If any of us three had had any doubts before as to whether we should escape, we now firmly believed that if we didn't take control and go over the wire we should never get out, and would more than likely end by pushing up mango trees right here in the swamp. I finished the very last of the tea and concluded that the more on edge and stressed we were, the better the tea tasted.

The new guards were all very cruel and rather unpredictable; they all roosted around where we usually sat, on the edge of the yard by the rubbish dump. They were competing with each other in trying to force a reaction out of us, squawking and flapping like an unkindness of ravens, pecking away at the last of our resolve. We just sat in a huddle, letting the abuse bounce off us. Sachin and Aditya were both close to their saturation limit now; Aditya especially was looking very ill and drawn, near to giving up. This place was fast becoming grossly unhealthy for all concerned.

Plooy, Noor and I needed to talk, so we pulled ourselves from the safety of our herd and started to lap the yard. Bob, Sachin and Aditya stayed put, sitting together in a small circle.

'I can't take this any more,' Plooy said quickly. Noor and I said nothing, just kept walking and thinking. Plooy spoke again. 'This lot couldn't organise a piss-up in a brewery; just look at the state Sachin and Aditya are in. I say we go tonight, before things in here get any worse for us.' Again Noor and I kept quiet, walking and thinking.

'Come on, are you two in or what?' A bit more walking and a bit more thinking.

'I'm in,' I said at last.

'OK,' said Noor.

The gentle throb signalled the arrival of another boat. A long canoe carrying one man and seven goats was chugging along at barely walking speed, powered by the tiniest outboard engine I had ever seen. The boat and the weary-looking owner were met by some of the guards, who hurried down to the river's edge to meet him. The weary-looking man tossed a line to the waiting guards who then pulled the canoe to the river bank, and its cargo of goats, strung together by rope around their necks, was led into the camp. The seven goats walked slowly in single file across the yard to a small piece of ground; hungry after their journey, they were quick to seek out some rough grazing. What we should have done now was to look a little more closely at the seven goats and what they represented. Goats are often used as sweeteners or even payment in West Africa for business deals, weddings or ransoms, and the Indians' ransom had already gone down the tubes so that really only left ours or Bob's. Perhaps something was lost in translation, they asked for boats and got goats, but our minds were too stressed, and tired, to join the necessary dots. A chopper flew overhead followed by gunfire splitting the air; the goats made a run for it, still tethered together. So did the old man, who with a blip of his throttle made like a snail to put as much distance as he could between the doomed goats and his canoe. We dived to the ground, hands over our heads, trying to block out the noise and festive chaos. Some of the guards who weren't firing at the chopper grabbed us by the arms, picked us up and rushed us inside, forcing us into our cells. The chaos the chopper caused didn't last long as it soon passed overhead, but the pumped-up guards took a lot longer to settle down; they just hated these choppers.

A fresh supply of drink and drugs had also been brought in with the goats, so the party started early. We stayed inside for the rest of the afternoon chatting quietly to each other about nothing in particular, trying to stay relaxed and positive and also to conserve our energies for tonight. I was hoping to get a last game of Frisbee or draughts in before bed, but the new guards were getting dangerously out of control; they made the old ones look like well-

278

meaning boy scouts, and we were missing them a lot. We didn't even want to give names to the new ones. Commander Jackson and the Lieutenants seemed to have lost interest in the discipline of the camp and what the guards and the goons were up to, resulting in a state of near-emergency.

The rest of the day was spent in our cells, killing time. The cook served us dinner as the last of the day's light disappeared below the jungle trees, our last supper of overcooked, stodgy rice. The three of us forced down two-thirds each of our meal, and then covertly stuffed the remainder of the rice into our empty plastic bottle to give us a little snack for when we were hiding out in the jungle. I hid the bottle up in the roof rafters of the cell.

As the evening drew on we went over our plan once again, so that we all knew what to do. At zero-two-thirty hours by Plooy's watch I would be first to leave. I was to say goodbye to my questionable mattress and make my way to the designated exit point, carrying the food and water. If I managed to get there safely without being compromised I was to wade out quietly, away from the bank, to deeper water, and wait with just my head above the surface for Plooy, who would follow five minutes later. I might even treat myself to a mudpack, to lose the shine to my face and help me get into character.

If he could, Plooy would pick up Commander Jackson's boots and then make his way out to join me in the river, where we would wait a further five minutes for Noor, who would bring along with him the machete blade, bits of rope and Bob's watch for navigation purposes. At no later than zero-two-fifty, and if all went according to plan, we would continue up-river and to freedom. If luck was on our side, a few days later it would be a hot bath, a cheeseburger and a pint.

With the breakdown of law and order the camp had become an even more frightening place to be. The atmosphere was one of hate and mutual loathing; the new guards just soaked this up and mixed it with a strong cocktail of drink and drugs, making them a very unpleasant bunch to be around. We hadn't even got the luxury of the Teacher's visits anymore; at least when he sat with us the mob would either join us for a civilised chat or stay away completely. Our level of fear was now at a constant high, and if you added to this my excitement and anxiety over the pending escape, then I was also not very pleasant to be around. I was like a five-year-old with ants in his pants.

'Sit still, Phil, for fuck's sake, you're making me feel uneasy,' said Plooy.

'What's the time?' I asked.

'It's just coming up to quarter to eight, five minutes since the last time you asked.'

'Let's walk then. We'll walk round the yard and keep an eye out for Commander Jackson's boots, and Noor can choose his moment to get the stuff out and hide it by the tree, ready for tonight.'

Bob had gone to bed, and Noor stayed by the rubbish dump to wait for any opportunity to squirrel some of our escape kit down to the tree that marked our exit point. Plooy and I walked a couple of laps of the yard before peeling off to chat to the guards, who were sitting under the shelter and already drinking heavily. It was the last thing either of us wanted to do, but we had to give Noor a chance to get our stuff over to the tree. Commander Jackson, BA and Denzel were there with a new guard, acting out the typical role of the rebel soldier. The new arrival looked battle-hardened but relaxed in these surroundings; he was leaning back on a moulded plastic chair with his AK leaning up against the table. The mood was flirting with hostility, but we had to engage and distract the enemy so Noor could do his thing. Plooy asked the new soldier what he was drinking, while I talked Commander Jackson out of a cigarette, lit it and enjoyed the reassuring smoke filling my lungs.

Plooy pressed the conversation with the guard. While I listened and smoked my cigarette, we learned that tonight's favoured tipple was Monkey Tail with a gunpowder mixer. You won't find this cocktail on any list next to Sex on the Beach or the Harvey Wallbanger, oh no. This was reserved strictly for those into warmongering and criminal insanity. But if you fancy knocking one up at home, simply pour a generous measure of kai-kai or Monkey Tail into a shaker, pull a round from an AK47 apart and drop in the powder and bullet tip, then shake – not stir – for about one minute. Make sure you discard the empty casing responsibly and then kick back and enjoy your refreshing libation with a few of your closest psychopaths. Pimm's it certainly was not – this stuff put the 'core' in to hardcore. The new soldier offered us some and, not wanting to offend, I gladly accepted.

'Plooy, what do you think?'

'Why not, what doesn't kill you only makes you stronger, right?'

The soldier poured two equal measures into dirty chipped mugs. Plooy and I looked at each other with a shrug as if to say, 'what the hell', clinked mugs, said cheers and then necked it in one. It wasn't a drink to savour and tasted exactly as you would expect. But according to juju law I was now bullet-proof, which would perhaps come in handy over the next twenty-four hours or so.

Plooy had taken advantage of the pissed-up state of Commander Jackson and managed to talk him out of two more cigarettes. I smoked one straight away; the other one I would save for before bed. Then Noor greeted us with a nod of the head that told us all had gone well, and that everything was in position for later; he had even had time to lace up those old boots with a couple of lengths of baler twine. For the rest of the evening we tried to stay out of everyone's way. We had no luck with the theft of Commander Jackson's boots, so Plooy had to prepare himself for the prospect of going on the run in his flip-flops. We also decided to let Bob hang on to his watch; we felt bad enough that we would have to leave him behind alone, and to a very uncertain fate. If we were also to mug him of his watch it would be the equivalent of a jolly good kick in the balls. Besides, none of us was exactly sure if the watch and sun navigation thing actually worked.

The sun had gone down on what I hoped would be my last day of captivity, day number seventeen. Not a long stretch by any means, but long enough for me. Some people who are taken hostage end up being held for months and months on end, and in some cases years. The very thought of spending years in that camp made me want to stop breathing altogether. I just didn't think I was cut out for this sort of caper. All around us the night's partying was beginning, the now highly sought-after gunpowder cocktails were being drunk in earnest, and big fat joints of smelly weed were being smoked by the dozen. Everyone apart from us was getting high. We walked the yard in a tight group, as sitting still was not an option; the mosquitoes were out in force and we were too much on edge. As we passed the goats nervously grazing sparse patches of greenery, I finished my last cigarette and decided to call it a night. Commander Jackson's boots were still laced up tight to his feet, so we gave up on them for good. Between us we had one good pair, mine, the old shitty pair that Noor had found, and the flip-flops. We decided that we could manage by rotating our footwear. Every half-hour of walking we would swap shoes to give the flip-flop wearer a rest. It was the best we could do.

A couple of un-aimed shots were fired up into the jungle canopy by a drunken guard, so we decided now was the best time to join Bob in our cell. Sachin and Aditya were already tucked up in bed. I would have liked to say goodbye to them and wish them luck, but to do that would only serve to hinder Operation Dick, and I thought poor old Dick already had enough going against him.

CHAPTER THIRTY-THREE

STARTING AGAIN...AGAIN

I had worked very hard for the last few years to turn my life around, and in one night I had turned it back to crap again, managing to lose my driver's licence for two years and saddle myself with some hefty court costs and compensation for the Constable I assaulted. At least I'd stayed out of prison, after much grovelling on my part and an understanding officer who played the whole thing down – I think he was a little embarrassed about being dropped in front of his mates. I'd written off my truck and fallen out with my boss, Big Dick, as I could no longer pick up the bait and get myself to The Newbrook. After one more massive argument I subsequently walked out on the best job I'd ever had (after leaving something unsavoury in his Incredible Hulk mug).

I felt I'd let everybody down: Sophie, my parents, even Alfie the little Jack Russell who seemed to have the hump with me. Alfie couldn't take the shame that I had brought once again to my family's doorstep, and two days later he ran away to join the French Foreign Legion. The poor little fucker only made it to the end of the road before he was put out of action by a careless driver, a drunken one no doubt.

I was devastated: my best mate and the dog I had named after him both killed in road traffic accidents. My old man took it the hardest, reduced from a big strong ex-fireman to a crumpled old wreck who just sat on the sofa for days on end, with that thousand-yard stare. Not because his son was in trouble again – he said I was big enough and ugly enough to look after myself – but he had grown so attached to little Alfie and missed him terribly. Mother couldn't even talk him into going down the pub at lunch-time to play cards with his mates.

Yet again I found myself in the position of having to sort my life out, and to make it up to the people I cared about. First I went out to get a new Jack Russell pup. It was a tight-knit community where I lived, so I managed to track down one of Alfie's sisters who'd had pups just that week, and took the last one that was left. He was definitely his uncle's nephew and looked just like Russell Crowe out of Gladiator, so we called him Maximus Decimus Meridius; Max for short but Maximus when he was naughty.

I rushed him straight round to the old man's as soon as I took delivery and said that Max could stay as often as Dad wanted. But that wasn't enough; the silly old sod wanted his own dog now. So I went to Big Dick and we put our differences aside for a bit; he had loads of Jack Russells and I was sure I could talk him out of one of them. After more grovelling and listening to what a prat I was, I managed to leave the house clutching a bewildered-looking bitch called Scrappy, and my last pay cheque. My old man was now happy, and so was Mum as he was leaving the house again and he even had a spring in his step.

Now all I had to do was find myself a well-paid job with good career prospects and good annual bonuses: no easy feat in our village, especially as I only had crab-fishing skills to offer. The last time I needed inspiration to find a good job I went down the pub, but as that was how I got into this mess, I was thinking perhaps I shouldn't push my luck. My brother came to my aid this time and found me a job with a small local building firm, so I tried my hand at labouring. The work was outdoors and physical, which I liked, and the other guys in the firm were fun to be with, but there was something missing, so I moved on to window-fitting.

Window-fitting was half-outdoor and half-indoor work. Sometimes half your body would be outside and half your body inside whilst working on a window, so you could say I had the best of both worlds; but I was soon bored. Next I tried carpet-fitting, which was all inside work, and I was definitely an outside type of guy. Yet again I enjoyed or tolerated the work but still found something to be missing. After a taste of working at sea, I found work on land just a bit dull. I was saltier than a big bag of salt now and I craved the ocean; not working at sea left me feeling quite empty.

One of our fitting jobs, however, found me at the house where I would seize my next opportunity. The job was laying a kitchen floor in a pleasant house in a nice village not too far from where I lived. The family that lived there were very friendly too, and I got along with them well. The lady of the house, Mrs B, would make me a pot of tea and Marmite on toast when I arrived in the morning, which I would eat at the breakfast table with the family whilst my boss got on with the work. On the mornings that I came in with a hangover, Mrs B would slip me a couple of aspirin to take the edge off.

The man of the house was a strong bloke with a happy-go-lucky character, and I liked him immediately. Some people I've met take no effort at all to get along with, and this man and his family were such people. I got talking to Mr B and asked him what he did for a living; I was curious, as he seemed to have a very capable and confident manner about him. I expected him to tell me that he was a jet pilot or a gun-runner, as he had that knowing smile on his face that I associated with a bit of skulduggery. His answer, however, blew me away: 'I'm a diver,' he said.

'What sort of diver?' I asked, my level of interest now at maximum.

'A mixed gas diver, saturation,' he replied, as if everyone knew what that was. I'd caught the diving bit, but he could have been talking in Hebrew about the other stuff.

I knew nothing about diving and had to find out more. I relentlessly interrogated Mr B, shushing my boss every time he asked if I was going to do any work today. Mr B answered all my questions and finished up by saying, 'It's just big nuts and bolts, boy.'

'I'm gonna do it,' I said, with total conviction.

'You what, boy?' he asked.

'I'm gonna do it,' I said again, left him and went back to join my boss Dobin and help him tidy up. My spirits were lifted and I had a plan already starting to take shape. I had a new direction to head in; I had a spring in my step now that made my old man look like a raspberry ripple.

I arrived home that evening a different person, very excited, jabbering about my new plans and annoying the shit out of everyone. Sophie had been with me long enough now and knew how to humour me, and was gently saying stuff like 'That's nice baby, sounds like fun', and 'So you're going to be a driver this time, eh, be careful, those roads are busy'. Her eyes never left the crossword she was close to finishing in her Take a Break magazine.

I got fed up with no-one taking me seriously, so I went to play a game of cards with George. My ban on playing with George unsupervised had been lifted just the month before, but only non-lethal games were allowed, like cards or Monopoly. Memories of the poor lad being blown up and shot were still raw in the grown-ups' minds. We jazzed these games up a notch or two though, by introducing forfeits for the loser that we kept a secret from the adults. These forfeits included a boiling hot spoon on the back of the hand, eating a spoonful of mustard, snorting lines of pepper or eating one of John's discarded fried egg whites out of the bin (he only liked the yolk). George loved the new jazzed-up versions of these games, especially when I was the loser.

The next day I set about finding out where to do a diving course, and was shocked to my very foundations when I found out how much they cost. The full course would take thirteen weeks to complete and would cost me just shy of ten grand. There was no way in hell I could afford that much: I was in debt now as it was, what with court fines, a mortgage to pay and my minimum wage as an apprentice carpet-fitter. Considering all that, I calculated it would take me about thirty-six years to save the money if I stopped going to the pub; I just didn't have that much determination or time. No, there had to be another way.

I carried on my investigation and tracked down a place in South Africa which did the full course for a third of the price. I'd always wanted to go to Africa anyway since reading novels by Wilbur Smith; I could even have some adventures while I studied. This was the place for me for sure, but I still didn't even have a third of the money. I thought about doing a stick-up in the village store, but the old lady behind the counter looked like she could handle herself, so I went to the bank in town to borrow some. I dressed up smartly and tried not to look too desperate, but the key to my success was the fact that I lied through my teeth. I told them that the house needed a new kitchen and that I was in permanent employment. Suckers! I hadn't lost the ability to lie like a cheap Spanish watch.

I came out of the bank with just enough to cover my mortgage for three months, the course fees, a plane ticket there and back, money for accommodation, a bit of spending money and a quick pint to celebrate in The Creeks End with Terry the landlord, who also liked to celebrate. I was on my way. The date for my departure and new adventure was the end of March 2006, and it came around fast. I had put all my eggs in the one basket, borrowing money up to and

287

well over my limit; it was a risk, but one worth taking. If my plan went belly-up and failed then I would be well and truly buried. I'd lose the house, lose Sophie, Max and my self-respect. But if I stayed and continued working in jobs that I didn't find fulfilling, the outcome would be the same, only it would take longer and be more painful.

When the day finally arrived for me to leave I said all my goodbyes: to my mum and Scrappy, John and George and then lastly to Sophie and Max. My old man was driving to Kent to deliver some wood carvings, so he was going to make a quick detour and drop me off at Heathrow. I loaded up the car with my bags and we set off. It was a bit of a drive from Devon, but we made it in good time, and as we pulled up outside Terminal Three I made myself ready for an emotional farewell. After I had pulled my bags from the boot, I turned to my old man and offered my hand. 'See you in three months then, Dad.'

The old man took my hand and said, 'Good luck with the driving course, son.'

'Diving, fucking diving. I'm going on a diving course, why the fuck would I be going to South Africa for a driving course? I haven't even got a licence.'

'Okay son, just you be careful,' he said as he turned back to the car.

I couldn't help but mutter, 'For fuck's sake,' as I watched him pull out into the traffic; then I turned and took myself inside the terminal to start my journey to Africa, the continent that is the mother of all fuck-ups.

CHAPTER THIRTY-FOUR

UNDER THE WIRE

Plooy nudged me from under our mosquito net with a ten-minute warning. It was zero-two-twenty by his watch. We could still hear voices and music, though. Not as many or as loud as earlier, but enough to get the nerves standing to attention. For the last four or five hours I had been listening, monitoring the activity from inside the net with Plooy, who also found sleep impossible. The alarm had just activated on his digital watch; we'd set it just in case we overslept on this most important of mornings. We didn't want to be late for our own escape.

I lay still next to Plooy, breathing slowly and deeply, trying hard to keep my heart rate from going through the roof, while the last few minutes ticked by. My night vision was good, and I could just make out Plooy's pale features and his slightly serious expression as the final minute counted down to zero-two-thirty. Time to go. I took one last sniff of my wretched bedding, shook Plooy by the hand, and we wished each other good luck. If the coast was indeed clear, I would see him in five minutes when we were up to our necks in the river. The bottle of rice and the bottle of water were stuffed into the deep side-pockets of my Nigerian-issued army trousers. I pulled my boots on and slipped silently from under the net and out of the door.

As I filed into the passageway with my back to the wall, I could hear the TV. It was on low but I could make out Ewan McGregor's voice.

'It's all in the grind, Sizemore. Can't be too fine, can't be too coarse. This, my friend, is a science.' A dull light from the TV flickered down the passage towards me. It was another re-run of Black Hawk Down, and there were half-a-dozen doped-up guards nodding off to it. Discarded joint butts and empty bottles lay at their feet. I took a couple of deep breaths and stood still for a moment, willing myself to be invisible. My heart was thumping. To me it sounded like a bass drum being beaten by a hyperactive chimp. It was irrational to think that the sound of my heart and breathing could alert the guards to my presence, but that was exactly what was running through my head and it took a little gentle persuasion on my part to get going again.

I walked slowly away from the TV room, trying to stay flat against the wall and keeping noise to an absolute minimum. I reached the open doorway that led outside and took another breather. This time I knelt down, making myself small before poking my head out to see if the coast was clear. It seemed to have taken an age to cover the five metres I had travelled, more than my allocated five minutes, anyway. I was expecting Plooy to come up my rear at any moment. Had to get a shifty on. There were just twenty-five metres left before I reached the water's edge and freedom beyond. The coast looked clear, so I took yet another deep breath and pushed on.

It was very dark down in that corner of the camp, but my eyes adjusted quite well to the gloom. The tree where we aired the mattresses, and in which our escape kit was hidden, came into view, which meant there were less than ten metres left to cover. As I made it past the tree I noticed several orange glows, and I could make out the dull monotone that only came from a person who was ridiculously strung out on dope and booze. I stood rooted to the spot, straining all my senses in the direction I wanted to go. A white flash. One of them must have smiled and then all of them; it was like several searchlights piercing the night. I could now make out a couple of outlines. Bollocks. They were sitting right where we had planned on making it out. Shit. We hadn't had time to do a recce since the new guards had turned up, to see where they parked themselves through the night.

I felt like a cat-burglar who had just been caught with the family silver; I turned to leave and make my way back to the cell, when a voice stopped me dead.

'What ya doing out here, fucking white man?'

It was said with the sort of confidence that only came from years of not being fucked with.

'I've just come to ease myself, boss,' I replied in the sort of submissive, sniffling tone that only came from a few days of jungle captivity.

Stepping into plain view, I counted five guys and waited for the man I'd just addressed to give me permission to pee. He let me stand there for a few more seconds before nodding his head towards the water's edge and carrying on his conversation, his rifle still pointing at me. I wasted no time in scurrying on past the group and up to my ankles in the river. My heart was banging in my ears as I emptied my bladder. Taking long, deep breaths I tried to think of another way out, but that meant changing the plan. I had to go back and tell the others.

I shook, zipped, and hurried back past the lads, making sure I didn't hold any eye contact. It took me only a few seconds to make it back to the cell, just in time to see Plooy's head emerge from under the mosquito net. I held up my fist just like they do in the movies, commanding an 'All stop', and whispered to him that we had a problem. Plooy ducked his head back under the net and I followed him on to the stinking mattress I had so hoped to leave behind. Explaining all that had happened, I noticed Plooy's shoulders slump and a look of disappointment pass across his face. He ducked under the net to pass the sad news to Noor, and to tell him to hold fast until further notice. We planned to give it half an hour, and then Plooy would go on his recce and hope by then the boys had gone to bed.

Half an hour passed slowly, we were so edgy. Plooy's forehead glowed green as he checked the time on his digital for the umpteenth time in the last five minutes. He made to leave, stopping only to give Noor a five-minute warning as he was next to go, leaving me to wait a further five minutes after that. I wasn't holding out much hope. Two or three minutes later I heard footsteps and then a few words spoken between Noor and Plooy, just before the net was lifted and a dejected Plooy plonked himself down, 'Ma se poes' were his only words. I guessed that was something rude in Afrikaans.

We carried on going to 'ease ourselves' every half-hour until four-thirty in the morning. It was too late to make good our escape before the rest of the camp came awake, so we aborted for the night; we would try again tomorrow and every night after that. Once we had stood ourselves down I slept soundly right up until Plooy nudged me awake.

'There's a lot of excitement out there.'

'I can't see why, it's not like we escaped or anything, is it?' I answered.

My head felt groggy and tired, my limbs heavy and slow. I was knackered and a little depressed, but then picked up my voice to try and sound cheery.

'What's going on then?' I asked.

Plooy crawled out to investigate, leaving me alone to reflect on another day in paradise. He was back after only a short while, with Noor in tow.

'Something has got the little bastards all riled up, but fuck knows what it is.' Noor spoke over Plooy's shoulder as they both crouched down under the net.

'The little fuckers are running about all over the shop, tidying up, servicing the guns; and one of the goats has just had his throat slit.'

'The General might be coming over; perhaps he has some more good news for Sachin and Aditya,' I offered as a solution.

'Nah,' replied Noor. 'The General's comings and goings have never got the camp this excited before; it must be something else.'

We couldn't face going outside yet, so we stayed under the net chatting about the possible reasons for all the fuss outside, and what a complete abortion last night's recces were. We were all for giving it another try again tonight, though, and we silently hoped for better luck.

'Out, out, out!' fired the Secretary through the window.

We left the privacy of the mosquito net and made to go outside into the morning air. With as little haste as we could muster we filed out into the sunshine and made our way over to the tip. By the rubbish dump we had a good view of all that was happening, and sure enough it did feel as if there was a different vibe to the camp this morning.

I could just make out the approaching *whup-whup-whup* sound of the rotor blades of an approaching chopper. And that was when merry hell broke loose. All the guards picked up their assault weapons and aimed them towards the sky. We crouched down lower and our arms instinctively rose, so our hands were just above our heads. All our movements were frozen like that as we waited for the chopper to come into view. I counted the seconds, one, two, and three, in my head and slapped my neck with the open palm of my hand as an insect took a bite. Just as the chopper flew overhead, all weapons erupted into a firing frenzy.

Dropping to my knees I looked up and caught a glimpse of the chopper racing overhead. Why the hell hadn't they changed their flight path yet? It could only be a matter of time before the militants got a lucky shot. Just then, and right on cue, two gunboats came tearing up the river, unloading their AKs into both sides of the river bank. It was like a scene from a low-budget action movie; the camp was under attack. I was up on one knee now, supporting myself with one hand, almost in a sprint start. I looked to Plooy, Bob and Noor to see what they were thinking, but they looked completely incredulous. Sachin and Aditya were cowering on the floor; Bob dropped to his knees and covered his ears.

I looked back to the boats and recognised no-one in the first, but the other was holding Commander Jackson and the rest. They were criss-crossing each other and seemed to be engaged in almost hand-to-hand combat.

'Run!' I heard Plooy shout. 'Forget our kit, just make it to the jungle!'

His voice penetrated my brain and I snapped out of my trance; a length of baler twine and a rusty old machete blade weren't going to help us out of this anyway. Keeping my head bowed and my eyes on the prize, I leapt forward and sprinted across the yard, zigzagging as I went. Just as we were within a few strides of the jungle several guards and many of the goons headed us off; I almost had my finger tips on the foliage.

The mob tackled us down into the dirt with their weapons and collected us together into a tight, pleading group. We were completely surrounded and once again escape was impossible. Bob, Sachin and Aditya, who hadn't managed to make a run for it, were dragged over and dumped down with us. The cheering militants started pulling at our clothes and we soon found ourselves nearly naked. It didn't look good, and I wondered if this was some weird game orchestrated by the sisters as their leaving present. That thought was soon dashed as more clothes from the Oxfam box were

294

thrown at us to be put on. Not much thought had gone into this, though, and in the chaos I was thrown Plooy's old shirt that he'd been wearing for the last few weeks and a pair of chinos that were too short in the leg and too loose in the waist. As we pulled on our new clothes the excited mob moved apart to let the crews from the boats through.

If I thought the Lieutenants from our snatch squad looked a little mad when dolled up in their battledress, well, they had nothing on this new crew. They had on the same black, red and white ribbons that were tied around their elbows, knees and ankles. But they had covered themselves in a white talcum powder-like substance from head to foot, and were wearing undergarments. With white wife-beater vests tucked into white Y-fronts, they looked ridiculously scary. Jabbering in their mother tongue, this new lot seemed to be taking control.

The mob motioned for us to get up and make our way over to the boats. We demanded to be told what was going on and looked about frantically for the Secretary or Commander Jackson, but saw neither. We started begging to know where we were being taken, and huddled in closer together. All I could think was that we were being sold to another group or, worse, being taken off by this new gang to be executed. In return for our begging they told us we were going to be killed, and once again we received the bony finger being drawn across the throat, backed up with some cheesy smiles.

The gunfire had all but stopped, just the odd isolated overhead shot making us flinch, as we were ordered to stand before being led towards the boats waiting on the muddy bank. The mob taunted us with death threats and slaps as we struggled to weave a safe passage to the water's edge. I caught a last glimpse of my dive booties as one shot out and connected behind Sachin's knee, causing him to stumble. Plooy steadied him over the last few metres to the water's edge. Once

295

there, we were ordered into the gunboats. Small packages were being thrown to the mob by the underpants gang, and a free-for-all followed as everyone clambered to catch one. Bob got knocked to the floor and we bent to help him up.

Plooy, Sachin and I were forced into the gunboat crewed by the lieutenants from our mob. Poor old Noor, Bob and Aditya were to be chaperoned to God knows where by the new gang in the pants. I climbed in with my legs feeling like boiled spaghetti, convinced that we were now being taken to the Niger Delta's abattoir, and that twenty-four hours from now every witchdoctor and juju man within a twenty-mile radius would be casting spells and feasting on our vitals. I kicked the thought from my head and instead wondered what was in those packages that nearly caused a riot. They must have been drugs or some other form of payment. This thought was also cut short, as the boat was kicked from the shore and eased out and away from Camp Horrid.

The Yamaha 115-hp outboards roared into life and carried us down-river, past the banks of the camp which were now lined with our ex-captors. I scanned the faces, still full of hatred for us, for one last time, and had a feeling that one way or another I would never be seeing them again. With a blip of the throttle the mango trees on the banks merged into one continuous green blur as we sped away, losing sight of the camp to our rear.

Forced low into the bilges of the gunboats we were once again catapulted into a hell-raising mystery tour. Five battle-hardened militants leaned into every bend the gunboat took. BA was sharp, but not in Frog Face's league when it came to manning the outboards. His steering was erratic with frightening last-minute adjustments – quite scary when you're going flat out. We three were covered by Eagle Eye's assault rifle, while the rest trained theirs on any threat that might come from any angle. They were all wearing their finest gear, Commander Jackson up front with a pair of binoculars round his neck and fake RayBan Aviators balancing on his bony nose. Plooy's boots, or rather Commander Jackson's boots, were polished to a high shine, and laced up tightly on his feet. Prada, just aft of him and ahead of us, wore double bandoliers that crossed at the chest, spare ammo for the big machine gun that Commander Jackson carried. Just behind us was Denzel, as always looking like the Hollywood movie star, bare-footed and jeans turned up. To look at him you wouldn't think he had a care in the world, talk about casual.

The front of the fast boat was riding high as the prop dug fiercely into the muddy waters, blocking any sight we might have had of what was coming up. Commander Jackson had to lean right over the barrel of his machine gun to keep some weight forward and stop the boat from riding up too high, which would compromise the handling. Then all of a sudden BA eased back on the throttle, the front of the boat dropped and we were met by a dead end, a wall of irrepressible jungle.

The gunboat behind, crewed by the Y-fronted hoodlums, also eased to a crawl, and for a few moments my heart sank and I felt a red-hot flush of fear, thinking, 'This is it. This is where we get a bullet to the brain and are dumped into the murky river, never to be seen again.'

I grabbed Plooy by the hand and whispered, 'I think this is it, mate.'

Plooy looked at me and nodded. I knew he was thinking the same, but then both boats fired up again and swung violently to the right, roaring off down a hidden creek. Both boats were racing flat out, taking lefts and rights. There was no way I could recover my sense of direction. The only thing I could say was that if we had chosen my plan of escape, Harry, then we would have been well and truly stuffed. Heading through this maze of swamps and jungle, with or without a compass, would have been the equivalent to pissing in a north-westerly force ten to eleven, gusting occasionally thirteen.

Life felt a little fragile being driven around by those lunatics; you just didn't know what was waiting to greet you round any bend. We had one more heart-stopping moment when both boats came to a standstill. It was at a place in the swamp which had the look of a big roundabout. Three or four waterways met at a small island in the middle, and at the edge of this overgrown island were several white flags and a stack of crates, five or six high, full of fizzy pop. There was Fanta, Coke, Dr Pepper and Sprite, none of your diet shit either. This was another of their offerings to the gods who frequented these parts. I was so thirsty and lacking in sugar, I could have drunk myself about thirteen Dr Peppers right there and then.

The boats chugged at a walking pace past the offerings and the militants started chanting respectfully. Plooy then turned to me, speaking softly.

'This must be our new home, Camp Horrid II.'

'Shit,' was about all I could mutter back as I scanned our new surroundings.

The island looked as if a terrible plague had forced everyone to abandon it many years ago, leaving nothing but a nasty smell in the air. The whole place sent a shiver down my spine, causing me to shake involuntarily. I think they call it 'out of the frying pan into the fire'. I would have done anything right then to have been taken back to Camp Horrid to see out the rest of my time; I did not want to stay here.

The boats drifted a little past the fizzy pop as I strained my neck to look further into the island, expecting to see some withered Robinson Crusoe hermit-type guy. I saw no sign of life; if anyone did live there, then they were very shy and not too keen on visitors. My head shot back on my strained neck as once again the boats pulled away and up to near-max speed in moments, for another ten-minute race about the rivers.

Taking another impossibly sharp left, our boat eased back. We were at the start of a waterway that was dead straight and nearly one hundred metres long; at the other end we could see two boats. Both our vessels were now side by side and Noor managed to flash me a quick smile. I was feeling tense but I flashed him one back. The two stationary boats grew larger as we crept closer. Although I could see many figures aboard these boats, they were still too far away to be identified.

I put a hand on Plooy's shoulder to steady myself as I made to stand for a better look, only to be helped back down by Eagle Eye's gun.

Sachin turned to us, looking a little pale himself, and said, 'There are white men up ahead.'

It was a little longer before I could see any skin, but sure enough, on the boat to my left were several white men, all staring right at us.

CHAPTER THIRTY-FIVE

FREEDOM

As the two boats at the end of the straight came into focus, I could now make out a few faces that appeared familiar. They were all sitting low in the boat looking very scared, drawn and haggard, but they were definitely our fellow co-workers, kidnapped with us nearly three weeks ago: there were the two guys from the anchor handler plus two Americans, an engineer, Shane the tower operator and a Nigerian rigger, plus another white male I didn't recognise, which made six hostages. Standing around them were three smartly-dressed Nigerians in traditional West African outfits of brightly-coloured, long flowing robes and matching hats.

The gunboat just off to the right was crowded with several of the General's most loyal bodyguards, all dripping with military hardware and serious-looking faces. And of course the General himself was standing erect in the middle, with an aura of menace. The three smartly-dressed Nigerians greeted us all warmly but with a no-nonsense attitude, and quickly ushered us aboard. Sachin and Plooy climbed into the boat as soon as we pulled alongside. Shane, the young American tower operator who had suffered a bloody leg during the early morning attack, helped me in by offering his hand.

'Fuck me, Phil, the food must have been good, you've put on weight.'

This was the Yank's attempt at sarcasm and I guess he pulled it off quite well. I returned Shane's friendly smile and replied, 'You look like shit, mate,' and he did. He probably had the best bushy beard, though, out of all of us. Everyone shuffled round to make more room for Noor, Bob and Aditya, and as we did so the militants closed in.

All the boats were now in close proximity, some gently bumping off each other in the natural movement of the river. As the last of the hostages were transferred, bundles of cash were pulled out from under the skirts of our Nigerian friends. It quickly dawned on me that we were being set free, and that feeling was like no other I could remember. Everyone in the boat started shaking hands, dishing out back-slaps and hugging each other with genuine man-love. We were all very much relieved.

The General, however, reminded us just how vulnerable we still were and started firing his pistol above our heads, demanding more and more money. I think the suits were trying to hold out on him and keep some for themselves, as more money miraculously appeared from under their skirts. This sparked up the underpants gang, who quickly reminded us with bursts of gunfire that they were being left out. In the next moment everyone with a gun was unloading into the river around our boat. This was about to go sideways. All parties were now shouting at each other between uncontrolled bursts of automatic gunfire. Once again we assumed the brace position we had learned so well during our time in the jungle. Hands on head, head between the knees, eyes shut tight.

The suits produced yet more Benjamin Franklins and started tossing them into the gunboats, all thoughts of any embezzlement replaced with ones of self-preservation. They were throwing money around like a diver on shore leave. The General, now placated with the amount of silver that had crossed his very greasy palm, called a halt to the gunfire. Money really did talk. The suits and the General exchanged a few choice words before his gunboat was coaxed alive and gone. Commander Jackson and his Lieutenants were just as quick to follow, leaving our boats pitching in their wake as they sped away to catch up with the General. There are no words to explain how it felt to see the back of them at last. Finally, we were safe – well, as safe as twelve hostages could be, miles from civilisation, deep in a militant stronghold, with only three suits for protection and a gang of strange men covered in talcum powder and wearing underpants. Were we safe? Or were these strange men to be our new masters? I checked out the underpants gang and received some reassuring smiles from each of them, apart from one who was probably smiling but no-one could tell, for he had changed a Manchester United beanie into a balaclava by pulling it over his face and cleverly cutting two holes for eyes. At least his eyes said he was smiling.

'Fucking hell, the guys that were looking after you were wound a bit tight, weren't they?' asked Shane, offering me a smoke.

'Thanks,' I said as I took one. 'I wouldn't exactly say they looked after us, but yes, they were a little highly strung,'

The suits asked if everyone was feeling okay and whether we were up for a little boat journey. They told us it would take a few hours to make it out of the swamp and back to the Governor's house for a meet and greet, a hot shower and some food. The suits received many nodding heads and a chorus of 'Just get us the fuck out of here', followed by lots of relieved laughter. With that we headed in the opposite direction to that of the General and began to make our way to safety, with our escort of heavily-armed men in battle-ready pants.

It was a perfectly calm night, with just a little breeze to freshen the normally stuffy air. Spirits were running very high as we managed to start putting miles between us and the General. We passed a few villages at cruising speed, and many of the villagers ran along the banks matching our speed, waving and cheering at us. We waved back. Noor and Bob, along with Sachin and Aditya, had been put in the stern. Plooy and I were up in the bow with Shane and one

302

other white face I didn't know. The rest of the guys were in the middle.

I was shocked to learn from Shane that the cause of his bloody leg was a gunshot. A bullet from one of the militants' AKs had fragmented, and a piece entered his calf when they opened fire at his feet in an effort to hurry him along. We tried to outdo each other by swapping horror stories to pass the time. I couldn't match the gunshot wound, though, so settled for showing him some of my scars left over from the mosquito bites; I was a little jealous of his bullet wound. The white face I didn't recognise, chatting to Plooy, was in fact a security advisor, kidnapped from the rig just down the way from us some three weeks before we were taken. In all twelve of us were released that day, our two Indian friends, Sachin and Aditya, the security advisor, and nine from our pipelay barge. The Nigerian rigger was taken off the barge accidentally on the morning of the attack. Shane told me that when they all got back to camp and the militants realised they had kidnapped one of their own by mistake they instantly set him free, but with no safe passage out he opted to stay and keep his co-workers company.

The underpants gang took time to say goodbye when they had journeyed as far as they could with us into fairly safe waters. It was especially good now to be completely lunatic-free. No more gun-toting militants for company, and half the distance already put behind us.

The sun started to sink behind the trees, casting a beautiful silhouette, and the stars were coming out in abundance. There was enough light to see by, though, even when the sun had completely set, due to the rather fat moon that night. Plooy and I sat with our backs resting against the backs of those behind us and looked up at the stars, feeling pretty chuffed with ourselves. Not only had we made it through with our lives and barely a scratch, but within a couple of hours our escorts would deliver us to the Governor's residence where we could have a hot bath, a shave and make a very emotional phone call home to the family.

Then the engine died. The two suits instantly began to chastise the young Nigerian boat driver they had brought along with them, who was frantically yanking on the pull-cord and willing the engine back to life. After pulling for all he was worth for a full five minutes he finally gave up, dropping back down on his arse totally exhausted. One of the suits piped up.

'I can't believe it, it is broken! How can this be?' The engineer from our barge had a quick look at the outboard and shook his head. For once I was completely speechless; this was the crappiest rescue ever. First they attempted to come into one of the most dangerous places on earth in a heap of shit with just one engine, and then tried to cream off some of the ransom money, nearly resulting in us all getting shot. But it got even better than that. Between the two suits and the boat driver they had one pay-as-you-go mobile which, unsurprisingly, wasn't receiving any signal, and probably didn't even have any credit.

After the unbelievable high earlier, everyone was now exhausted and the once very cheery faces were all looking rather glum. We were drifting with the flow of the river, about a knot, but at least in the right direction. We were not yet out of pirate-infested waters so the mood was once again a little tense. All we could do now was sit and wait.

A couple of hours had passed and Plooy and I were halfway through yet another game of 'I Spy'. In the distance we heard the low rumble of an outboard heading our way. Everyone was on tenterhooks, waiting to see what would come round the bend. You could literally hear the proverbial pin drop. I never did get to find out what Plooy had spied beginning with 'C & W', for the noise of the engine was getting louder as it neared the bend in the river. One of the suits sounded a little like a Nigerian Michael Caine as he delivered an absolute peach.

'Hold on a minute, lads, I've got a great idea!'

CHAPTER THIRTY-SIX

A COLD ONE IN THE TAVERN

The suit's idea was rubbish. He proposed that all the white men hid in the bottom of the boat whilst they called over the passing vessel, and they would then force them to tow us to safety. How do you hide twelve white men in a boat designed for four people? We stuck out like a dozen pork chops at a Saudi wedding, and who in their right mind would stop and offer assistance to sixteen desperate-looking men on a darkened river? Not surprisingly, the approaching boat took one look at us desperadoes and took off like a cat being chased by a pit bull. It was close to eight hours later that we were finally rescued, slightly dehydrated and totally exhausted. I didn't think we were ever going to get out of that swamp. A trade boat passing in the opposite direction and travelling even more slowly than us eventually got word sent that we were in the shit, and that we needed a lift. Two fast boats came and picked us up and took us to a nearby village, where they dropped us ashore into the protection of Nigeria's Joint Task Force. They lined the jetty, heavily armed, and for the first time in a while I was glad to see men with guns. As soon as we set foot on dry land we were ushered into a waiting luxury coach with blackened privacy glass.

The mood among us hostages changed as the coach pulled away under a heavy escort. At last we felt safe and we all relaxed visibly, letting the tension of the past weeks evaporate. The coach had turned into a party bus and we were on a mystery trip to who cared where, because anywhere was better than where we had just been.

After a relatively short ride through some of the Delta's worst slums we arrived at the Governor's house; he had the unfortunate job of overseeing this vast shit-hole. The protection around this man's house was immense. Soldiers were positioned on the gate, on the walls and in the street. There were searchlights, razor-wired walls and fortified watchtowers with 50-calibre machine guns pointing in all directions. All this just to keep his constituents out! And I could see why. Outside these walls was abject poverty, where average life expectancy could be as low as forty and where living on just two dollars a day was considered extravagant.

Inside the walls things were a little more comfortable. The Governor didn't just have one plush manor, he had about fifty, and all built to a very high spec. Seeing this contrast did go a little way in helping me understand why some young men form gangs and turn to kidnapping. There is, after all, lots of money in the pot; it's just about how you get your share.

TV crews and the Nigerian press were waiting inside the main house for the party bus to disgorge its sorry-looking cargo of hostages, bedraggled, unkempt but in high spirits. The press conference was held and a statement was read out by the Governor. 'Today, 11th June, MEND has released from captivity all twelve hostages being held. No ransom was paid. MEND released all twelve hostages as a goodwill gesture, to give the Nigerian Government more time to bring roads, medical centres and schools to the Rivers State people.'

This statement received a raucous round of applause and lots of flash photography. I felt like coughing and shouting at the same time, 'BULLSHIT!', but instead my award-winning smile was playing up to the paparazzi. As far as I was concerned they had got me out, they could say what they liked and I would just nod; I still needed to get home.

We never found out how much money was handed over for our safe return. Certainly not the five hundred million dollars and some boats demanded by the General, but we did see some goats and bundles of cash changing hands. Shane, who was being held at another of the General's camps, said that he saw three duffel-type bags full of money, but I think they were more than likely filled with rice and beans - to go with the goats. I won't waste my time trying to guess the true amount. As for 'a goodwill gesture' by MEND, well, I'm sure when they first formed only two years previously in 2005 they had honourable intentions, but these had muddied somewhat as time went by. They may have set out to be a bunch of Robin Hoods with God on their side, but no money they made from any of their kidnappings went back into the communities for healthcare, education or anything else. All the money made from this shady industry went on fuelling the war, drugs, arms and the General's beloved boats.

A banquet was laid on and for a moment all I could do was stare. After being deprived for so long of food that possessed any form of colour or taste, the feast before me was a sight to behold. I stood clutching my plate, drooling like a Great Dane staring at a Scooby snack. It was like an ocean up-welling: there was a selection of shellfish peppered between fillets of fresh fish, brought to the table on a warm current of sliced meats, rich pastas, potatoes, pastries and cakes, lots of cakes; it was all there and it was all for the taking.

After we could eat no more we were given mobile phones to call our families. I phoned Sophie; it was three in the morning but I didn't think she'd care. It wasn't quite the call that I had been dreaming about for the last three weeks. The line was crackly, with a long delay on my end, but we managed a few well-chosen words. Next I phoned Mum and Dad, and again we managed a few snatched words with white noise for a backdrop. I ended up shouting 'I'll phone from the airport', and of course a big fat 'sorry for all the fuss'. It was the only time in my life that the response wasn't 'Well, Philip, sometimes sorry isn't enough,' or 'You can't just keep saying sorry and expect everything to be all right.' This time it was 'It's all right, son, just get yourself home.'

We were split into four groups of three and given a house for the night. Hot baths and lots of drinking followed. Now it was time to get drunk, not just tidily fudged but out-and-out smashed on a Biblical scale. Plooy and Noor were my housemates, but Shane dropped by for a drink and ended up crashing.

I awoke early, still clutching a half-finished bottle of fine cognac, with not the slightest of hangovers; I was still riding my euphoric high, but I would no doubt pay for it at some stage. As I rolled over I bumped into my new bed-partner, Shane. Plooy had made it to his own bed; I missed him, but it was time to move on. Cognac for breakfast, this was the life.

Before I was smuggled out of Nigeria on a BA flight to Heathrow, we had another night at a hotel in Port Harcourt. We said goodbye to Noor here, as he was catching an earlier flight. It was a happy goodbye, as we were all still jubilant and we knew we would see each other again. The diving community is quite small and we all run into each other from time to time on various jobs. I said my goodbyes to Plooy at Lagos Airport.

'Well, Plooy, if I ever get kidnapped again I can't think of anyone I'd rather be banged up with.' We shook hands.

'Me too,' he said while we were still shaking hands. 'We did OK.'

'We did more than OK,' I replied.

'Phil, if those militants hadn't been right by where we planned to escape the other night, you, me and Noor would still be wandering around in circles out in the jungle looking for scraps to eat and dodging bad guys.'

'I know, Plooy, I don't even want to think about it.' I let go of his hand and watched him turn and walk down towards his boarding gate.

'See you, mate,' I said. He raised his hand without looking back, before he was swallowed up by the throng heading for the same flight. His flight was one hour before mine, so that left me alone to contemplate my reunion with my family over a pint. It felt strange but nice to be on my own after living so closely with others for so long.

I was asleep before the wheels left the runway, and woke again just before touchdown in England, glorious Blighty. Sophie was there to greet me at Arrivals and drive me back to Devon. I don't know why, but I was nervous about seeing her. I stopped just inside the arrivals door and took a few deep breaths. I needn't have worried, though; as soon as she saw me she threw herself into my arms, buried her head in my neck and we hung on tight, Sophie letting go a few quiet sobs before lifting her face up to look at me.

'Are you OK?' she sniffed.

'I'm fine, baby, I just need a little TLC.' Sophie looked at me and gave a happy laugh before saying, 'Are you sure? You look like crap.'

We had plenty to talk about on the journey home, and Sophie had an instantly calming and comforting effect on me. She filled me in on all that had been happening whilst I'd been away. It was a happy moment for me just being back in her company and chatting normally, not worrying about being beaten or shot. I didn't want this exhilarating high I was feeling ever to go; I was utterly exhausted and it was the only thing that was keeping me going.

I arrived to an overwhelming welcome at the Torcross Tavern. Sally had put on a bit of a do for friends and family. It felt surreal to be sitting at the bar, surrounded by my loved ones at last, laughing, joking, and just being in the company of normal, non-threatening people. I had made it, I was safe and back home where I belonged, and that was when it hit me. I had lost my euphoric high; I wasn't feeling happy any more, I was coming down and crashing fast. I looked around the bar and saw everyone I knew having a good time, but I could no longer join in. I had held myself together for so long, but not anymore; I was about to let go. I slipped away from the bar and went to the toilets for a wee. At the urinals I found myself alone and just started crying. A dam had burst in my head, and all my emotions started pouring out of the floodgates. I couldn't help it and I couldn't stop, I was shaking so much; my wee was going all over the place. I had snot and tears streaming down my cheeks. The British stiff upper lip I had been wearing for the last few weeks and had been so proud of was going south, fast turning into the quivering bottom lip. This was going to be embarrassing. That's when I heard my old man at my back. 'Come on, son, let's get you home before you cause a scene.'

My old man went to take a step towards me and give me a man-hug and then hesitated; he obviously didn't want to get snot and urine on his going-out clothes. He then changed his mind again, thinking 'it's only my son's snot and urine', and completed the transaction, giving me the hug I so desperately needed. We stayed like that for a minute or so. It had been a long time since my dad and I had had a cuddle.

'Son,' he said, breaking the spell, 'you could at least put your willy away.' We pulled apart.

'Sorry, dad,' I said, wiping my nose with my sleeve. I zipped myself up as he steered me out of the toilets and through a side door into a waiting car, where my mum had the engine already purring. I didn't look back at the bar where my friends and family were still enjoying the night, for fear of causing that scene, but instead offered a silent 'Thank you' to everyone who had been thinking of me and supporting my family over the past few weeks. Oh, and I hoped they enjoyed the drink on me; I had put that fifty quid I owed my brother behind the bar.

WHAT HAPPENED NEXT?

Alhaji Dokubo-Asari was released from prison on the 14th June, 2007, three days after our formal release. He immediately began talks with the then government to call a halt to all militant attacks in the Delta, severely pissing off the rest of the militant factions. He washed his hands of MEND after his release, criticising its other reported leaders.

MEND accepted the government's June 2009 offer of amnesty and consequent ceasefire. The group remained quiet until the 4th February, 2012, when they blew up an AGIP trunk line in Bayelsa State. They are now threatening to up the ante, calling on political leaders to free Henry Okah, another reported leader who was arrested in Angola in 2007 and extradited to Nigeria a year later. Both oil and non-oil infrastructures are now under threat of attack, as the underlying causes of unrest are still not being dealt with.

Camp Horrid and its denizens: what may their future have been? Pure speculation.

THE GENERAL gave up warlording and invested his share of our ransom money in a low-level political campaign in Bayelsa State.

THE SOMALI is currently working at the Pink Shrimp in downtown Port Harcourt as a transgender lap-dancer. He/she struggles to make ends meet, but is at least earning an honest wage.

THE TEACHER is undergoing treatment for alcohol and drugs problems at a secret location rumoured to be one of the Delta's most prestigious clinics, courtesy of one Alhaji Dokubo-Asari.

THE SECRETARY worked as the General's political spin doctor, but was stabbed to death in a bar brawl while defending the General's good name.

COMMANDER JACKSON was killed in action by a stray bullet to the back while leading the assault on a jack-up drilling rig off the Delta coast in 2011. It seems that the bullet was fired from an AK47 by one of his own men.

PRADA was killed in 2009 by one of his own home-made bombs, taking one goon with him and injuring two others.

BA & DENZEL were arrested for armed robbery in Port Harcourt in 2009, after crashing their getaway van into an illegally parked Humvee. They are currently serving fifteen years each.

FROG FACE died from malaria in 2007.

THE PREACHER is now a popular pastor at the Holy Trivial Church, keeping his foot-long and circus balls in check while delivering his sermons.

GASTRO POD was burned to death while bunkering. An explosion occurred after fourteen militants hot-tapped illegally into a 24" pipeline with a blow-torch and discovered that it was a gas line. The three sisters were among the dead.

EAGLE EYE found his voice, and took control after the mysterious death in 2011 of Commander Jackson. He is now leading his own snatch squad and is spreading fear across the Delta waterways. He goes by the name of Commander Eagle Eye.

THE MISSING MONEY stolen from the Indians' paymasters by the shady doctor was used to start up and fund his own terror and kidnap business. Known as RMEND, the Real Movement for the Emancipation of the Niger Delta, it is a splinter group which has not yet opened up dialogue with the Government.

ME, I married my sweetheart Sophie. I continue to work as a diver and went back to work in Nigeria, telling my loved ones I was working somewhere else so they didn't worry. That didn't work out too well for me either.